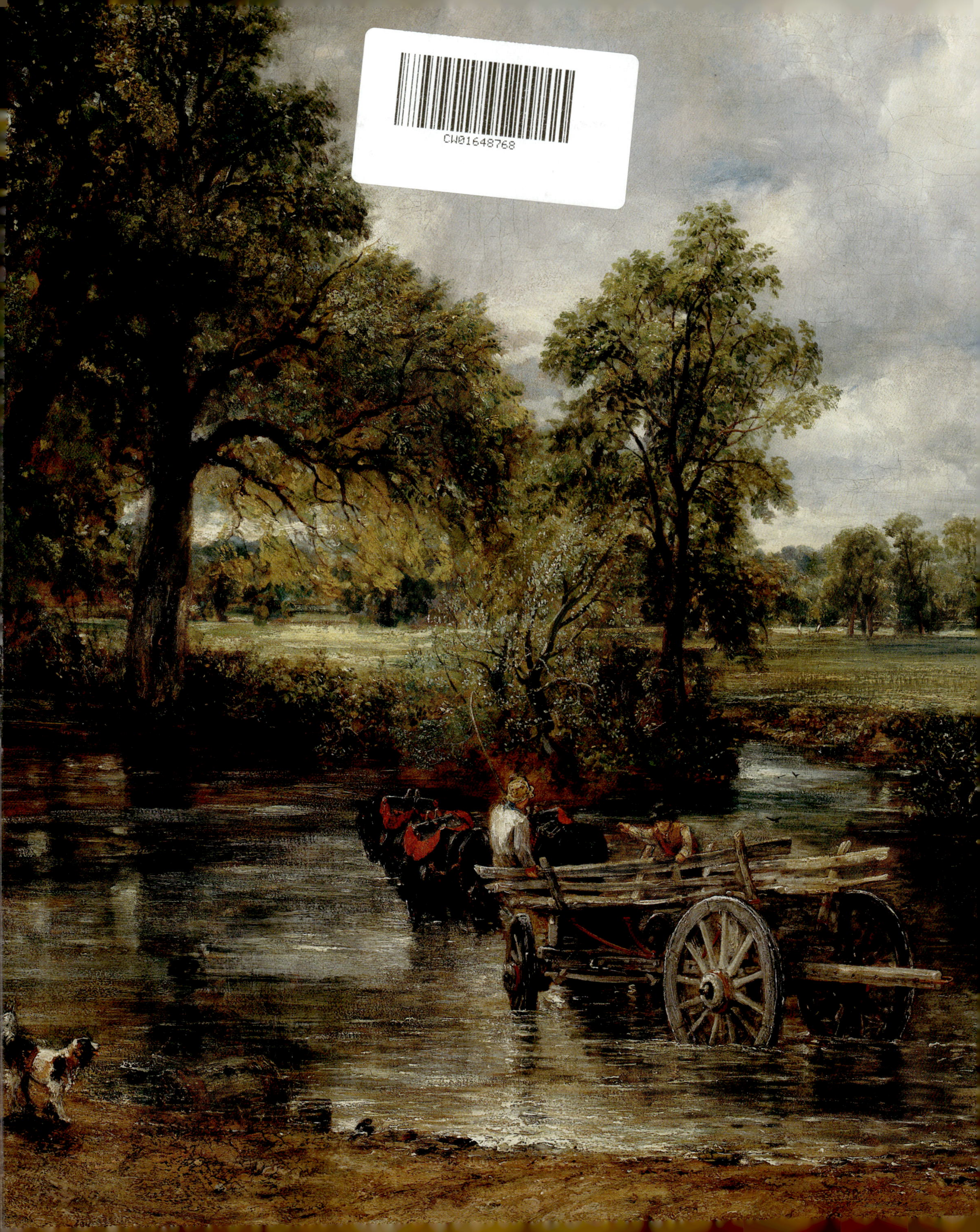

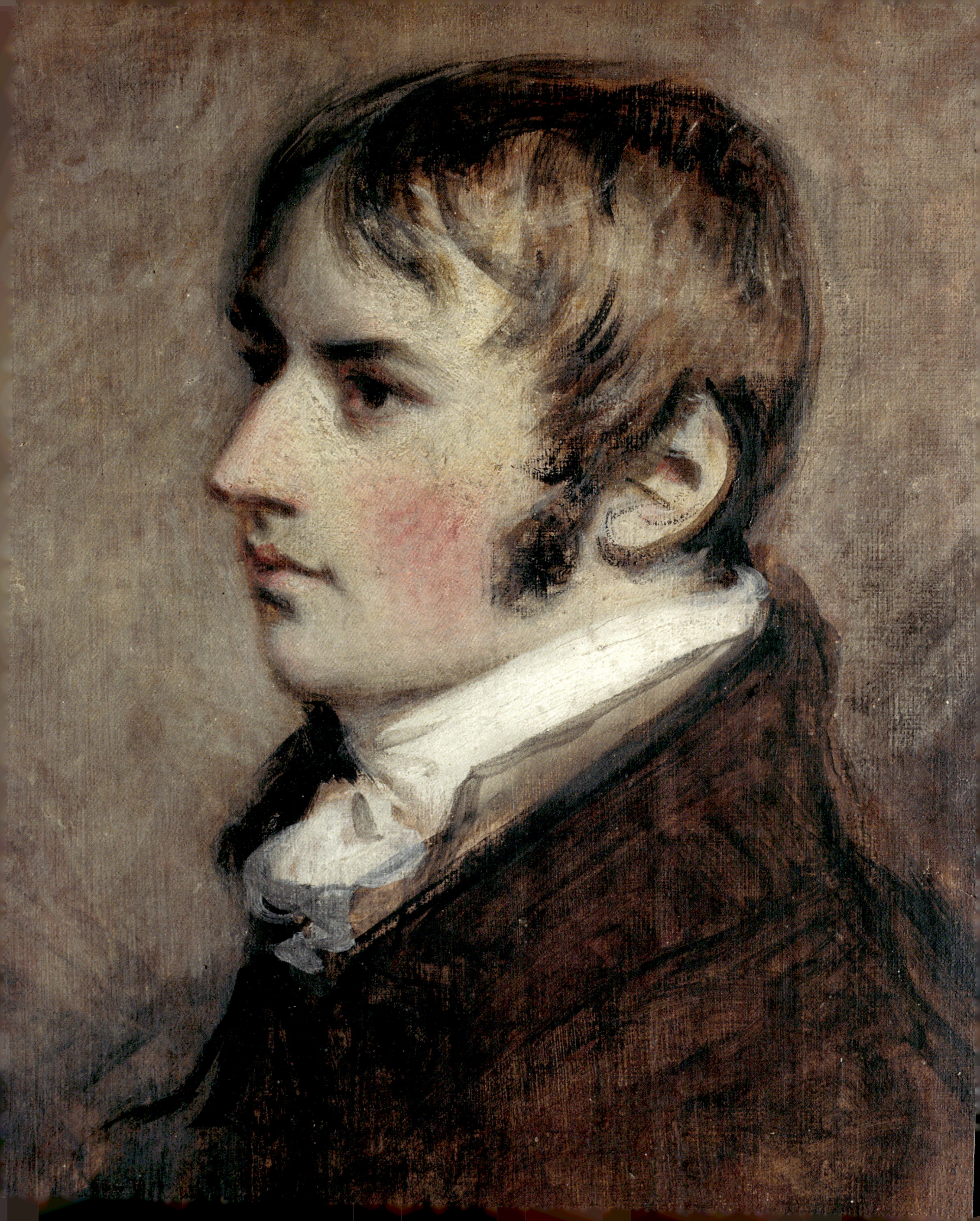

DISCOVER CONSTABLE & THE HAY WAIN

CHRISTINE RIDING AND MARY MCMAHON
WITH CONTRIBUTIONS BY JENNY GASCHKE,
ANNE LYLES AND EMMA ROODHOUSE

NATIONAL GALLERY GLOBAL, LONDON
DISTRIBUTED BY YALE UNIVERSITY PRESS

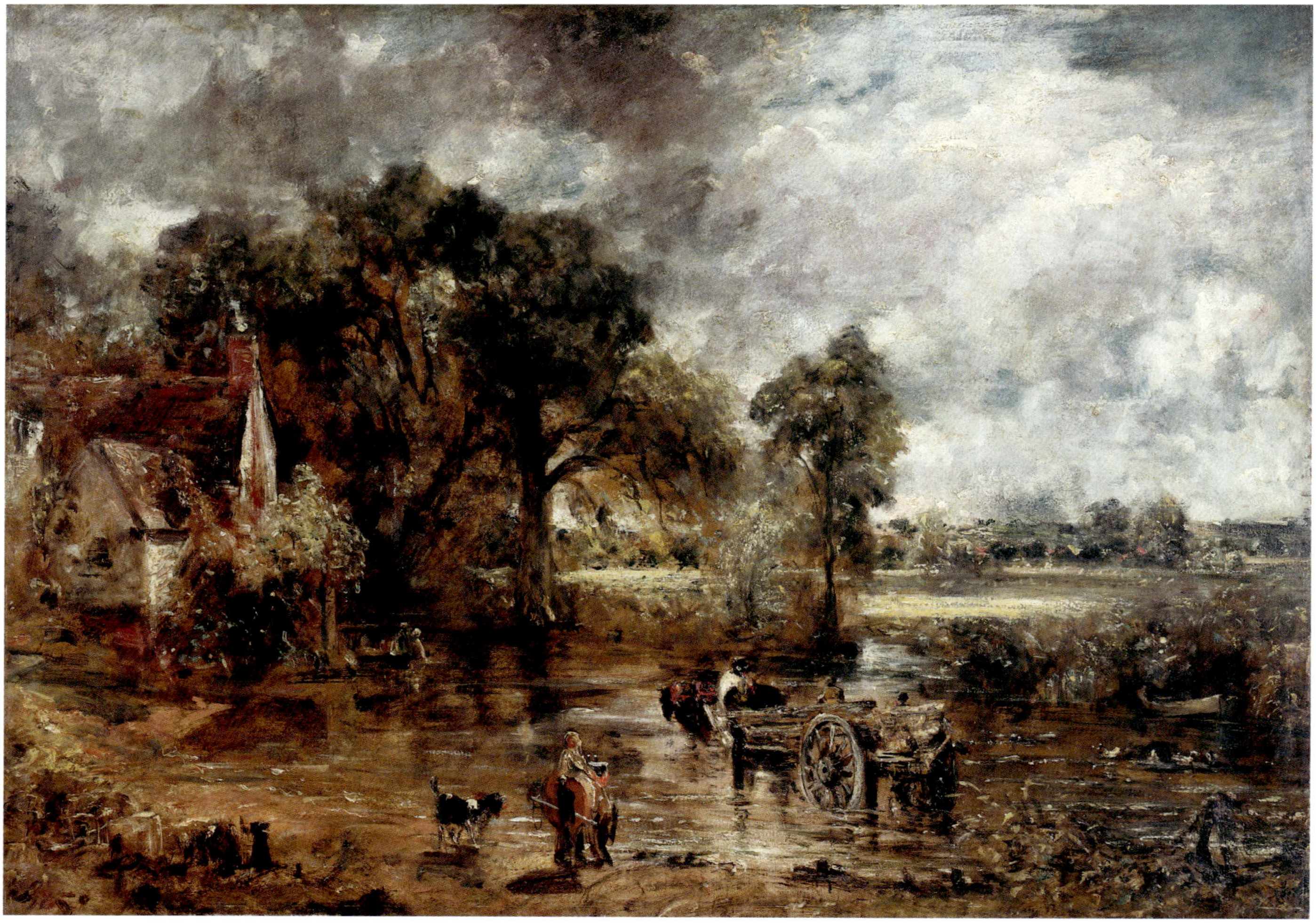

Fig. 1
Full-scale study for
The Hay Wain, about 1821
Oil on canvas, 137 × 188 cm
Victoria and Albert Museum,
London

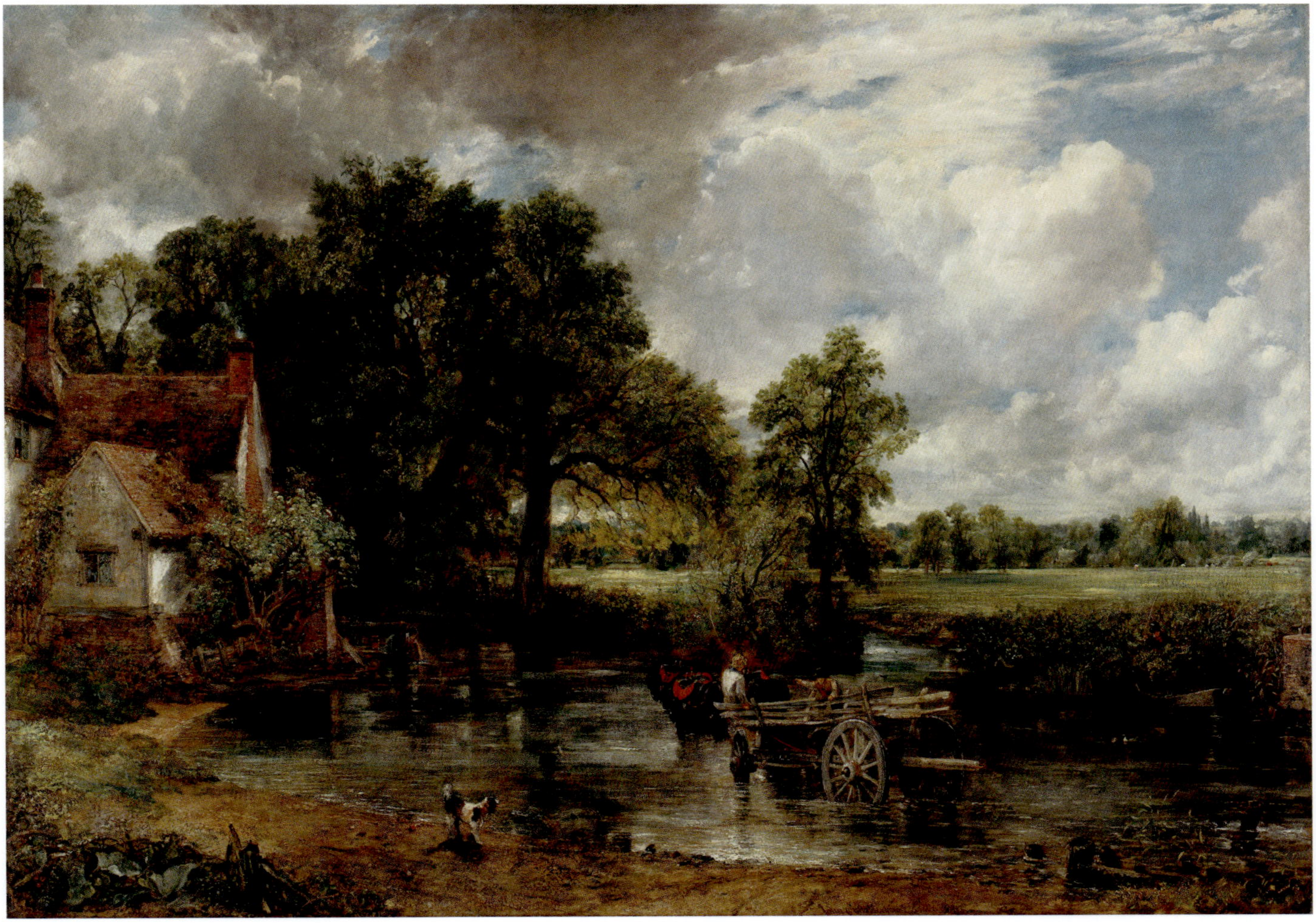

Fig. 2
The Hay Wain, 1821
Oil on canvas, 130.2 × 185.4 cm
The National Gallery, London

Published to accompany the exhibition:

Discover Constable & The Hay Wain
The National Gallery, London
17 October 2024–2 February 2025

Exhibition curated by
Christine Riding
Mary McMahon

Exhibition supported by

The Thompson Family Charitable Trust

BOODLES
1798

The Sunley Room exhibition programme is supported by the Bernard Sunley Foundation

In celebration of the National Gallery's Bicentenary this catalogue has been supported by the Finnis Scott Foundation

The Finnis Scott Foundation

This exhibition has been made possible by the provision of insurance through the Government Indemnity Scheme. The National Gallery would like to thank HM Government for providing Government Indemnity and the Department for Culture, Media and Sport and Arts Council England for arranging the indemnity.

NG200
200 YEARS OF THE NATIONAL GALLERY

First published in 2024 by
National Gallery Global Limited
Trafalgar Square
London WC2N 5DN
www.shop.nationalgallery.org.uk

ISBN: 978 1 85709 721 4
1053824

British Library Cataloguing-in-Publication Data
A catalogue record is available from the British Library

Publisher: Laura Lappin
Project Editor: Catherine Hooper
Copy-editor: Jenny Wilson
Proofreader: Robert Davies
Picture Researcher: Suzanne Bosman
Production: Jane Hyne

Designed by Sandra Zellmer
Cover design by Sonia D'Orsi
Origination by DL Imaging, London
Printed in Belgium by Graphius

All works are by John Constable (1776–1837) unless otherwise stated.

All measurements give height before width.

Front cover and p. 1: *The Hay Wain* (detail from fig. 2)
Back cover: *Cloud Study: Horizon of Trees* (detail from fig. 85)
p. 2: *John Constable, RA, at the Age of Twenty* (detail from fig. 11)
p. 8: Alexis Joseph Depaulis (1792–1867)
Front and reverse of the gold medal awarded by Charles X of France to John Constable, 1824.
Gold or gold-plated with silk ribbon, 4.5 × 4.5 cm
The National Gallery, London
pp. 76–7: *The Hay Wain* (detail from fig. 2)
p. 119: *Golding Constable's Kitchen Garden* (detail from fig. 64)

MIX
Paper | Supporting responsible forestry
FSC® C014767

Director's Foreword 9

Introduction: Nature and Nation 10
CHRISTINE RIDING

'Pure nature's soul':
The Emergence of a Natural Painter 26
EMMA ROODHOUSE

'Rather a more novel look than I expected':
The Making of *The Hay Wain* 38
ANNE LYLES

'Landscape not merely as seen, but as experienced':
Constable and Europe 52
JENNY GASCHKE

From 'dull replica' to 'national treasure':
The Afterlife of *The Hay Wain* 62
MARY MCMAHON

PLATES

Landscapes of Tradition and Innovation 78

Constable before *The Hay Wain* 92

Making *The Hay Wain* 97

After *The Hay Wain* 110

NOTES 112

BIBLIOGRAPHY 114

LIST OF EXHIBITED WORKS 116

LIST OF LENDERS 117

ACKNOWLEDGEMENTS 118

PHOTOGRAPHIC CREDITS 120

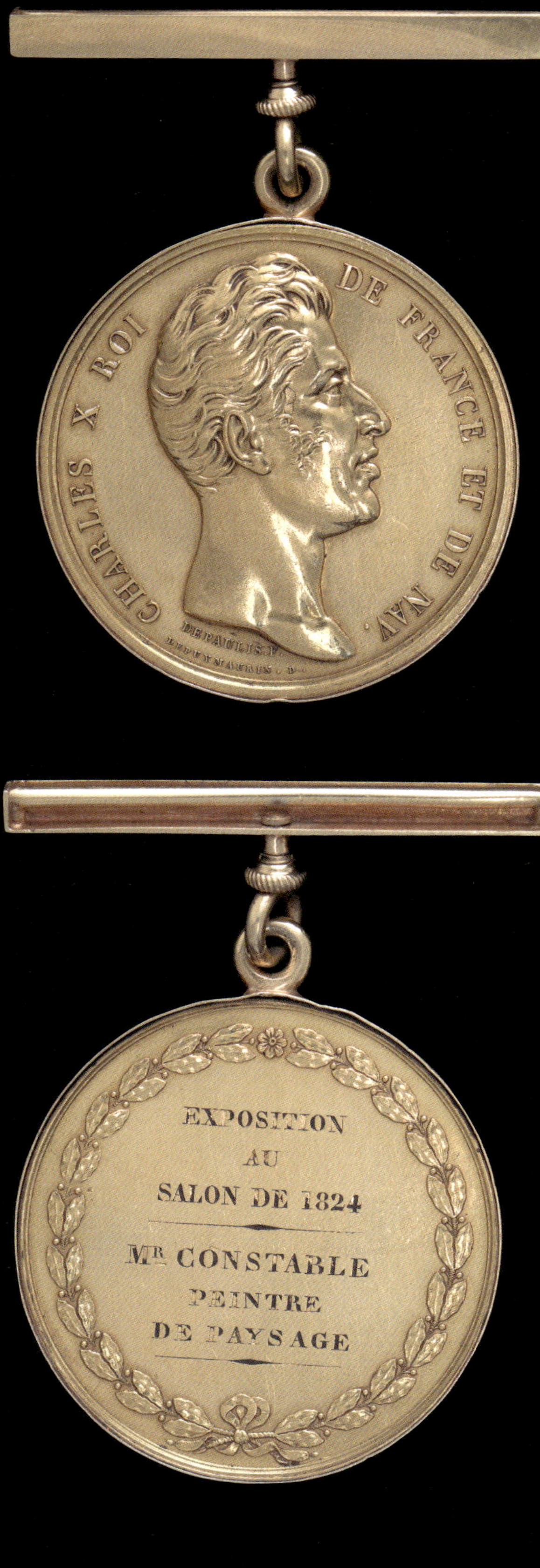
CHARLES X ROI DE FRANCE ET DE NAV.
EXPOSITION
AU
SALON DE 1824
Mr CONSTABLE
PEINTRE
DE PAYSAGE

DIRECTOR'S FOREWORD

Discover Constable & The Hay Wain centres on what is undoubtedly one of the most admired paintings in British art. Surprisingly, perhaps, it is the first loan exhibition at the National Gallery on the work of John Constable, but the timing – during the Gallery's Bicentenary – is highly appropriate: 1824, the year when the Gallery opened its doors to the public, is also the year *The Hay Wain* received international acclaim at the Paris Salon. On that occasion Constable was awarded a gold medal by King Charles X of France (which is also in the Gallery's collection, see opposite), and the Director of the Louvre tried but failed to acquire the painting for the French nation.

The Hay Wain represents the river Stour and the land that ran alongside Flatford Mill, which Constable's father owned. It is the most successful of the artist's 'six-footers', as they are now known, depicting the area around the Essex–Suffolk border in which he grew up. His regular portrayal of the places he felt deeply attached to would see Suffolk referred to as 'Constable Country' even within his lifetime. On its first showing at the Royal Academy in London in 1821, *The Hay Wain* garnered mixed reviews, with some critics finding it a radical reimagining of the landscape tradition. On Constable's death in 1837, *The Hay Wain* was in a French collection and, following its passage through a succession of collections, it was donated to the National Gallery in 1886 by art collector Henry Vaughan. That is when the public's love story with the painting really began.

This exhibition brings together works by Constable's British predecessors and contemporaries to reveal how his notion of natural painting diverged from the conventions of his time. It considers the personal context in which the artist was working and how he approached the creation of his celebrated masterpiece. The catalogue, with contributions by authors Emma Roodhouse, Anne Lyles, Jenny Gaschke, and the exhibition's co-curator, Mary McMahon, Associate Curator NG200 Collections at the National Gallery, also discusses the afterlife of the painting and Constable's posthumous reputation.

The exhibition was conceived by Christine Riding when she was the Jacob Rothschild Head of the Curatorial Department in Trafalgar Square. She has since become Director of Collections and Research, and I am grateful to her for the skilful commitment she has brought to this project. I wish to thank all the lenders and institutions who have generously contributed to the exhibition. I would like to express my gratitude to the Bernard Sunley Foundation for their long-standing support of the Sunley Room exhibition programme and to the Thompson Family Charitable Trust for their continued generosity. I am also grateful to Boodles for their sponsorship of *Discover Constable & The Hay Wain*, and to the Trustees of the Finnis Scott Foundation for their support of this catalogue in celebration of our Bicentenary year.

Gabriele Finaldi
Director, The National Gallery

CHRISTINE RIDING

Introduction: Nature and Nation

We step from rural Nature herself with as much satisfaction
to view Mr. CONSTABLE's Landscape by Noon,
as we do to see her ever charming scenes in the company
even with Ruysdaal and Hobbima.

The New Monthly Magazine, July 1821

The artistic identity of John Constable (1776–1837), as promoted by himself and his critics and supporters, was founded on the notion of a 'natural' and (in time) a 'national' painter. In early nineteenth-century Britain, rural naturalism was characterised by scenes of everyday country life painted in a relatively realist manner, often touched with sentiment. Foremost in this regard is Constable's *The Hay Wain*, first exhibited at the Royal Academy in 1821 (see fig. 2). In fact, so identified was he with the area of Suffolk, in the east of England, depicted in the painting that it was referred to as 'Constable Country' even during his lifetime.[1]

The succeeding 200 years since its creation have only served to persuade us that *The Hay Wain* is, categorically, a truthful and authentic representation of rural England. Moreover, the familiarity of this image today means that it is almost impossible for us to appreciate its originality, and thus its impact on first audiences. At that time, few art patrons and commentators in Britain challenged the long-standing hierarchy of the traditional genres, with history

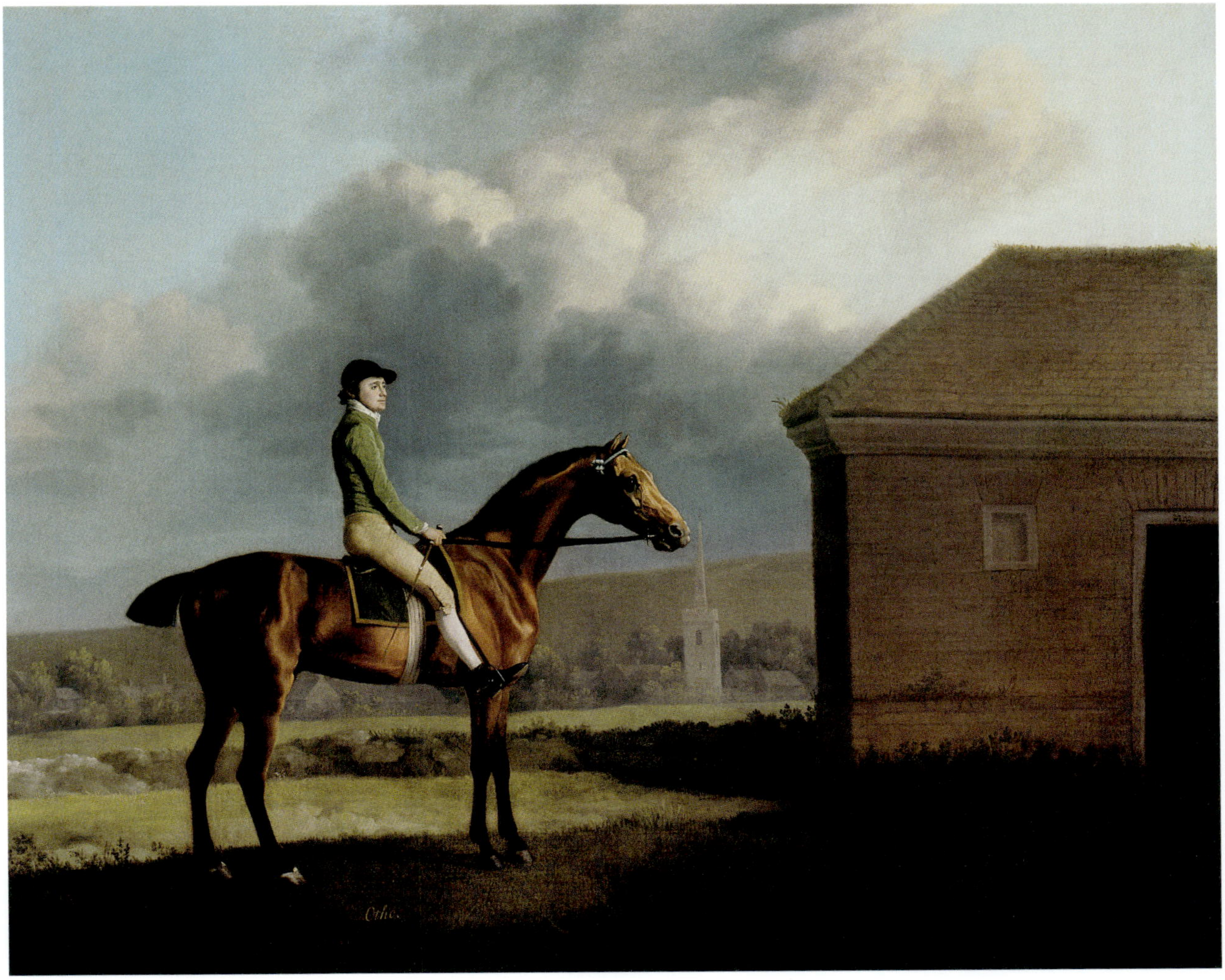

Fig. 3
George Stubbs (1724–1806)
Otho, with John Larkin up, 1768
Oil on canvas, 101.3 × 127 cm
Tate, London

painting as pre-eminent: the notion that British artists had largely failed in this field was also broadly accepted.[2] Even so, the 'lower' genres, such as portraiture, landscape and 'genre scenes' of daily life that dominated early nineteenth-century British art, were increasingly admired and promoted, not least because painters, to varying degrees, applied the formal conventions and elevated meanings associated with the European 'old master' tradition. At the same time, the so-called Romantic period (around 1780–1840) saw artists creating ever-more expressive and complex landscapes that expanded their own imaginative scope. Diversity and innovation, rather than strict conformity, categorised Romanticism's approach to nature. Ranging from the naturalistic to the visionary, its collective legacy was felt for many decades to come. In Constable's case, his particular brand of pictorial naturalism not only influenced French Romantic art but has also been seen as a precursor to that most transformative of art movements, Impressionism.[3]

Beyond the art world, the truly momentous international event of 1821, only days before the Royal Academy exhibition opened, was the death of Napoleon Bonaparte, former Emperor of France, who had been exiled after his defeat by allied forces at the Battle of Waterloo only six years previously. Over 20 years of conflict, collectively known as the Napoleonic Wars (1792–1815), then followed by economic and social crises that affected town and country alike, had a profound effect on Constable and his contemporaries, as both artists and citizens. Under these circumstances the British landscape could not be viewed as a neutral space devoid of politics and patriotism, privilege and discrimination. This is worth remembering if only to question how artists such as Constable interpreted contemporary rural life, including how much they chose to conceal or reveal.

Between art and nature

In practice, Constable never adopted a straightforwardly naturalistic style. His guiding principle, shared by other artists, was the close observation of the natural world, integrating the resulting sketches (whether pencil or oil) into strong, formal compositions that were informed by past and present artistic exemplars. What set Constable apart was how he interpreted 'naturalism', firstly through ever looser, more expressive handling of paint: it was his unorthodox technique, rather than his subjects and compositions, that divided his critics.[4] Secondly, he focused almost exclusively on the 'commonplace', as the term was then understood, and locations to which he felt personally and emotionally connected – above all, the Suffolk landscape of his boyhood. Less concerned with strict imitation of nature or artistic precedents, Constable sought to develop his own style, with landscape as a way of expressing 'truth' and 'feeling'.[5]

However, the sheer variety and complexity of approach exhibited by his exact contemporary, J.M.W. Turner (1775–1851), offers a striking counterpoint. With all the artistic traditions and conventions at his fingertips, Turner adroitly blended historical and contemporary practice and associations, from Italian *vedute* (views) and French classicism to Dutch and Flemish 'naturalism', as well as mastering oil, watercolour and engraving media, while deftly navigating the contrasting aesthetics of the sublime, the beautiful and the picturesque, and in addition forging a powerful identity as an intrepid artist-traveller. In comparison, Constable's single-minded 'stay at home' dedication to his subject, only occasionally self-identifying as a 'picturesque' artist (notwithstanding the concept's poetic and artistic associations), necessarily resulted in a narrower scope for his art. This allowed him, justly or not, to be more easily relegated to the second tier traditionally assigned to 'mere' painters of rural landscape.[6]

In consequence, Constable gained the reputation, both in his time and since, of being progressive – avant-garde, even – but within limits.[7] This assessment can seem at odds with his conservative attitudes more generally to politics, religion and society, as is evident from his correspondence with friends and family.[8] Unusually for a British landscape painter, Constable was intimately connected to his subject matter from a position of privilege, as the son of a wealthy mill owner and corn merchant who 'had adopted the lifestyle and attitudes of a paternalistic country squire'.[9] Whether this conditioned his artistic outlook is a matter of conjecture. But Constable's preoccupation with the Suffolk landscape has often been explained away, by subsequent commentators, as nostalgic for a way of life that was changing before his eyes, courtesy of rapid industrialisation, urbanisation and agitation for political reform – with an increasingly educated and proactive working and labouring class, including within rural communities – all of which he fervently resisted.[10] This is why the urban mills and modern factories, steam power and (eventually) railways, which regularly feature in Turner's work, are largely absent from Constable's. While this preference for the status quo (chiefly within the political realm) reflected the world view of most wealthy landowners and rural employers, it was not universal: Henry 'Orator' Hunt (1773–1835), a prosperous gentleman farmer from Wiltshire, and William Cobbett (1763–1835), fellow farmer and political radical from Farnham, Surrey, were both leading advocates of parliamentary reform.[11]

In addition, Constable's family ties to landownership – hence his assumed affinity with employers over labourers – are important to the subject of landscape painting, because the two were so intimately connected in Britain.[12] After all, it was the drive to improve and enlarge estates that saw country house and estate portraiture flourish from the 1680s, initially as practised by Jan Siberechts (1627–1700/3) and other itinerant Netherlandish artists, later by British and Irish painters such as George Barret (about 1730–1784), and then by Turner (see fig. 57), and occasionally Constable himself, such as his painting of Wivenhoe Park, Essex (now at the National Gallery of Art, Washington, DC), exhibited in 1817. Likewise, country pursuits often separated the rural elite by law from the urban professional class: only those who possessed land worth £100 or more, for instance, could participate in hunting. British sporting art, representing blood sports, horse-breeding and racing, was therefore entirely dependent on the landed gentry and aristocracy, exemplified by such images as *Otho, with John Larkin up* (fig. 3), set in Newmarket, Suffolk, by the leading exponent of the genre, George Stubbs.[13]

For British landscape and genre painters, engaging with the style and subjects of the revered European tradition, particularly in those works designated as 'old masters', was an absolute necessity in order to progress artistically and to respond to market expectations. That contemporary painters, as a matter of course, were compared and contrasted with their artistic forebears is underlined by the published review of *The Hay Wain* quoted at the beginning of this essay, during its inaugural exhibition at the Royal Academy, which judged the painting favourably (if condescendingly) as being in company 'even' with the Dutchmen Jacob van Ruisdael (1628/9–1682; see fig. 26) and Meindert Hobbema (1638–1709).[14] Moreover, the classical bias of British aristocratic culture – demonstrated above all by the 'Grand Tour', with Rome and its environs as the *locus classicus* – meant that eighteenth-century patrons focused on contemporary Venetian

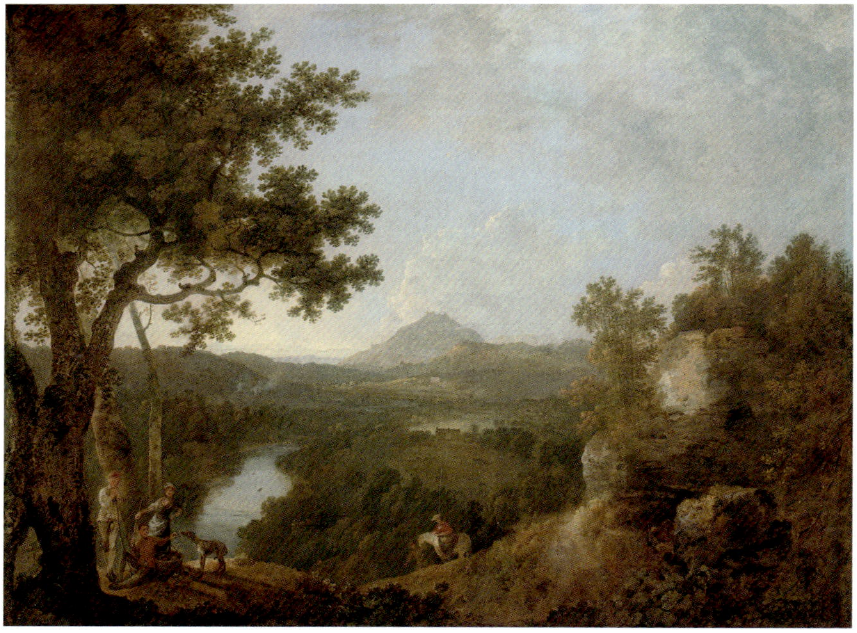

Fig. 4
Richard Wilson (1713/14–1782)
View near Wynnstay, the Seat of Sir Watkin Williams-Wynn, fourth Bt., 1770–1
Oil on canvas, 180.3 × 244.8 cm
Yale Center for British Art, Paul Mellon Collection, New Haven

or Roman-based landscapists, such as Antonio Canaletto (1697–1768) and Claude-Joseph Vernet (1714–1789). More desirable still were the works of celebrated seventeenth-century French masters Claude (1604/5?–1682) and Gaspard Dughet (1615–1675), as well as the images of dark, untamed nature by the Neapolitan Salvator Rosa (1615–1673). Their paintings, incorporating mythological and biblical themes and narratives, set a standard in historical landscape that British artists were thought artistically and intellectually incapable of emulating – a long-held bias that was only just beginning to wane during Constable's lifetime. And it was these broad traditions (and prejudices) that Richard Wilson (1713/14–1782) and Thomas Gainsborough (1727–1788) inherited and, against all the odds, naturalised into British landscape art, with Gainsborough leaning towards the Netherlandish tradition, and Wilson, the classical. Both artists were esteemed by Constable and his fellow painters as innovators and founders of a distinctly British school of landscape.[15]

Of course, Gainsborough through commercial necessity conducted his career primarily as a portraitist, only painting landscapes and rural scenes as a 'sideline', with examples exhibited speculatively in London from the late 1760s. Some, like *The Watering Place* (see fig. 8),[16] despite its echoes of Claude and Peter Paul Rubens (1577–1640), remained unsold at his death.[17] Wilson, in contrast, succeeded in becoming the first British-born artist to specialise solely in landscape, and the most elevated kind at that. By adapting the classicising tradition, inspired by an extended stay in Italy in the 1750s, Wilson not only produced landscapes that aimed to rival, rather than pastiche, those of Claude, Dughet and Rosa, he also then applied this culturally potent formula to representations of British scenery and country estates. A pre-eminent example is his *View near Wynnstay* (fig. 4), the estate of fellow Welshman Sir Watkin Williams-Wynn, painted just after the latter's return from the Grand Tour.[18] Such images also came to define the growing emphasis on the 'picturesque' (meaning, literally, 'like a picture') and the pictorial quality increasingly evident in British literature, especially poetry, from James Thomson's highly influential *The Seasons* (1726–30) to William Wordsworth's *The Prelude or, Growth of a Poet's Mind* (1798–1805, published 1850). Consequently, the appreciation of actual landscapes was filtered through the artifice of landscape painting, particularly those works by Claude, because he offered a model of refinement through formal harmony and subtle luminosity, his compositions gracefully framed by trees, with the viewer's eye guided via classical architecture to distant horizons, the foreground often populated by idle shepherds and nymphs.[19]

The lie of the land

Evidently, the appeal of the Claudean landscape came from its 'improvement' of the natural world. Its influence also went beyond picture making, by shaping the practice of generations of landscape designers, most famously Lancelot 'Capability' Brown (1716–1783), who transformed parks and gardens surrounding British country houses, often displacing whole villages, dwellings, woodlands and arable land. Many commentators at the time were critical of this trend and its more negative consequences, one of the most prominent being Oliver Goldsmith (1728–1774), the Anglo-Irish author and playwright, whose popular poem 'The Deserted Village' (1770) includes the lines: 'The man of wealth and pride/Takes up a space that many poor supplied;/Space for his lake, his park's extended bounds,/Space for his horses, equipage, and hounds'.[20] The evident impact on lives and livelihoods, including migration to towns and overseas, also mirrored the concurrent process of enclosure of common land and the associated phenomenon of engrossing (the merging of small farms to make larger, more commercially efficient ones).[21]

That the picturesque conditioned experiences of the landscape per se – whether lowland, mountainous or coastal – is underscored by the vogue for the picturesque tour and the almost mandatory 'Claude glass': this convex mirror was used by artists, connoisseurs and sightseers, as the Revd William Gilpin (1724–1804) noted, to 'give the objects of nature a soft, mellow tinge, like the colouring of that master'.[22] In sum, the concept of the picturesque embraced everything from painting and poetry to landscape, architecture and domestic tourism. It became the subject of fierce debate during the 1790s, in response to the writings of Gilpin, followed by those of Sir Uvedale Price (1747–1829), a Herefordshire landowner, and Richard Payne Knight (1751–1824), classical scholar and author of *The Landscape: A Didactic Poem* (1794). By the early nineteenth century, its influence over the mindset of the landed and leisured classes made it increasingly the target of satire: for example, in Jane Austen's *Pride and Prejudice* (1813) and *Northanger Abbey* (1817), and, from 1809, in William Combe's *The Tour of Doctor Syntax in Search of the Picturesque*,

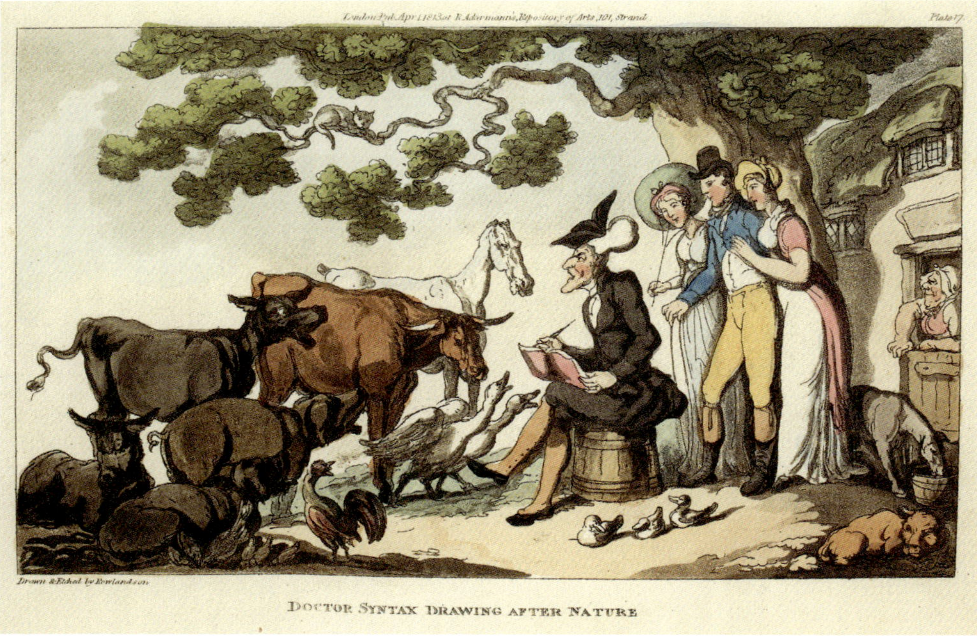

Fig. 5
Thomas Rowlandson (1757–1827)
Doctor Syntax drawing after Nature, 1 May 1812
Hand-coloured etching with aquatint on paper, 10.8 × 18.7 cm
The British Library, London

illustrated by Thomas Rowlandson (fig. 5), which followed the travels, and travails, of a hapless rural schoolmaster.[23]

All of this may seem a far cry from Constable's ambitions as a 'natural' painter. But if he took a dim view of such a formulaic and pretentious way of engaging with nature, he surely appreciated that Gilpin and others were making rural Britain their focus and, in so doing, were also challenging the ideology of the Grand Tour with its stress on continental travel.[24] From Constable's perspective, this shift might encourage a potential market for, and appreciation of, his English views. Similarly, the aesthetic of the picturesque, with its emphasis on rusticity and 'accidental irregularity', sitting somewhere between the 'shock and awe' of the sublime and the more patrician ideal of beauty, laid the groundwork for a wider appreciation of the naturalism of Dutch and Flemish painting for which Constable, like Gainsborough before him, had a genuine affinity. Indeed, Gainsborough, who was also born in Suffolk, led the way for Constable, with such early masterpieces as *Cornard Wood* (see fig. 47), a work indebted to Ruisdael as well as closely representative of its Suffolk location.

Importantly, the stock subjects and motifs in Dutch and Flemish landscapes were the domestic and working buildings – village inns, mills, cottages, farmhouses, navigable rivers and canals – that also featured, of course, in actual English landscapes, alongside their human inhabitants and livestock. Another key Netherlandish tradition was the depiction of the seasons or months with the associated activities of rural communities, whether hunting, haymaking or herding, by the likes of Pieter Bruegel the Elder (active 1550/1; died 1569).[25] Consequently, they were all incorporated seamlessly into British painting, by Gainsborough, Francis Wheatley (1747–1801), George Morland (1763–1804; see fig. 48) and many others. Such was the demand among collectors for Morland's rural scenes that they became a subject for the caricaturist James Gillray in 1807 (see fig. 49).[26] Indeed, their popularity within the British art market may well explain why Stubbs from the 1780s pivoted away from horse portraiture towards rural subjects in a sequence of paired pictures entitled *Haymakers* and *Reapers* (see fig. 46), the latter showing dignified, well-dressed field workers, overseen by a mounted gentleman farmer.[27]

For Constable, more immediate exemplars of Flemish art came with the arrival in London in 1803 of two masterpieces by Rubens, *The Rainbow Landscape* (about 1636; Wallace Collection, London) and its companion, *An Autumn Landscape with a View of Het Steen in the Early Morning* (see fig. 27), the latter acquired by Sir George Beaumont, Constable's early mentor. Their influence on *The Hay Wain* has long been acknowledged. But perhaps less remarked upon is that Rubens painted them for his own pleasure, as a successful artist and a proud, patriotic landowner.[28] Critically in this regard, the Netherlandish and classicist traditions aligned with two revered poetic ones, the pastoral and the georgic, associated with the Ancient Greek poet Hesiod and his Roman successor Virgil, the latter renowned in Britain for his *Eclogues* (or *Bucolics*) and *Georgics*.[29] Some measure of the latter's continuing influence across society, including among

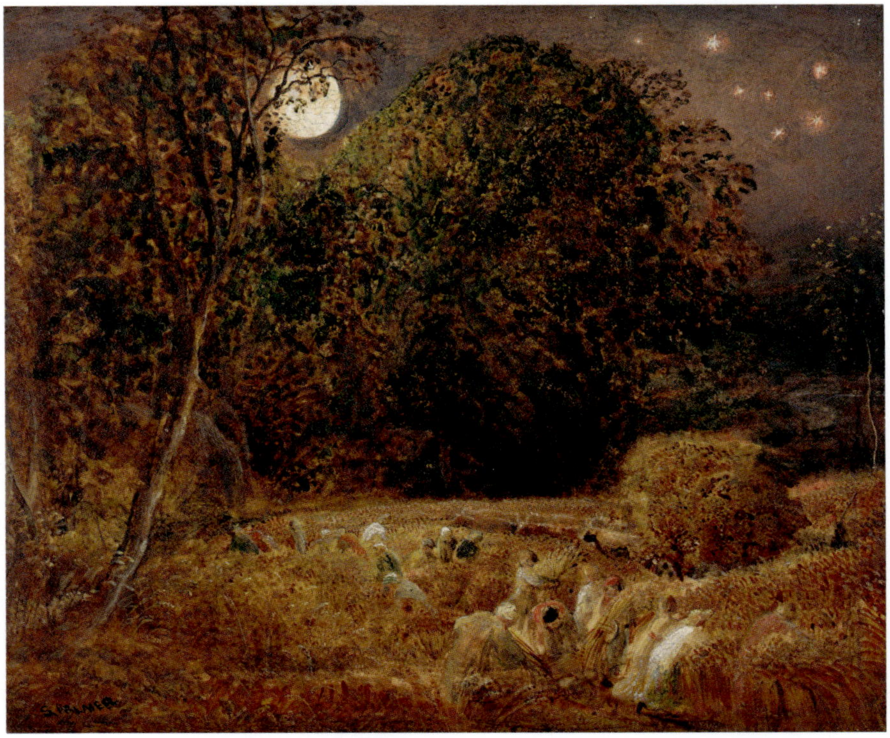

Fig. 6
Samuel Palmer (1805–1881)
The Harvest Moon, about 1833
Oil on paper, laid on panel,
22.2 × 27.6 cm
Yale Center for British Art, Paul Mellon Collection, New Haven

schoolchildren, is the publication in 1821 of Robert John Thornton's *The Pastorals of Virgil*, which includes small woodcut illustrations by William Blake (see fig. 54) that proved highly influential on British landscape art.[30] While the essence of the pastoral (and by association the Claudean) was the languid world of the Arcadian shepherd, the georgic celebrated the virtues of agriculture and good husbandry. This in turn offered an appealing cultural framework for the representation of rural life in contemporary Britain, as orderly, productive and contented, irrespective of (and often at odds with) the reality. It thus neatly aligned with the fashionable 'cult of sensibility', evident in society portraiture from the 1760s, one of the hallmarks of which was an affinity with the natural world alongside a refined sympathy with the plight of the rural poor.[31] Such images as Constable's *The Wheat Field* (see fig. 66) and *The Hay Wain*, and the overtly spiritual *The Harvest Moon* (fig. 6) by Samuel Palmer (a devoted follower of Blake), certainly showed rural workers behaving as their employers hoped, rather than engaging in the drunkenness and lechery that was widely supposed to occur, whether during work or leisure time, as in Rowlandson's 'Rural sports. Or a pleasant way of making hay' (see fig. 50) of 1814.

Importantly, Virgil's approach and influence were already fully integrated into British poetry, through Thomson, Wordsworth and – as an example of word and image combined – 'The Shepherd', one of three poems in the pastoral tradition from Blake's *Songs of Innocence* (see fig. 53). Another homegrown poet, Robert Bloomfield (1766–1823), had made his reputation in 1800 with the publication of his long poem, *The Farmer's Boy*. Unlike the others (Constable included), Bloomfield, a native of Suffolk, could lay claim to an alternative, uniquely authentic perspective, given his lived experience and ancestry as a member of the rural labouring class. In this he can be related to the Scottish poet and lyricist Robert Burns (1759–1796) and, more directly, with the so-called 'Northamptonshire peasant poet' John Clare (1793–1864), whose *Poems Descriptive of Rural Life and Scenery* were published to acclaim in 1820. Many British painters appended (particularly in exhibition catalogues) excerpts from classical and modern poetry to their paintings, in the time-honoured spirit of *ut pictura poesis* (as painting is, so is poetry).[32] Constable did so only rarely but tellingly: on one such occasion, in 1817, he chose lines from Bloomfield's celebrated poem to accompany *The Wheat Field*. And he returned to this poem in the 1830s, transcribing lines from 'Winter' below an appropriately atmospheric cloud study (fig. 7). In so doing, Constable stressed that his response to the great poetic and pictorial traditions, both past and present, was at heart a thoroughly English one, with its roots in the land, culture and heritage of Suffolk.[33]

War and peace

The drive for a truly national rather than derivative landscape art underpinned Constable's whole approach. For similar reasons, eighteenth- and early nineteenth-century artists from East Anglia shared his empathy with seventeenth-century

Fig. 7
Cloud Study with Verses from Bloomfield, 1830s
Ink on paper, 33.7 × 21.3 cm
Tate, London

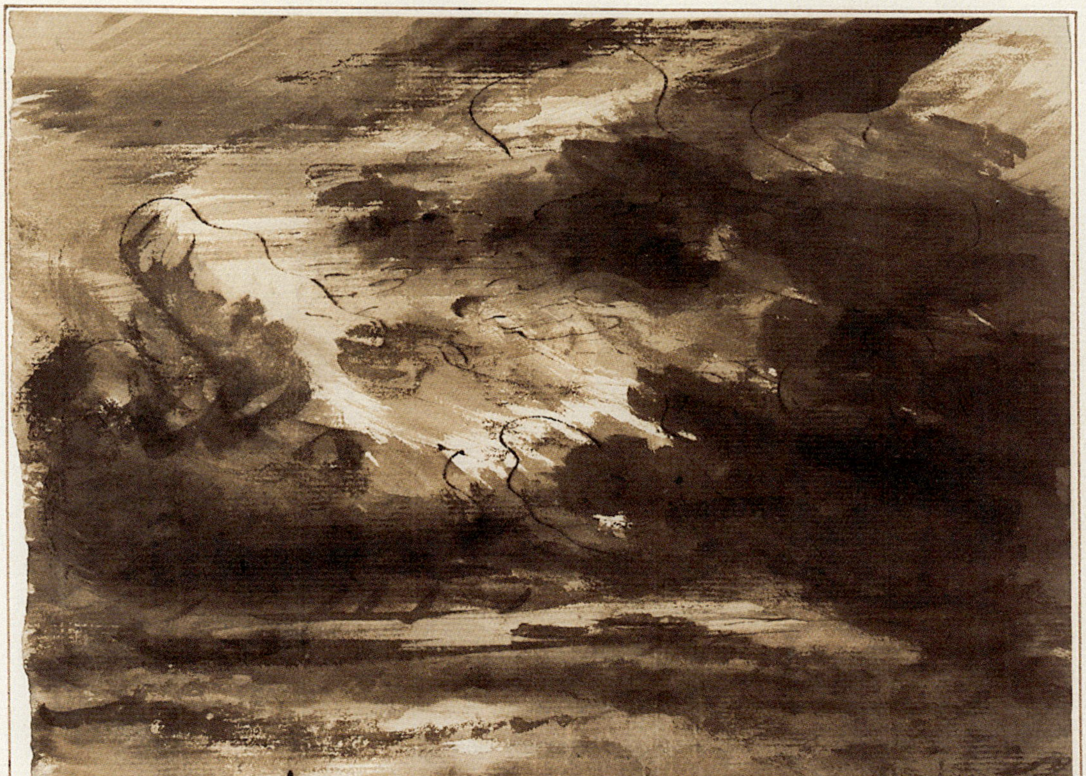

With sauntering step he climbs the distant stile,
~~Whilst~~ Yet all around him wears a placid smile;
~~There~~ Thence views the white-rob'd clouds in clusters driven
And all the glorious pageantry of Heaven.
Low – on the utmost boundary of the sight,
The rising vapours catch the silver light;
Thence fancy measures – as they portray fly,
Which first will throw its shadow on the ~~[illegible]~~ eye
Passing the source of light; and thence away
Succeeded quick by brighter still than they.
Far yet above these wafted clouds are seen
(In a remoter sky still more serene)
Others, detach'd in ranges through the air,
Spotless as snow and countless as they're fair;
Scatter'd immensely wide from east to west, –
The beauteous semblance of a flock at rest.
These to the raptured mind – aloud proclaim
Their mighty shepheard's everlasting name.

Dutch artists, particularly Rembrandt, Ruisdael, Hobbema and Aelbert Cuyp, partly because they had successfully established a national landscape tradition through scenes and subjects inspired by their own country, rather than foreign or imagined lands.[34] Tellingly, the first art movement outside London, the Norwich School of painters, was founded in Norfolk (the county to the north of Suffolk) in 1803, by John Crome (dubbed 'the English Hobbema'; see fig. 56) and John Sell Cotman (1782–1842).[35] This was soon followed in the late 1810s by the so-called Bristol School, who specialised in genre scenes and naturalistic landscapes centred on the Avon Gorge in the West of England, the group initially led by the Irishman Francis Danby (see figs 58 and 59).[36]

Of course, the context for this artistic momentum is the French Revolution (1789–99) and Napoleonic Wars, which had dominated Constable's life from his teenage years. Initially, many Britons were sympathetic to the Revolutionaries, including writers and artists such as Wordsworth, Blake and Gillray. As events turned ever more bloody and threatening, as signalled by Louis XVI's execution in 1793 during the Reign of Terror, and the rise of Napoleon (from French consul, to military commander, to emperor, by 1804), the national mood changed: effectively, any attempt at social, political and above all parliamentary reform in favour of the disenfranchised majority was branded as French-style revolution by an increasingly reactionary Tory government.[37] But there were some winners, not least within the art world. For example, works of art from disbanded royal, aristocratic and ecclesiastical collections from France, Italy and beyond made their way across the Channel for sale, with London now rivalling Paris and Amsterdam as the centre of the old master market. Many masterpieces purchased in London at this time, such as *An Autumn Landscape with a View of Het Steen in the Early Morning* by Rubens (see fig. 27), subsequently entered the collection of the National Gallery.[38]

The founding of the National Gallery in 1824 was but one outcome of British wartime and post-war pride and patriotism. Equally important was how the zeitgeist offered an unprecedented opportunity for contemporary British art to take centre stage. This was not only because the extended period of conflict presented a plethora of topical subjects, across all genres; it also assisted in moving critical and public opinion towards the idea that British art could now hold its own with the long-established European schools, including (most poignantly at this time) that of France.[39] An example of this is the founding of the British Institution in 1805 by a group of wealthy collectors and connoisseurs, including Sir George Beaumont.[40] As a philanthropic organisation, the Institution both complemented and rivalled the activities of the Royal Academy by seeking to promote and influence contemporary British art. For this reason, it initially showcased contemporary British painting; the first exhibition held in 1806 comprised some 250 works, including two by Turner and seven by Stubbs, who had died that year, one of which was an enamel version of *Haymakers*. From 1813, it hosted annual displays of British artists from previous generations, starting with the first President of the Royal

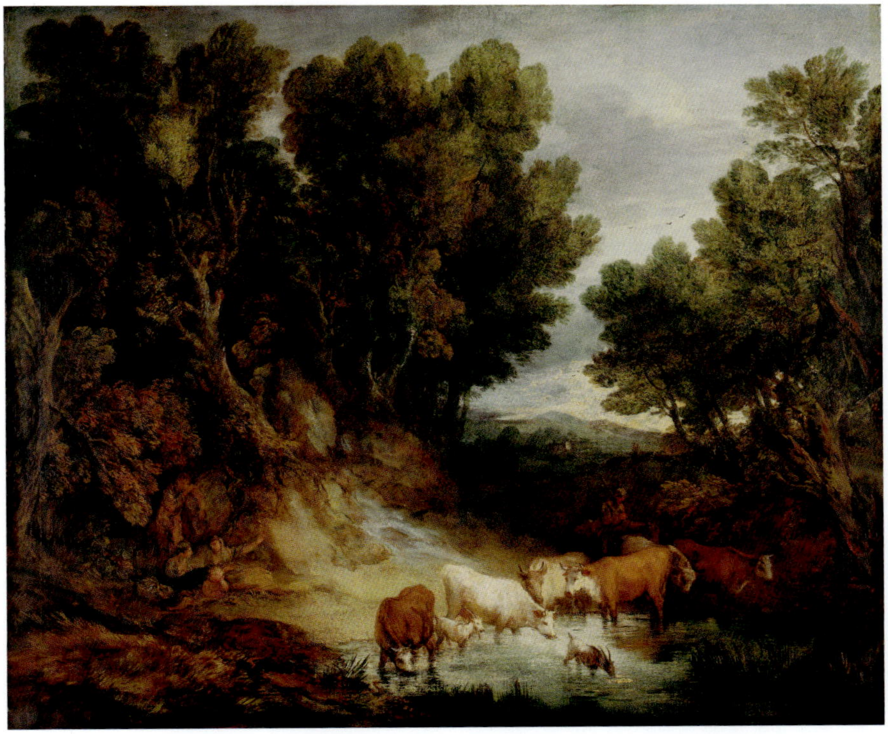

Fig. 8
Thomas Gainsborough
(1727–1788)
The Watering Place, before 1777
Oil on canvas, 147.3 × 180.3 cm
The National Gallery, London

Academy, Sir Joshua Reynolds (1723–1792). In 1814, the exhibition included Gainsborough's *Cornard Wood* (then in the possession of David Pike Watts, Constable's uncle) and *The Watering Place* (fig. 8), and in 1817, the exhibits included portraits, genre scenes and landscapes by Stubbs, Gainsborough, Morland, Wilson and Joseph Wright 'of Derby' (1734–1797).[41] From 1815, the Institution pioneered regular temporary exhibitions of European old masters from private collections (normally accessible only to a select few), beginning with Dutch and Flemish paintings, thus giving a broader art-interested public the opportunity for the first time to make direct comparisons between the art of the past and that of the present.[42]

An important context for landscape and rural imagery, by Constable and others, was that the years following the Napoleonic Wars saw an acute economic depression, with high levels of unemployment and unprecedented harvest failure across Western Europe due in large part to the 'Year without a Summer' of 1816, caused by a volcanic eruption in Indonesia.[43] Despite expanding industrialisation, accompanied by the introduction of income tax in 1799, the nation's economy still depended on agriculture – a point that Rowlandson made in 'The Sign of the Four Alls' (see fig. 51), in reference to the ongoing war effort. In Britain, the situation was exacerbated by the Corn Laws, first introduced in 1815, which imposed tariffs on foreign imports, with the aim of protecting English grain producers, and thus of interest to the Constable family business (the word 'corn' in Britain denoted all cereal

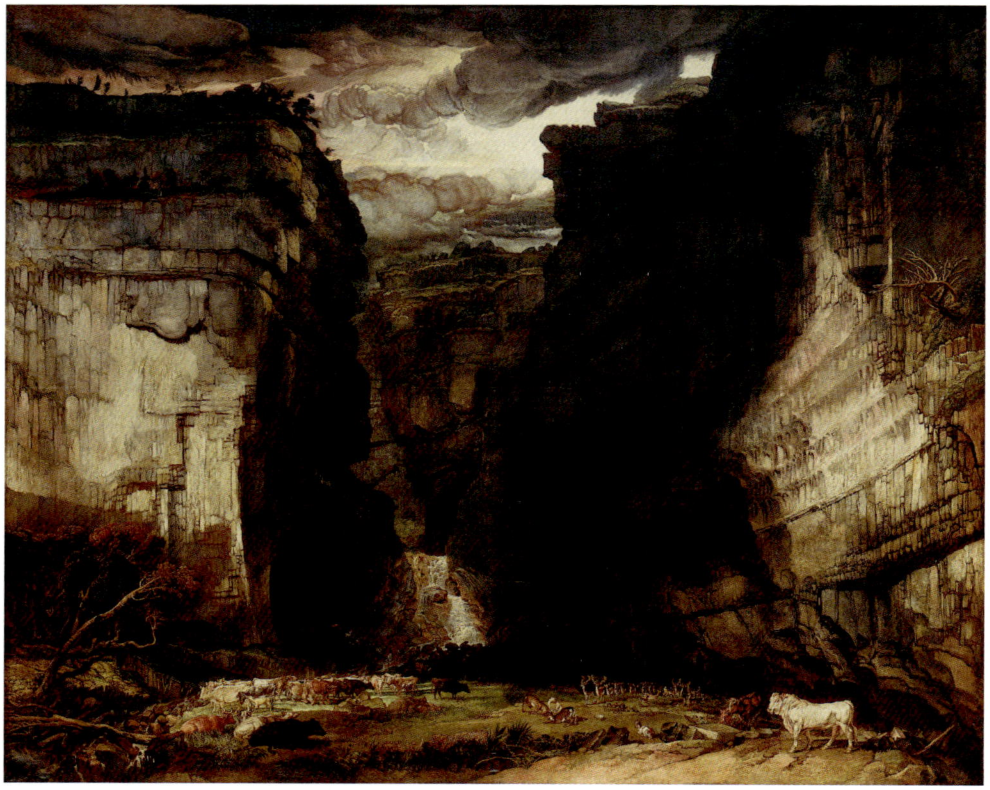

Fig. 9
James Ward (1769–1859)
Gordale Scar (A View of Gordale, in the Manor of East Malham in Craven, Yorkshire, the Property of Lord Ribblesdale), ?1812–14, exhibited 1815
Oil on canvas, 332.7 × 421.6 cm
Tate, London

grains, including wheat, oats and barley). With food shortages and rising prices for basics such as bread, the labouring and working classes were doubly hit. Charles Williams's satire of 1816, 'Political Balance' (see fig. 52), was one of many to highlight the distress and inequality caused, which ultimately brought the demand for political reform to a heightened pitch across the UK.[44]

It was under these complex and socially divisive circumstances that the Royal Academy exhibition opened on 7 May 1821 at its premises in Somerset House. The display included more than 1,000 exhibits by some 600 artists and architects, professionals and amateurs, veterans and newcomers, with the painter Sir Thomas Lawrence (1769–1830) participating as the recently elected President, having succeeded Benjamin West (1738–1820). The exhibition walls continued to be dominated by portraiture, submitted by Lawrence, Henry Raeburn, Thomas Phillips and many others, with fewer examples representing subject categories, whether allegorical, historical or contemporary genre, and a range of landscapes and townscapes, coastal scenes and seascapes, by Constable and his exact contemporaries Augustus Wall Callcott and William Collins, alongside submissions by younger painters, including Francis Danby, John Linnell (see fig. 60) and Constable's early biographer, C.R. Leslie.[45]

Unusually, Turner did not show at the Royal Academy that year. One explanation for this temporary absence is that he had alighted on an alternative and highly lucrative forum for his work in watercolour – that is, a succession of topographical print projects, including estate portraiture, financed by wealthy individuals, such as *The Vale of Ashburnham* (see fig. 57) for John Fuller's 'Views in Sussex' series, or organised as commercial enterprises by professional engraver-publishers. This reflected a broader trend in the print market for specifically British subjects, bolstered by limited opportunities for foreign travel during the extended war period, and the related growth in domestic tourism, previously discussed.[46] At the same time, the medium itself was popularised for both professionals and amateurs, and increasingly promoted as a distinctly English 'national art' – a notion supported by such initiatives as the formation of the Society of Painters in Watercolour in 1804. Unprecedented in their breadth and quality, Turner's own watercolours were, from 1819, reaching a wider audience beyond the Academy through privately staged exhibitions.[47]

Meanwhile, Constable had demonstrated in recent years his growing confidence and ambition by exhibiting progressively larger works, starting with *A Summerland* (private collection) in 1814 to his largest work to date, *Flatford Mill* (see fig. 16) in 1817, while still resolutely drawing inspiration from his first-hand knowledge of the landscape and rural workers of his native Suffolk. Since the inauguration of public art exhibitions in London, particularly at the Society of Artists in 1761 and the Royal Academy in 1769, audiences for art had expanded well beyond connoisseurs and patrons. The resulting emphasis on spectacle within the crowded and competitive environment of exhibition spaces meant that artists were now openly vying for attention. Consequently, the material scale or size of an artwork was as decisive a factor as palette and handling. A case in point is the vast, brooding picture of Gordale Scar in North Yorkshire by James Ward (fig. 9), exhibited at the Royal Academy in 1815. At over three metres high by four metres wide, its scale was unprecedented at that date in British landscape painting, and, as a recognisable English location, treated in a heroic manner, it was more than a hint to Constable, whose career at the time (despite his being almost 40 years of age) was only just launching. Four years later, *The White Horse* (see fig. 21) – the first of Constable's great landscape canvasses (or 'six-footers') representing the river Stour – was exhibited, ensuring his election as an Associate Royal Academician.[48] This was followed in 1820 by the second of that series, *Stratford Mill* (see fig. 40). Constable submitted four oil paintings the year after, including two small-scale views of Harrow and Hampstead Heath, and his third 'six-footer', the latter evoking an everyday, rural scene during the harvest season, featuring an empty wooden wagon (or wain) crossing a mill stream at Flatford, with a meadow beyond and haymakers in the distance.[49] It was a location that Constable had known from childhood, and had sketched and painted from different viewpoints for over a decade. Simply titled 'Landscape: Noon' in the accompanying exhibition catalogue – albeit privately referred to by Constable and his friend John Fisher as 'Hay Wain' – this large-scale painting hung not in the crowded display of the Great Room but in an adjoining, more modest space.[50]

A tale of two cities

The critical response to *The Hay Wain* was largely favourable, if qualified.[51] Surprisingly, perhaps, given its current status as a much-loved icon of British art, it was not the most acclaimed painting of 1821. In fact, judging by the volume of published reviews, Constable's masterpiece, as we see it, was relatively speaking overshadowed by other, mainly figurative, paintings (some long forgotten) by the likes of Sir David Wilkie, William Mulready (see fig. 61) and William Etty.[52] This in part reflects the attitude of the reviewers, who tended to esteem figure paintings over landscapes, especially if the latter (in the opinion of one reviewer, referring to *The Hay Wain*) was a 'lowly scene, faithfully executed in the modest colouring of nature'.[53] Moreover, the season's acknowledged 'picture of the year' was John Martin's richly coloured biblical epic, *Belshazzar's Feast* (fig. 10, copy of original) – a highly theatrical exhibition piece *par excellence* – which had for some months been drawing large crowds, not at the Academy, but at the nearby British Institution on Pall Mall.[54]

While the Napoleonic Wars had shaped (and would continue to shape) the lives of all British citizens, the 1821 exhibition unusually made little direct reference to recent events. This was not the case in other years. Turner's *Field of Waterloo* (now at Tate), exhibited in 1818, presented the grim aftermath of the battle, and Wilkie's *Chelsea Pensioners reading the Waterloo Dispatch* (Apsley House), painted for the victorious allied commander, the Duke of Wellington, caused a sensation in 1822. Both were bold statements on the impact of the war on the lives of everyday people.[55] In comparison, Constable's *Hay Wain* was an understated, naturalistic English scene of rural labour, seemingly undisturbed by the tumultuous events of the recent past or present – in many ways, a kind of parallel universe. But the post-war period itself was marked by economic, social and political crises, emblematic of which was the 'Peterloo Massacre' of 1819 – the brutal suppression of a mass meeting at St Peter's Field, Manchester, calling for parliamentary reform (the majority of the 60,000 who came to hear Henry Hunt were workers from across urban and rural Lancashire).[56] In this context, perhaps what Constable aimed to offer his first audience, only 16 months later, was a vision of the British landscape as a reassuringly constant and serene presence in a time of continual change and uncertainty.

The Hay Wain remained unsold when the Royal Academy exhibition closed in July. Constable sent the painting to the British Institution's sale exhibition the following year. There it was seen by the dealer John Arrowsmith, who eventually purchased and then sent it, together with Constable's *View on the Stour near Dedham* (see fig. 28) and a small sea piece of Yarmouth, to the so-called 'British' Salon of 1824, held at the Louvre in Paris. Constable was honoured with a gold medal (see p. 8), alongside fellow Englishmen Richard Parkes Bonington (see fig. 62) and the watercolourist Copley Fielding (1787–1855). All three had exhibited landscapes.[57]

Interest in Constable had been growing in France since 1821, fanned by the enthusiasm of influential French writers and artists, such as Charles Nodier and

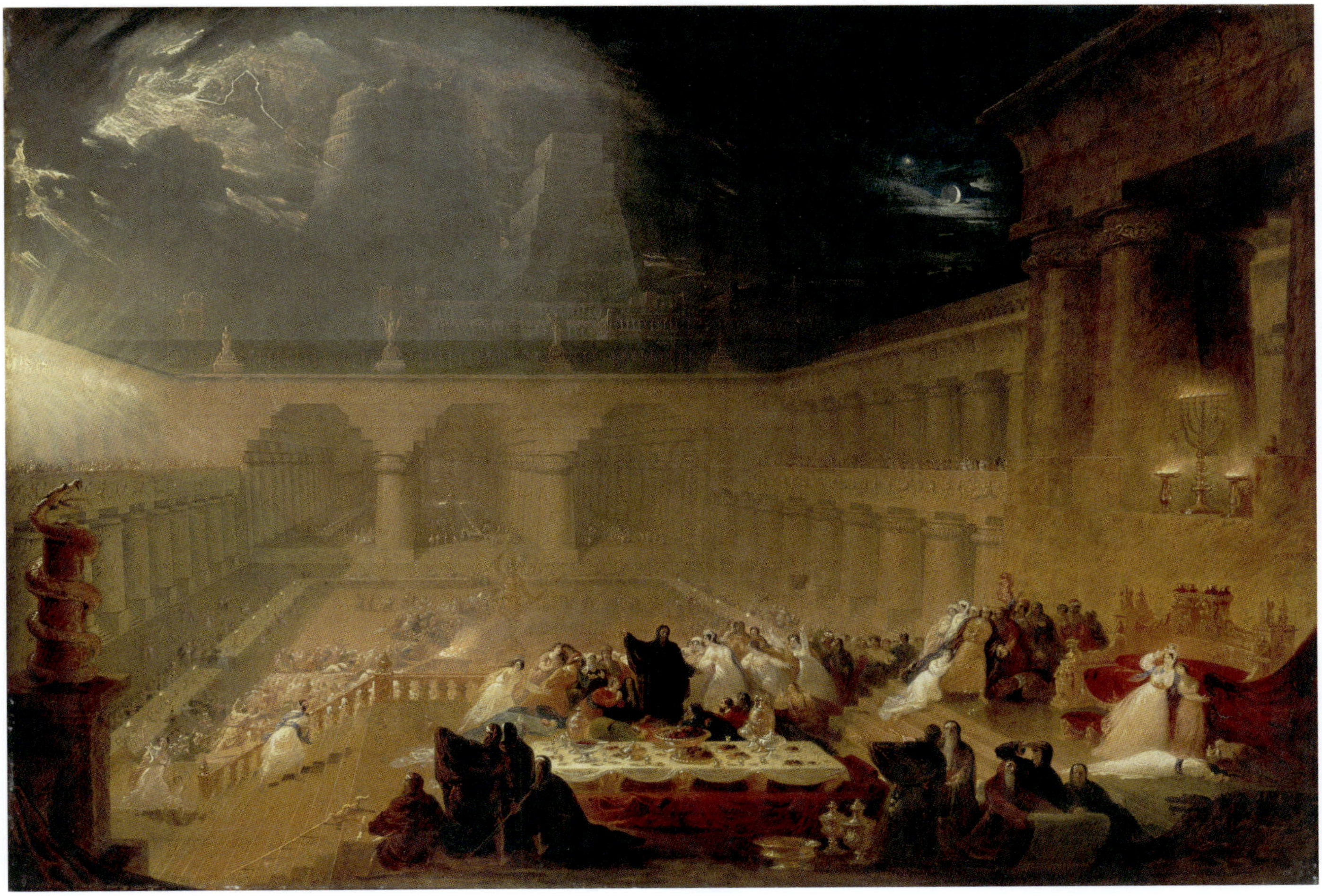

Fig. 10
John Martin (1789–1854)
Belshazzar's Feast, 1820
Oil on canvas, 80 × 120.7 cm
Yale Center for British Art, Paul Mellon Collection, New Haven

Théodore Géricault (1791–1824), who, during their visits to London, had admired *The Hay Wain* principally because of Constable's innovative approach to pictorial naturalism. Given the potential market for his paintings on the Continent, Constable was both amused by and welcoming of the unprecedented attention and debate his paintings had provoked across the Channel. Indeed, so different was the reception between London and Paris that the claim has often been made that it was the French who 'discovered' Constable during the 1820s, while his quiet radicalism went unrecognised in England. Constable himself was often frustrated and disappointed by his contemporaries' inability (as he saw it) to fully appreciate his novel approach to landscape art.[58] But he was not ignored. In fact, Constable had been exhibiting almost 20 years before *The Hay Wain* appeared in 1821. Anyone interested in art, therefore, had had ample opportunity in London to follow his artistic journey. The opposite was true for the French. Consequently, for those seeking new directions in post-war Paris, *The Hay Wain* came as a revelation.

EMMA ROODHOUSE

'Pure nature's soul': The Emergence of a Natural Painter

In January 1799, the 23-year-old aspiring artist John Constable (fig. 11) was staying at the Manor House in Ipswich, home of the wealthy John and Elizabeth Cobbold, friends of his parents. For the Constable family, Ipswich was a place of business, banking and recreation, and for young John, in particular, it was a place where he could meet like-minded people who might encourage his work as an artist. The scientist, artist and poet Elizabeth Cobbold (1765–1824) took an interest in nurturing local talent and could provide a wide network of contacts.[1] During Constable's stay, Elizabeth introduced him to Priscilla Wakefield (1750–1832), the Quaker writer and philanthropist – a pivotal meeting that would furnish him with an introduction to the London art scene, through a letter to the artist Joseph Farington (1747–1821) and entry to the Royal Academy Schools in London: 'Spent the evening at Mrs. Cobbold's ... met there Mr. J. Constable a pleasing modest young man – who had a natural genius for painting.'[2] More importantly, Elizabeth and Priscilla's assistance would finally convince Constable's parents to let him pursue his training as an artist – a career choice they had not envisioned for their son.

At the newly built East Bergholt House in Suffolk, 28-year-old Ann Constable (1748–1815; fig. 12) had given birth to her fourth child on 11 June 1776. Her husband, Golding Constable (1739–1816), immediately sent for his close friend the Revd Walter Wren Driffield, clerk of Feering, to baptise the baby, as it seemed he would not survive. The infant John Constable did live, however, and soon joined his three siblings, eight-year-old Ann, seven-year-old Martha and two-year-old Golding. (Two more children would join John in later years, Mary and Abram.) The Constable family had lived in East Anglia

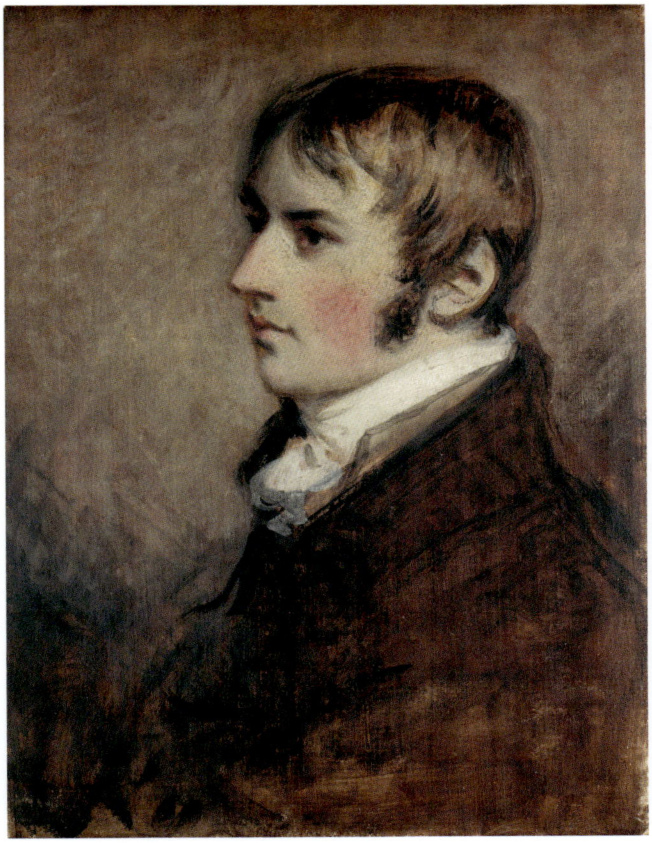

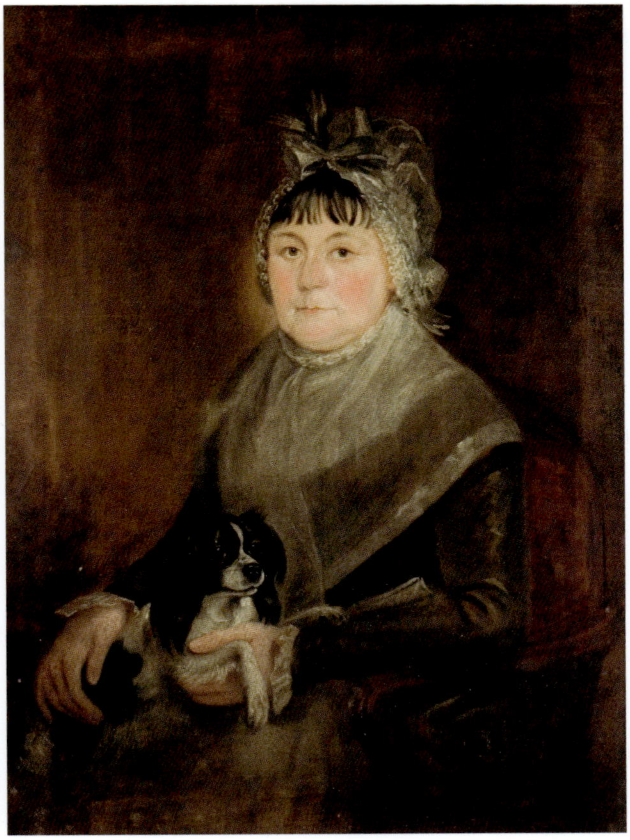

Fig. 11
Daniel Gardner (1750–1805)
John Constable, RA, at the Age of Twenty, 1796
Tempera on canvas, 69.6 × 57.4 cm
Victoria and Albert Museum, London

Fig. 12
Ann Constable, the Artist's Mother, about 1800–5
Oil on canvas, 90 × 69 cm
Colchester & Ipswich Museums: Colchester City Council

for generations, and Golding and Ann occupied a prominent place in the local community through their ownership of mills, barges and land. At the age of 26, Golding had been fortunate enough to inherit a substantial bequest from his father's uncle Abram. This inheritance included stocks in trade and shipping, around £3,000 in cash and government securities, furniture, and property in East Bergholt. The will also presented a home for Golding and his future wife, through the tenancy of Flatford Mill. The location and the industry along the banks of the river Stour later provided their son John with endless subject matter for drawing and painting.

Golding and Ann had originally hoped that John would enter the Church, and they ensured he received an appropriate education at the grammar school in Dedham. Constable would walk from East Bergholt House, passing the church of St Mary, where the family had its own pew. Descending down Fen Lane, past the cornfields following the river Stour, he continued towards Dedham, crossing over the county border into Essex. The cottage Constable passed every day on his way to and from school featured in two later paintings (for one example, see fig. 65). This routine walk, taken in all seasons, provided constant inspiration to draw and paint, and rather less for academic study:

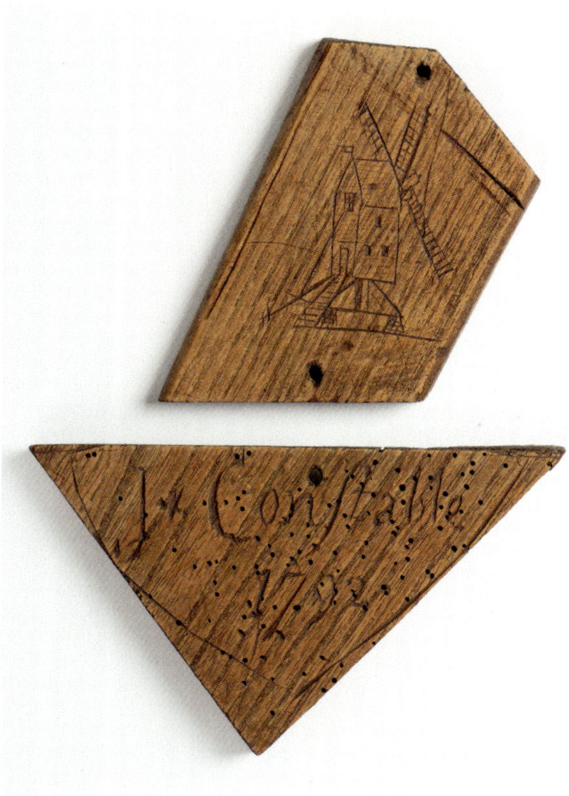

Fig. 13
Fragments of Pitt's Mill, East Bergholt, with carvings by John Constable, 1792.
Wood, 12.4 × 8.5 cm; 9.5 × 17 cm
Colchester & Ipswich Museums: Colchester City Council

> During his French lessons a long pause would frequently occur, which his master would be the first to break, saying, 'Go on, I am not asleep: Oh! now I see you are in your painting-room.'[3]

Constable was brought up in a household with conservative views on class and the existing social strata of rural life, alongside a deep belief in the importance of the Anglican Church. Ann and Golding not only wanted their son to honour these values, but they also encouraged him to take on the family business and work in his father's mills. The fact that he carved a depiction of Pitt's Mill on one of the timbers while he was working there as a teenager (fig. 13) suggests that his attention often strayed away from the occupation of milling. Fortuitously Constable's younger brother Abram (1783–1862) eventually took on the business, allowing John the freedom to pursue his career in London and providing financial stability for the wider family. However, John would retain these conventional family values throughout his life, even in the pursuit of a radical approach to art.

Constable was very fortunate to have a neighbour who could provide artistic companionship and encouragement. John Dunthorne Sr (1770–1844) was somewhat older than Constable. He was a working-class painter – commissioned to produce inn signs and hatchments – and a skilled woodworker, especially in making musical instruments. Dunthorne's marriage to Hannah Bird, a widow 13 years his senior, had brought him to East Bergholt. The couple had four children, one of whom, John, became Constable's only studio assistant.

The elder Dunthorne and Constable would walk, sketch and discuss approaches to art. When Constable was finally able to progress his art career at the Academy Schools in London, the letters he wrote to Dunthorne are honest and open about his true feelings regarding the art world:

> Still Nature is the fountain's head, the source from whence all originally must spring – ... I am come to a determination to make no idle visits this summer or to give up my time to common place people. I shall shortly return to Bergholt where I shall make some laborious studies from nature ... there is room enough for a natural painter.[4]

This pursuit of being a 'natural painter' was to inform how Constable approached creating pictures of his native scenes (see fig. 72), and even though it was not fashionable he was determined to continue on this path.

Ann Constable realised that if her son wanted to pursue a career as an artist, he would need connections of a higher social status than Dunthorne. She turned to Lady Rachel Beaumont (1717/18–1814), who lived in Dedham, and her son Sir George Howland Beaumont (1753–1827), an amateur painter, patron of the arts and collector of old masters. On one of the artist's visits to Dedham, the latter showed him the small richly painted oil of *Landscape with Hagar and the Angel* by Claude, now in the National Gallery.[5] It was a moment of revelation, in which Constable saw how he wanted to approach landscape painting, and Claude's work certainly influenced his depictions of Dedham Vale. Beaumont also allowed Constable to study the old masters at his London house, where the artist made copies of paintings by the influential landscape artist Richard Wilson[6] and the watercolourist Thomas Girtin (1775–1802). The influence of Beaumont and his collection was acknowledged by Constable later in his life, when he wrote to William Wordsworth: 'I feel that I am indebted to him for what I am as an artist.'[7]

In 1796, Constable's parents advocated a visit to his maternal aunt Jane and her husband, the brewer Thomas Allen, in Edmonton, London. The aim of the visit was perhaps to encourage Constable to see the virtue of family-run businesses. Instead, the trip introduced him to John Thomas Smith (1766–1833), a commercial printmaker, and the painter John Cranch (1751–1821), who would furnish him with a cultural reading list, instructions for printmaking and guidance on art techniques.

Constable was eager to impress his new mentors and quickly took to sketching country cottages, in assistance of Smith's forthcoming publication *Remarks on Rural Scenery*. St Mary's Church in East Bergholt also seemed a suitable subject for experimentation (fig. 14): 'I shall soon send you our Church, I was thinking of painting it in oil, would it suit you as well to etch from?'[8] Smith responded enthusiastically and even wrote to Constable's

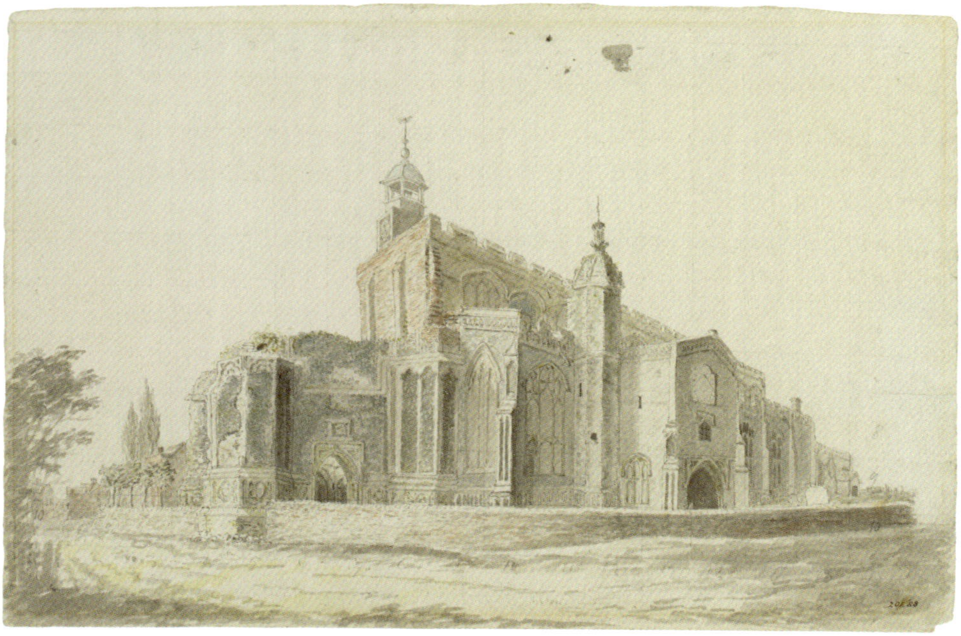

Fig. 14
East Bergholt Church: The Exterior from the South-West, about 1796–9
Pen, ink and watercolour on paper, 25.8 × 39.7 cm
Victoria and Albert Museum, London

mother to commend him. It was through Smith that Constable began to research the important Suffolk artist Thomas Gainsborough, in Ipswich, where the artist had lived from 1752 to 1759: 'There is a place up the river side where he often sat to sketch, on account of the beauty of the landscape, its extensiveness, and richness in variety, both in fore and back grounds.'[9]

Constable sought out the self-taught artist George Frost (1744/5–1821), a Gainsborough collector who ran the coaches from Ipswich to London. He would regularly go out walking with his drawing materials and sketch in the same locations as had Gainsborough, along the river Orwell – a practice Frost also encouraged in Constable. Constable wrote to Smith, 'I believe I may be here a fortnight longer. It is a most delightful country for a painter. I fancy I see Gainsborough in every hedge and hollow tree.'[10]

In the years when Constable was in Ipswich (1802–3) he often visited Elizabeth Cobbold and went out walking with Frost, sketching the ships and warehouses at Ipswich docks. Constable treasured these early friendships and retained at least 27 Frost drawings for his own collection in London. His time with Frost also established his habit of drawing on the move and always carrying a sketchbook in his pocket, ready to dash out spontaneous observations (see fig. 67). This approach of quick sketching in the open landscape later informed his work in watercolour and oils, ultimately providing the source material for his larger-scale Academy paintings.

In 1802, Constable achieved his first acceptance for the Academy exhibition – a landscape. There was still family pressure to find paid work, however, and through the Suffolk friendship of Dr John Fisher (1748–1825), rector of Langham in Essex and future Bishop of Salisbury, Constable found himself applying for a job as drawing master at the Royal Military College in Great Marlow. Fortunately, he was steered away from the position by advice from Joseph Farington and the President of the Academy, Benjamin West. Fisher would remain an early patron, and introduced Constable to his nephew, the Revd John Fisher (1788–1832), with whom the artist developed a deep friendship and could correspond on art, poetry and their shared faith in the Anglican Church.

From June 1802, Constable was beginning to establish his pattern of returning to East Bergholt in the summer months, to sketch and paint, and then taking these studies back to London for the winter. On one of these visits home, he met and subsequently fell in love with Maria Bicknell (1788–1828), granddaughter of the Revd Dr Durand Rhudde, rector of East Bergholt. It was a long courtship, drawn out by Rhudde's opposition, with the couple writing many letters to each other. Constable painted views towards the rectory, where Maria would stay, amid richly coloured sunsets over Dedham Vale, expressing his feelings more strongly than he was able to do with words. He was becoming more skilled in the use of oils, employing a wider range of colours in an effort to elevate his depictions of his beloved Stour Valley, as well as his renown as an artist (fig. 15):

> From the window where I am writing, I see all those sweet fields where we have passed so many happy hours together. It is with a melancholy pleasure that I revisit those scenes that once saw us so happy – yet it is gratifying to me to think that the scenes of my boyish days should have witnessed by far the most affecting event of my life.[11]

Early in 1815 the American war of 1812 finally ended with the signing of the Treaty of Ghent, and that summer also brought about the longed-for victory over Napoleon at the Battle of Waterloo – a war in which Constable's cousins were involved, and one died, through their deployment with the army and navy. As for Constable, he was six years into his courtship with Maria and had still not been elected an Associate of the Academy, and so he returned to the East Bergholt family home. In March of that year, Ann Constable had collapsed in her flower garden and died shortly thereafter. Constable did not attend the funeral. By summer, his father was seriously ill, and the Constable children faced a future without either of their strong-willed parents. During this time, Constable created two highly personal works as a tribute to his parents and the world of his childhood. The two small paintings, *Golding Constable's Flower Garden* (see fig. 63) and *Golding Constable's Kitchen Garden* (see fig. 64), encompass all the aspects of the landscape he loved best, while also alluding to his parents' interests. Despite the title of its picture, the flower garden had been created and nurtured by Ann, for her own pleasure. It is shown in deep shade, while the view of the kitchen garden reflects Golding's cultivation of and commercial profit from the land.

The garden paintings were not created for London audiences. Rather, they were to remain with Constable for the rest of his life. He had realised that artworks created for the commercial world needed to make a powerful impact, and one way to achieve that effect was to work on a much larger scale in an effort to capture the true natural landscape. Constable no doubt also hoped that a commercial success would help him obtain one of those elusive Associateship places at the Academy, and so prove to his father that he had made something of himself. As he wrote to Maria:

> I have been so much out, endeavouring to catch the last of this beautifull [*sic*] year ... I have put rather a larger landscape on hand than ever I did before and this it is my wish to secure in a great measure before I leave this place.[12]

In pursuance of this goal, Constable returned to the locations he knew and loved best, writing to Dunthorne, 'I am determined to finish a small picture on the spot for every one I intend to make in future.'[13]

Flatford, East Bergholt, Dedham, and particularly the area around Willy Lott's House, or 'Gibbeon's Gate Farm' as it was then known, were his favoured locations. The Lotts were a farming family who had leased Valley Farm since the eighteenth century. They were well known to the Constables through business dealings. William 'Willy' Lott (1761–1849) had grown up in Flatford, and, although uneducated due to poor health as a child, he would ultimately manage to raise enough money to buy the house that would later bear his name (fig. 18), and the surrounding land, in 1825. When Abram and sister Mary moved into the house at Flatford Mill, after their parents' death, they would become very friendly with their neighbours, the Lotts. Willy lived to the age of 88; his grave remains in East Bergholt churchyard.

The house is a feature of *The Mill Stream* (see fig. 74). Painted much earlier than *The Hay Wain*, it would contain foundational elements – the gable end of the house with a woman bending down to the stream, reflections and churning water. Earlier sketches would be scaled up for transfer to this larger canvas as Constable experimented with the composition and pushed himself as an artist. He thought highly enough of this image to use it as the basis for one of the mezzotints included in the 'English Landscape' series of 1831.

On 14 May 1816, Golding Constable died at the age of 78. He did not live to see his son married, or recognised by the Academy. Abram Constable now took on the family businesses, selling East Bergholt House and dividing up the income between his siblings. Constable found solace in painting an oil sketch of Willy Lott's House, with the ivy creeping towards the roof and the roses climbing around the fence, a trail of smoke drifting out of the chimney (see fig. 75). He dated this work 29 July 1816 – the day of the death of his uncle David Pike Watts, who had helped him early in his career. This oil sketch, painted outdoors, was another important visual aid he employed during the creation of *The Hay Wain*.

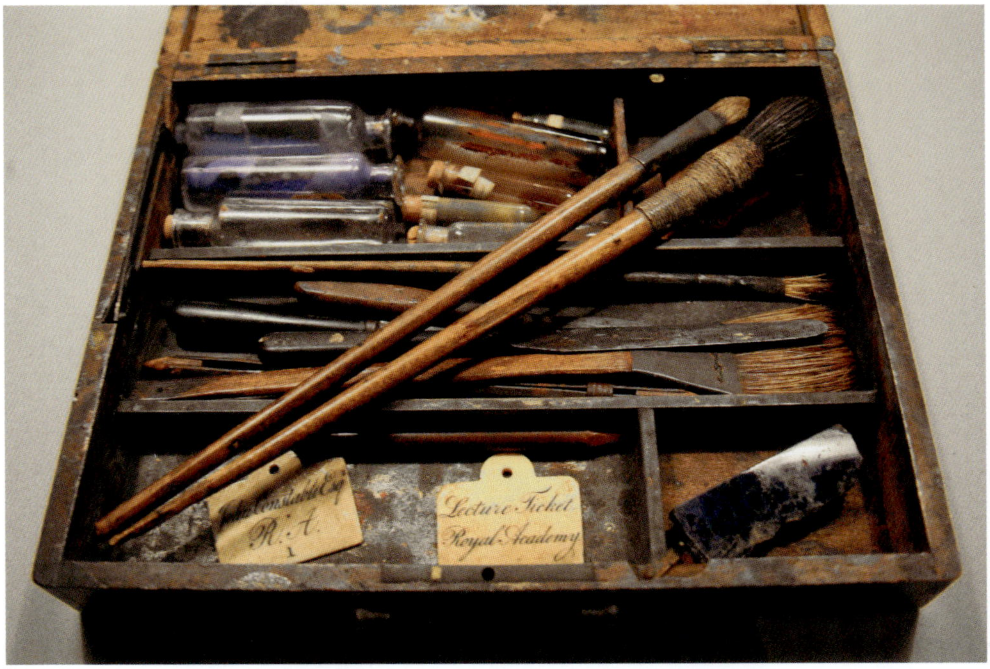

Fig. 15
John Constable's wooden portable sketching box (detail)
23 × 30 cm
On loan to Gainsborough House from the Constable family

Change and grief followed the Constable family during these years. Britain had been through a turbulent period, with the end of the Napoleonic Wars in 1815 and the great social unrest that ensued. In East Bergholt, there was protest against the Enclosure Act, which divided up formerly common land, with Constable commenting to Maria:

> The village has been quite in a bustle about the division of our Common ... Some amongst us have shown such extreme greediness and rapacity to 'lay field to field' as to make themselves obnoxious. That thank God is not our case ...[14]

With increased income from the family businesses after the death of his father, a flurry of painting commissions, and enthusiastic encouragement from his close friend John Fisher, Constable decided that now was the time he could propose marriage to Maria Bicknell. On 2 October 1816, the Revd Fisher conducted the marriage ceremony at St Martin-in-the-Fields and the couple finally began their life together. After a honeymoon in Dorset with the Fishers, the newlyweds returned to London. There, Constable continued his preparations for the largest painting depicting the working river he had ever submitted to the Academy. *Flatford Mill ('Scene on a Navigable River')* was an ambitious painting to undertake with his practice of painting outdoors and would push his development further in creating large-scale canvases worthy of exhibition (fig. 16): 'I am now in the midst of a large picture here which I had contemplated for the next Exhibition – it would have made my mind easy had it been forwarder ...'[15]

The painting would return to London for further finishing and even after the Academy show Constable altered the entire sky and trees. The imagery of *Flatford Mill* still derives from earlier sketchbook studies and observations. It includes key details of the scenes Constable had noted since boyhood, looking down the tow path towards the mill, with Valley Farm in the distance, the locks, barges, working horses, and labourers in the fields, and the red brick of Flatford Mill standing amid the woodland. Constable had high hopes for this painting, anticipating that it would propel him to the Associateship of the Academy. He playfully added his signature as if it had been scratched into the baked earth of the tow path.

Unfortunately, he was not successful. Instead, he found refuge in his new family: Maria gave birth to a baby boy on 4 December 1817, and he was named John Charles. Constable's later life was spent mostly in London, but his familial and spiritual ties in East Anglia continued to draw him back over the years, and these later visits always refreshed his visual memory of his beloved Suffolk landscapes:

> I have been this morning a walk up the Langham Hills, and through a number of beautifull feilds [*sic*] & by the side of the river – and in my life I never saw Nature more lovely ... I was at Ipswich yesterday, this afternoon, I am going to walk to Holton Hall with Abram, to see the Cooks ...[16]

It may have been one of these visits back to Suffolk, as well as the impending birth of their second child, Maria Louisa (Minna) on 19 July 1819, that persuaded the Constables to seek out Hampstead for their health during the summer months. They finally settled in Well Walk from 1827. It was a place that could provide inspiration, with its elevated views across the capital and its relatively clear, unpolluted skies. This unleashed a flurry of outdoor oil sketches depicting the changing weather, and these highlight Constable's wider interests in meteorology and natural sciences, which would assist in his aspiration to be a 'natural painter':

> Painting is a science and should be pursued as an inquiry into the laws of nature. Why, then, may not a landscape be considered as a branch of natural philosophy, of which pictures are but experiments.[17]

Finally, at the age of 43 and now a married man and father of two, in November 1819, Constable 'was last night by a large majority elected an Associate of the Royal Academy'.[18] Immediately writing to his brother Abram, he added this momentous news almost as a postscript. After years of patient perseverance with his Suffolk scenes, he had achieved recognition by the Academy.

Constable now concentrated on creating his 'six-footer' series of paintings, building up to *The Hay Wain*. He still returned to East Bergholt, Colchester and Ipswich from time to time, to visit friends and family, and as late as 1821

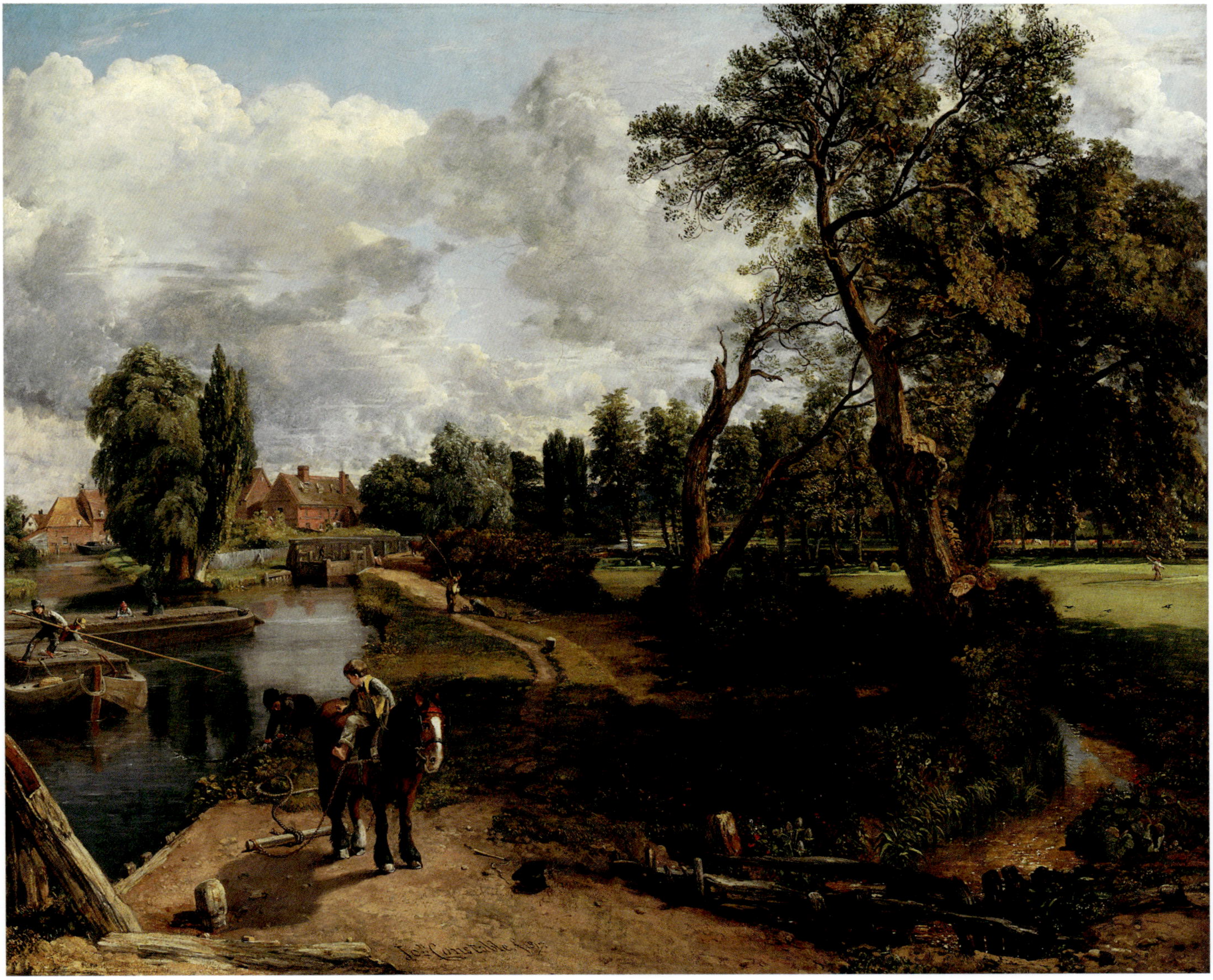

Fig. 16
Flatford Mill ('Scene on a Navigable River'), 1816–17
Oil on canvas, 101.6 × 127 cm
Tate, London

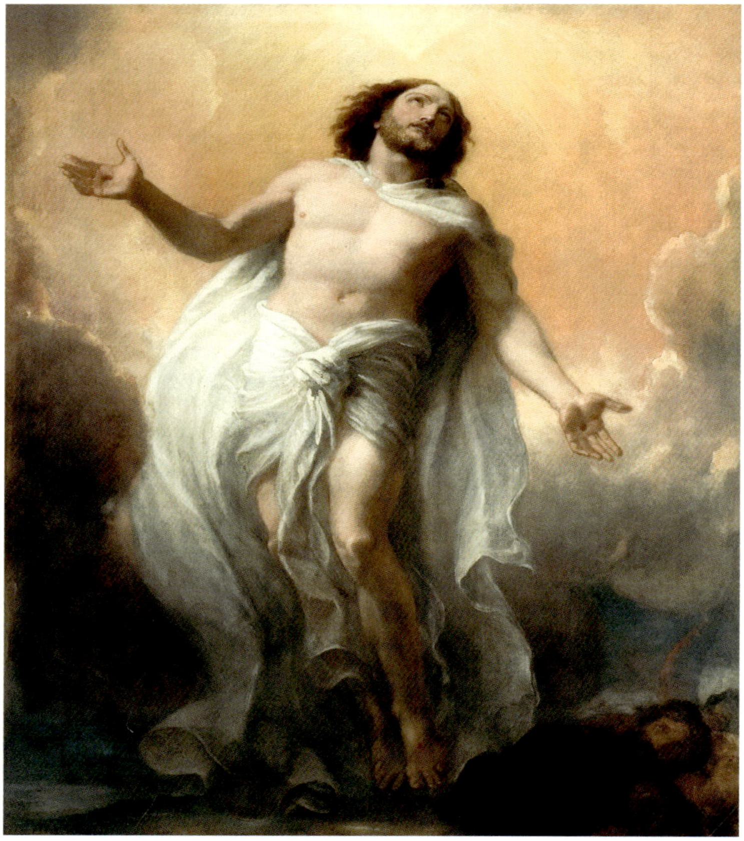

Fig. 17
The Ascension, 1821–2
Oil on canvas, 162.5 × 127 cm
The Constable Trust

Fig. 18
Detail from *The Hay Wain* (fig. 2), showing Willy Lott's House.

he took a commission for a church painting. Shortly after *The Hay Wain* was exhibited (July 1821), Edward Alston, a brewer who was distantly related to the Constables, approached him to create a painting for the parish church of St Michael at Manningtree (now on display in St Mary's Church, Dedham; fig. 17). It was to be Constable's final religious commission. Previous such works had been completed for St Michael's Church in Brantham (*Christ blessing the Children*, 1805) and St James's Church in Nayland (*Christ blessing the Elements*, 1810). The 1821 painting amounted to an attempt to win the favour of the Revd John Jefferson, Archdeacon of Colchester, who had the power to grant or deny licensing to public houses. It was a commercial project for Constable, although eventually he ended up paying for it himself as Jefferson died before its completion. At this stage in his career, Constable did not need this commission, but he took it probably in the service of the values with which he had been brought up – family, church and livelihood. The landscape of his childhood had inspired him as an artist, but it was his family, friends and early mentors who had formed who he was as a person.

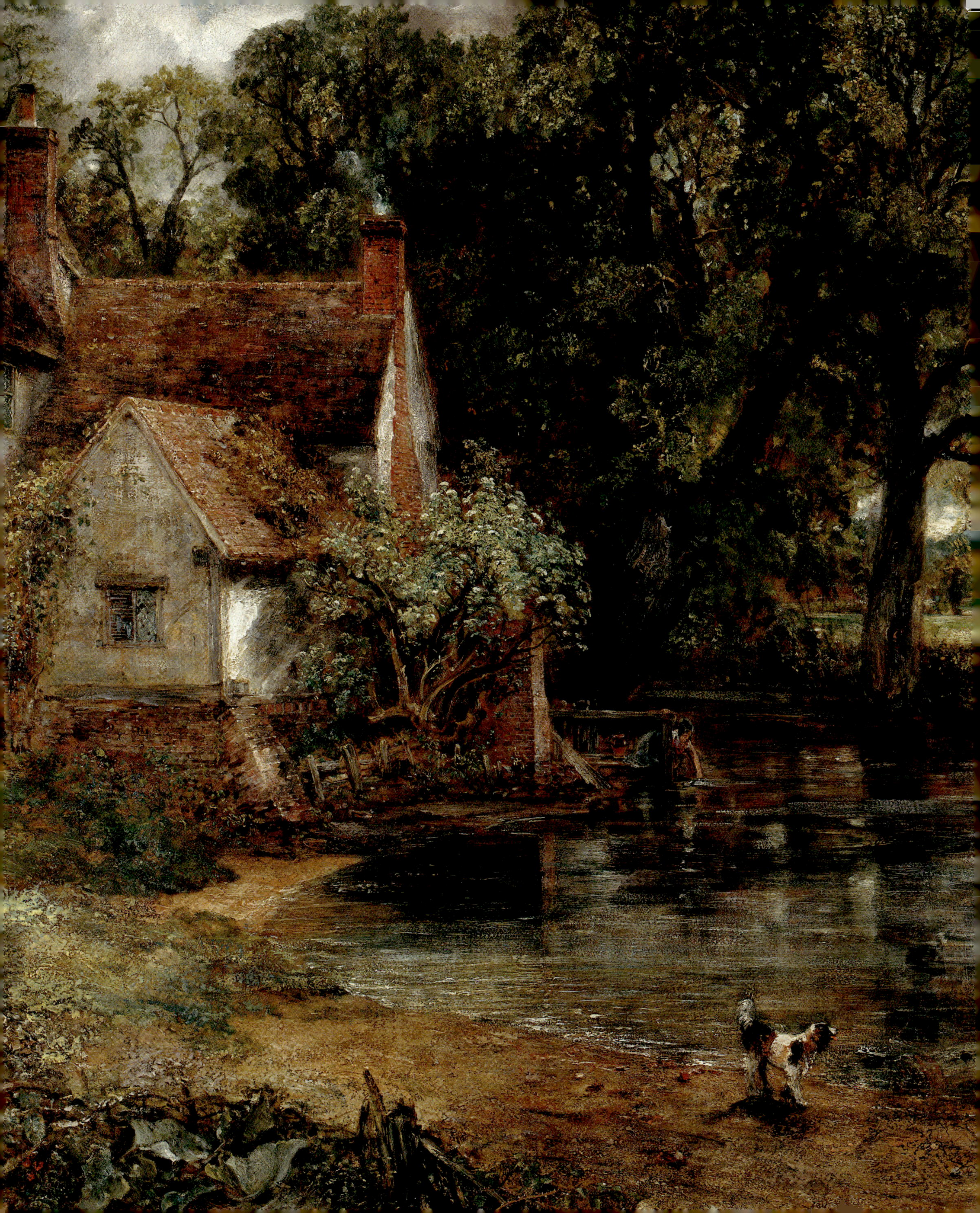

ANNE LYLES

'Rather a more novel look than I expected': The Making of *The Hay Wain*

Visitors to 'Constable Country' today usually find the highlight of their visit to be the moment when they reach the site shown in Constable's painting, *The Hay Wain* (see fig. 2). Having arrived at a position immediately behind Flatford Mill, at a point where the tail water from the mill used to flow into the mill stream, they see the familiar outline of Willy Lott's House to the left, and its surrounding landscape opening out on the right more or less unchanged since Constable's day, if a little more enclosed. The act of recognition is immediate. Generations of visitors have paused here to have themselves photographed against the familiar backdrop.

Indeed, such is the similarity of the scene today to that shown in *The Hay Wain*, and so faithfully has Constable apparently transposed it onto canvas, that it is not hard for many of those visitors to imagine that the artist painted the National Gallery picture in front of the view itself; and also, perhaps, to assume that he did so more or less effortlessly. This is, however, far from the case. *The Hay Wain* was actually painted by Constable in London in his studio, over a little less than five months, worked up – in stages – from several preliminary sketches. Moreover, despite the picture's air of truth to appearances, it in fact owes an important – if subtle – debt to the work of the old masters, especially to Dutch and Flemish painters of the seventeenth century.

Constable tends to be remembered today, thanks in great part to his biographer C.R. Leslie, as Britain's quintessential 'natural painter'. Leslie emphasised that one of the artist's most cherished painterly aims was 'truth to nature'.[1] It is indeed the case that, in the first half of his career in particular, Constable made many oil sketches directly in front of the motif. Furthermore, in the period 1814–17, Constable even attempted to paint pictures – ones he

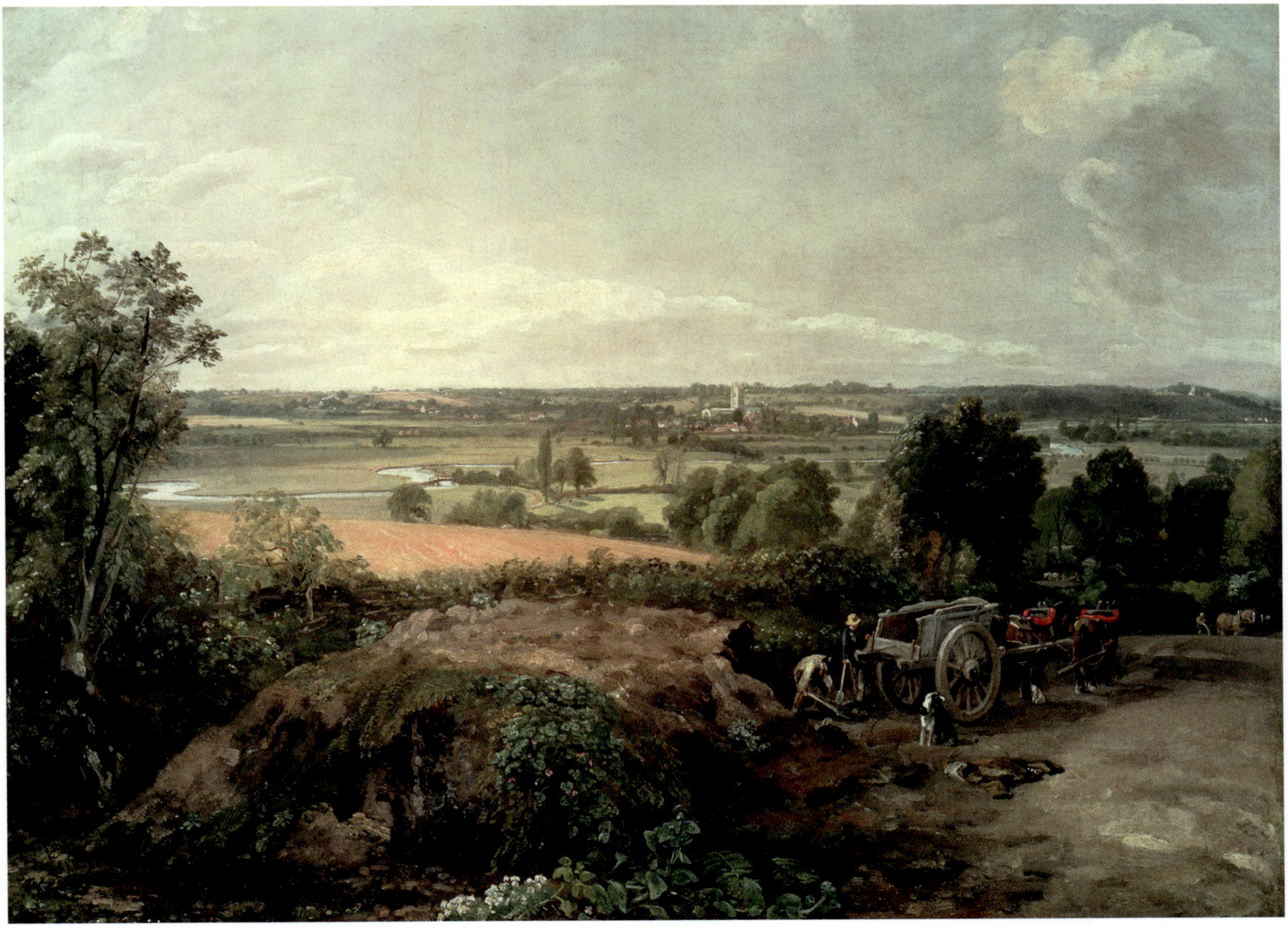

Fig. 19
Stour Valley and Dedham Church, about 1815
Oil on canvas, 55.6 × 77.8 cm
Museum of Fine Arts, Boston

intended to exhibit at the Royal Academy – substantially in the open air, a revolutionary practice for the period. *Stour Valley and Dedham Church* (fig. 19) is such an example, painted by Constable for the most part in front of the motif during the fine summer and early autumn mornings of 1814, and exhibited at the Academy the following year.

However, it is not always appreciated quite to what extent Constable's methods of working changed after his marriage to Maria Bicknell in the autumn of 1816. Thenceforward he lived and worked almost entirely in London, rather than spending long summers in Suffolk with his family. As he no longer had direct access to those rural scenes that were to remain the cornerstone of his art, he now had to recreate his Suffolk material synthetically in the studio. He was of course able to refer back to sketches he had made in earlier years on site. However, increasingly he found he needed to paint additional, purpose-made composition sketches to test out his ideas.

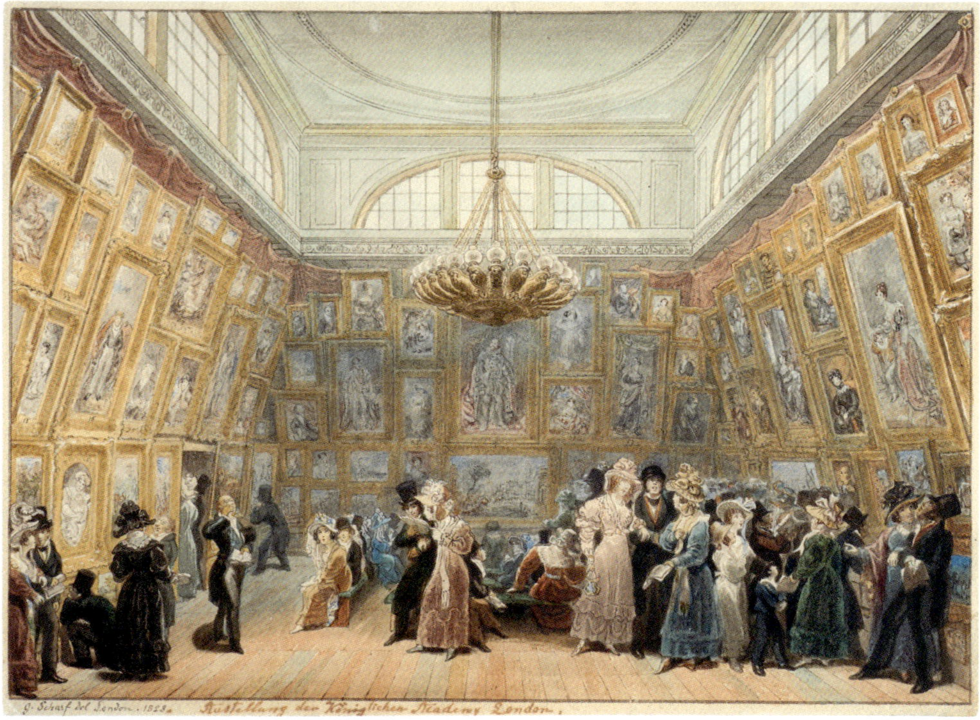

Fig. 20
George Scharf (1820–1895)
The Royal Academy Exhibition of 1828, 1828
Watercolour on paper, 18.4 × 26 cm
Museum of London

Fig. 21
The White Horse, 1819
Oil on canvas, 131.4 × 188.3 cm
The Frick Collection, New York

Moreover, from around 1818 Constable started to nurture an ambition to paint landscape on a much larger scale. He now began to paint on a canvas some six feet in width (or height) – something that would have been impractical in front of the motif. He was well aware that some of his key predecessors in landscape – Rubens, Ruisdael and Claude, for example – had often painted on this scale, and no doubt had their example partly in mind. In addition, after his marriage and permanent move to London, Constable was determined to ensure his work would make a more powerful impact at the annual exhibitions at the Royal Academy. He knew that a larger painting was more likely to stand out among the many pictures of varying sizes hung frame to frame in the exhibition spaces designed by William Chambers at Somerset House (fig. 20).

Constable's new strategy to paint on a larger scale was to pay immediate dividends. The first 'six-footer' he exhibited at the Academy, in 1819, *The White Horse* (fig. 21) was sufficiently well received that it helped secure his long-delayed election as an Associate Academician towards the end of that year. From now on, and for the rest of his career, Constable resolved to try to paint a large picture for every annual Academy exhibition, alongside some smaller pictures he knew would prove more saleable. The next five large canvases he painted for exhibition at the Academy, between 1820 and 1825, followed the example of *The White Horse* in showing scenes relating to the working life of the river Stour on or near Flatford Mill – subjects all taken from within a small geographical radius of about three miles. Together these six canvases are today generally regarded as a series. *The Hay Wain*, exhibited in 1821, is the third in the series, following *The White Horse* in 1819 and *Stratford Mill* (see fig. 40) exhibited in 1820. It was followed in 1822 by *View on the Stour near Dedham* (see fig. 28). After a break in the series in 1823 when, due to ill health, Constable was unable to paint a large landscape for the Academy exhibition, two more paintings of Suffolk river scenes were to follow over the next two years: *The Lock* (1824, private collection) and *The Leaping Horse* (1825, Royal Academy of Arts, London).

The Hay Wain is a painting that, of course, can be appreciated on its own terms, for its own inherent qualities. Yet it is also important to bear in mind its position in the series. For when examined as a group, it is clear that – as the series progresses – these large paintings of river Stour subjects gain in

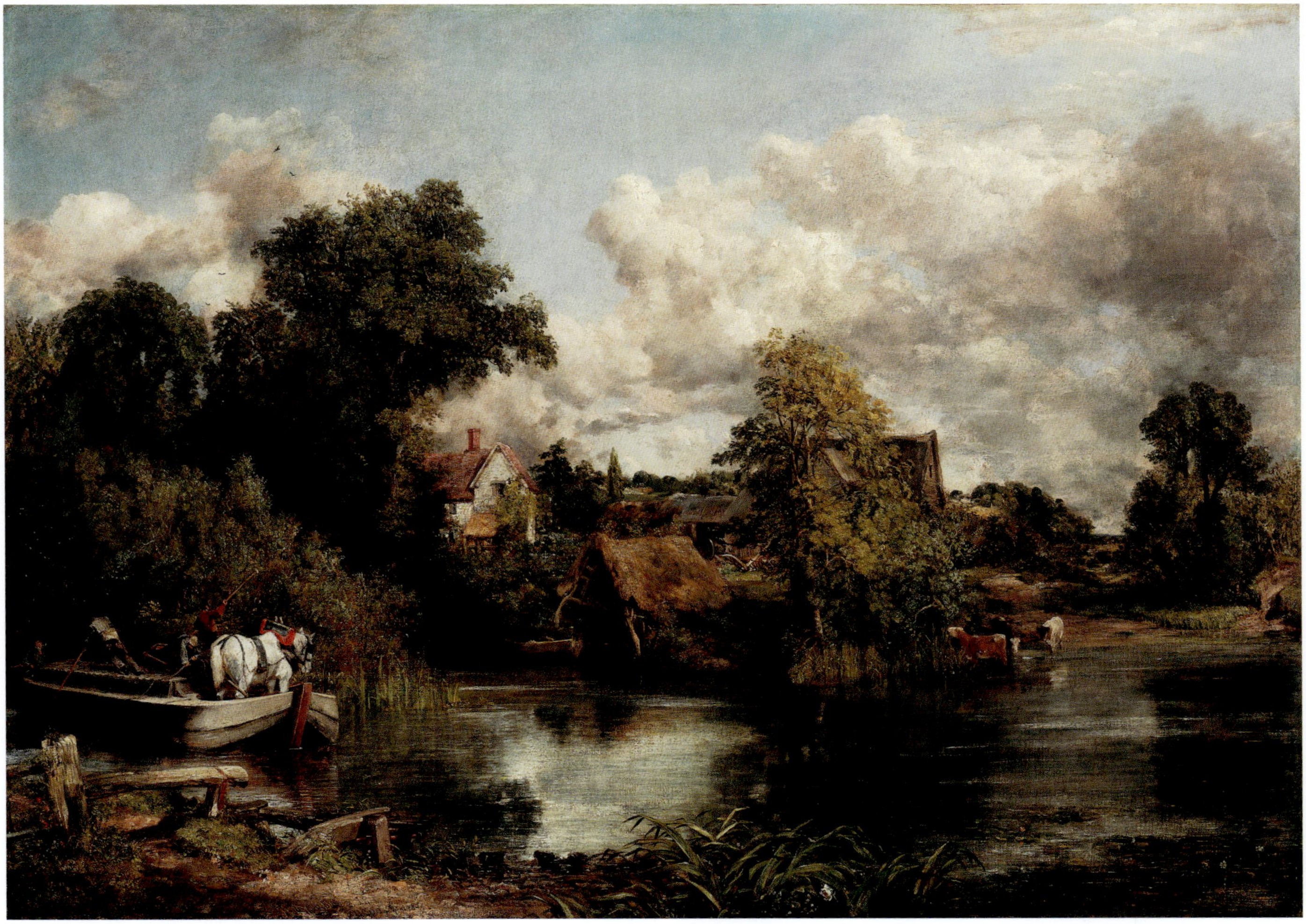

visual coherence and also in dramatic force. The first picture in the series, *The White Horse*, shows a tow horse (a heavy horse used for towing barges) being ferried across the river to join the opposite bank. Yet this, the chief narrative episode of the picture, is relegated to the far left-hand side of the picture. Furthermore, the composition itself is somewhat disjointed, breaking up too easily into three separate parts.[2] The second painting in the series, *Stratford Mill*, showing a water-mill just two miles upstream from Flatford, has a more unified composition, but here the viewer's attention is somewhat torn between the scattered figures of the rider, the anglers and the bargemen.[3] With *The Hay Wain*, by contrast, the viewer's attention is immediately drawn to the central narrative episode of the hay cart briefly pausing before making its way through the shallow mill stream to the hay fields beyond.

Meanwhile, the remaining three large river Stour compositions all deal with more dramatic narrative incidents associated with the river traffic of a partially canalised waterway. In *View on the Stour near Dedham*, a barge is energetically poled into the middle of the stream away from a barge behind it; in *The Lock*, a lock-keeper strains forward with his capstan to open the lock-gate at Flatford; and in *The Leaping Horse*, the last picture in the series, a young boy encourages a horse to leap over one of the barriers on the tow path, while his anxious mother watches on. Constable's *Hay Wain* may be lacking in the sort of dramatic incidents found in these three subsequent river Stour six-footers. However, what it loses in drama it gains in a sense of serenity and self-containment. How did Constable, with *The Hay Wain*, arrive at such a fully resolved composition, one where every element seems so perfectly judged and to have found its rightful place?

Given the amount of time it took Constable to paint these large pictures, he generally liked to start planning them during the autumn preceding the spring of the following year, when he intended to send them to the Academy for exhibition. Although the spring exhibitions would usually not open until the first week of May, paintings submitted for inclusion would generally be sent in around early April. While we do not always know exactly when Constable started on a given 'six-footer', we do know that *The Hay Wain* was painted under more time pressure than most of the others in the series, owing to his late change of mind over the subject. He had originally intended to send in a view of London's Waterloo Bridge seen from Whitehall Stairs for his 1821 Academy exhibit. However, in late November the Academician and famous diarist Joseph Farington advised him to continue with another river Stour subject instead.[4] This gave Constable a month or two less than he usually allowed himself for the preparation of a large picture.

When planning to paint a large exhibition canvas, Constable did not generally work intuitively, as he did when painting in the open air. Rather he worked methodically, making progress on his large compositions only via a number of distinct stages. In the first instance, he might turn to some earlier sketches made in Suffolk, in oils or pencil, to provide him with ideas for a larger composition. At the same time he would experiment with new landscape designs, using small composition sketches in oil. For his six-foot paintings, meanwhile, he devised an additional procedure, which was to paint a preparatory compositional sketch on the same scale as the picture he intended to finish. These large, 'full-scale' composition sketches – which survive for all six river Stour six-foot canvases – allowed Constable to experiment with the composition's distribution of light and shade and its masses, and to try out the position of figures and other narrative ingredients.[5] To paint a full-scale sketch – in addition to the final picture – was of course a very laborious and time-consuming exercise for Constable. However, it enabled him to resolve – or at least more or less to resolve – the composition without overworking the surface of the finished picture itself.

Constable seems to have first experimented with the idea for a landscape painting closely resembling *The Hay Wain* in a small composition sketch now in the Yale Center for British Art, dateable to around 1820 (see fig. 76). Most of the key ingredients found in the final picture in the National Gallery are already in place in this small sketch, including Constable's central idea of showing a horse-drawn cart fording the shallow mill stream at a point close to Willy Lott's House (Flatford had, after all, taken its name from this so-called 'flat ford'). Even the idea of the woman bending down by the side of the house to fill a water jug (or perhaps do some washing), in front of a flowering elder bush, is already in place here, and was in fact borrowed by Constable from an earlier plein-air oil sketch of around 1811 (see fig. 73) – a motif similarly recycled in his earlier paintings of *The Mill Stream* and *Willy Lott's House* of 1816 (see figs 74 and 75). One feature included in the Yale Center sketch, which is absent in the final painting, however, is a sailing barge with a yellowish-orange sail on the water beyond the bank that separates the mill stream from the main course of the river. In the final painting, Constable was to drop the barge from this position, opening out the composition on the right to include – in the far-distant fields – tiny figures busily working on bringing in the hay harvest (see pp. 76–7).

Having established the key ingredients of the composition for *The Hay Wain* in the small sketch in the Yale Center, Constable now needed to transfer his design to a canvas of a size corresponding with that of the final picture – and this he did in a full-scale sketch now held in the Victoria and Albert Museum (see fig. 1). This large composition sketch shows how Constable has extended the foreground area, to which he has added – on the path close to the water's edge – figurative elements taken from earlier plein-air sketches he had in the studio: a black and white sheep dog running along the bank, from the same 1811 sketch that features the woman bending down by the side of Willy Lott's House, and a horse from another sketch Constable made on the back of this one, to which – in the full-size sketch – he added a rider, a young boy. A small, moored rowing boat on the right-hand edge of the picture, meanwhile, was taken by him from an earlier drawing of around 1809 (see fig. 71).

In the full-scale sketch for *The Hay Wain*, Constable also began to define the composition's chief element, the hay cart, more clearly. When painting Suffolk carts in earlier pictures or studies, Constable had generally depicted the local, two-wheeled tumbril – a type of cart designed to tilt backwards to empty its load. An oil study by him of one of these carts, pulled by two horses, also survives in the collections of the Victoria and Albert Museum (fig. 22). Indeed, Constable closely followed the latter study when depicting the cart in *Stour Valley and Dedham Church* (see fig. 19). This painting features a large dung heap, of a type known locally as a 'runover dungle' because a tumbril could be run up it to empty its load and then run down the other side.[6] It would appear that Constable painted the same nimble vehicle, a tumbril, in a recently authenticated composition sketch of around 1820, *Willy Lott's House with a Horse-Drawn Cart and Distant Hay Harvest*, which shows a similar scene to that featured in *The Hay Wain* but from the opposite direction (fig. 23).[7] In fact, it now seems likely that Constable's first idea for including a hay harvest in the distance of *The Hay Wain*, and juxtaposing this with a prominent horse-drawn cart presumably destined to carry the hay, may well originally derive from this very composition.

However, when it came to resolving his ideas for the cart in *The Hay Wain* itself, Constable realised that he should replace a tumbril with a larger wagon more suitable for carrying loads of hay. So he decided instead to show a cart adapted from a timber wagon, that is to say one made suitable for carrying hay by the addition of wooden boards (or 'raves') on either side. Constable may have remembered that such carts had often been used in the vicinity of Flatford

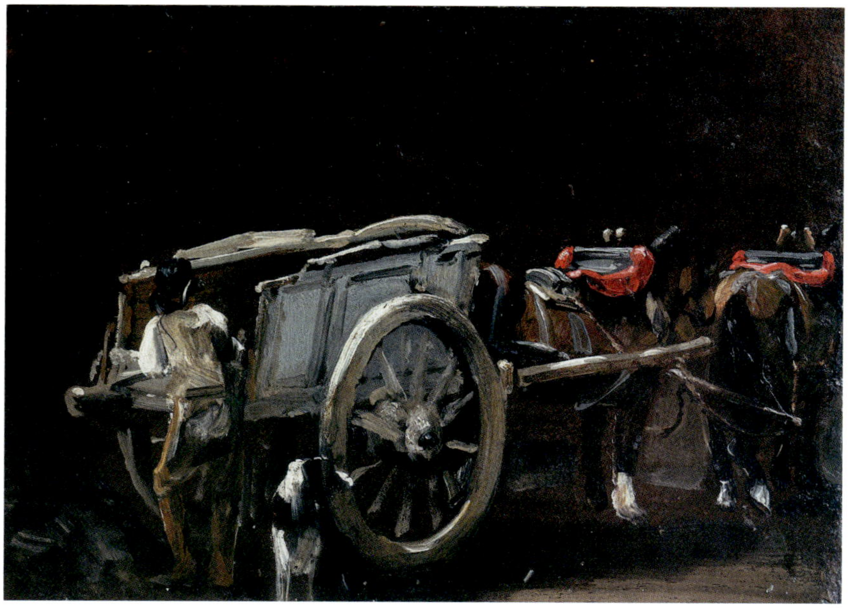

Fig. 22
Study of a cart and horses, with a carter and a dog, 1814
Oil on paper, 16.5 × 23.8 cm
Victoria and Albert Museum, London

Fig. 23
Willy Lott's House with a Horse-Drawn Cart and Distant Hay Harvest, about 1818–20
Oil on canvas, 40.6 × 55.9 cm
Private collection

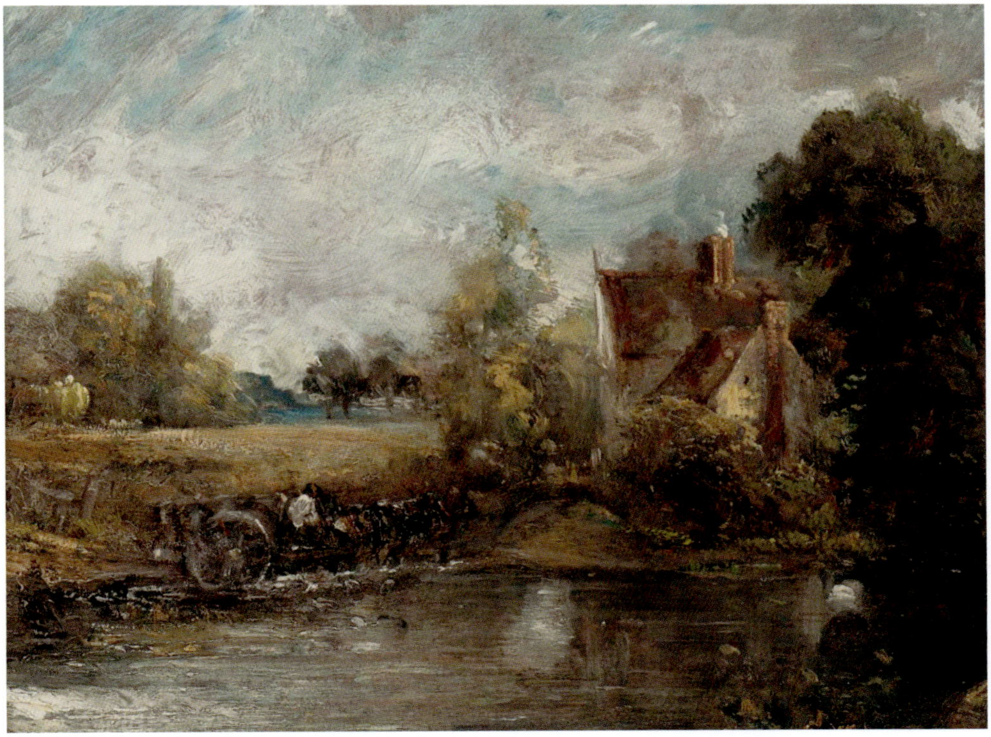

during the hay harvest; or perhaps – it has been suggested – he decided to include this lower-sided cart (lower, that is, than a true hay cart) for aesthetic reasons.[8] Whatever the explanation, when Constable realised that he had no suitable sketch of his own for this sort of cart, he asked his brother Abram to contact his old friend John Dunthorne in Suffolk to enquire if the latter's son, also John, could provide him with a suitable sketch 'of a scrave or harvest waggon'.[9] By late February 1821 Dunthorne's sketch was ready to be sent to Constable from Suffolk, and we can assume it was delivered to him – although it no longer survives.

Constable's representation of the adapted timber wagon in *The Hay Wain* can be seen especially well in the final painting in the National Gallery (see p. 1). The planks added to the cart's sides are clearly visible here, as is the central undercarriage beam (projecting at the back of the cart) – along which the rear axle and wheels were moved – designed to carry different lengths of timber.[10] Three horses seem to be pulling the cart. It is also evident from the representation of the cart in both the full-scale sketch and the final painting that it has just started to turn its front wheels with the intention of swinging round to the right, in order to weave its way through the ford to reach the main course of the river and thence up the shallow bank onto the field where it will shortly join the harvesters in the distance. It has also been suggested that the cart in *The Hay Wain* may briefly have halted in the shallow water to cool its wheels, with a view to preserving the contact between the wood and iron in their structure.[11]

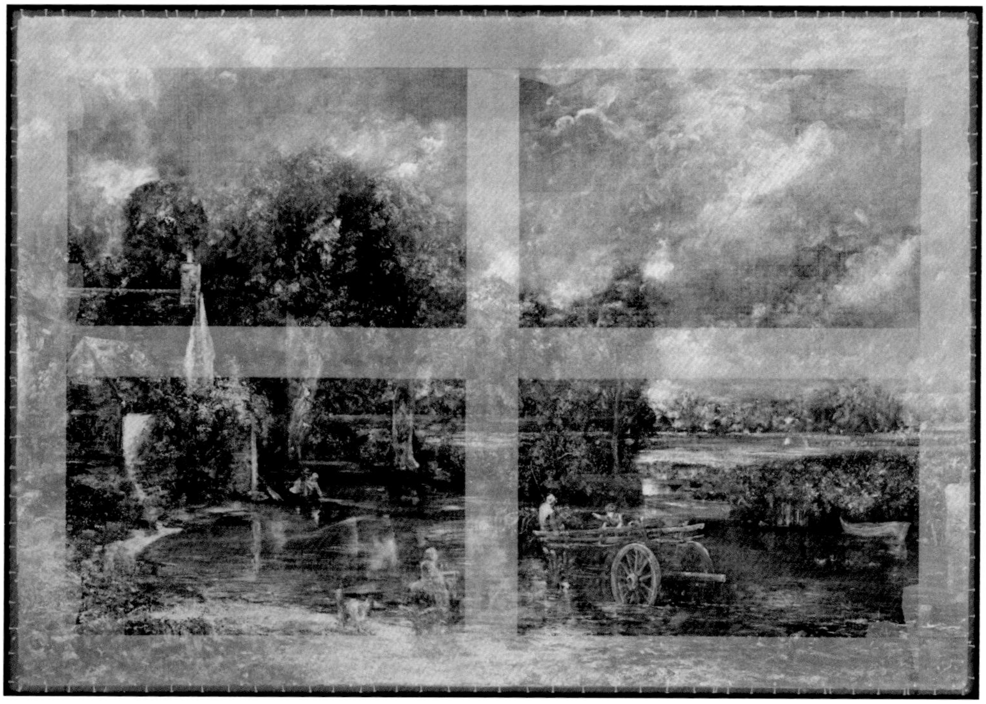

Fig. 24
X-radiograph of *The Hay Wain*
The National Gallery, London

Fig. 25
Hampstead Heath, about 1821
Oil on canvas, 54 × 76.9 cm
The Fitzwilliam Museum, Cambridge

Given all the careful preparation Constable had put into *The Hay Wain* composition so far, one might have assumed he would then only have made minimal changes between the full-scale sketch and the final work – apart, of course, from bringing details into sharper focus in the exhibition picture. However, this is evidently not the case. The full-scale sketch, as we have seen, includes a young boy on a horse, and Constable did originally paint this detail into the National Gallery picture. However, he subsequently painted this out, substituting the boy and horse with a barrel, which he then painted out in turn. The ghostly shadows of their shapes can still be made out in the National Gallery picture with the naked eye, where the paint has become more transparent with age. Their forms can be made out even more clearly in the X-radiograph of *The Hay Wain* (fig. 24).

A closer examination of the X-ray reveals another fascinating change of mind that Constable made at quite a late stage with the final composition. For the X-ray reveals that he considered including a barge with sail in the narrow channel of water on the left just beyond the woman bending down.[12] Even though he had not painted the barge in the full-scale sketch, he must have remembered experimenting with the idea in the small sketch in the Yale Center, albeit in that study he had placed the barge on the right-hand side. Why Constable should have changed his mind again about the barge at this late stage – and painted it out – is not clear. However, had he originally painted its sail in the same yellowish-orange as in the Yale Center sketch, he might have feared the bright touch of colour in this location would have proved distracting. As it was to transpire, the only obvious note of bright warm colour in the final picture was to come from the touches of red representing the fringes on the leather collars of the 'housen' attached to the horses' harnesses.[13]

Making these sorts of late changes to his pictures was a risky business on Constable's part, especially when the deadline for the spring Academy exhibition was fast approaching. As paintings conservator and technical art historian Sarah Cove has pointed out, there was only so much progress Constable could make on a picture in a day, given the time needed for paint to dry, not to mention other commitments, whether relating to his work or family.[14] Between the autumn of 1820 and the spring of 1821 when Constable was working on *The Hay Wain*, he was also juggling portrait commissions as well as trying to finish three other landscape paintings destined for inclusion at the 1821 Academy exhibition, 'Hampstead Heath' (perhaps identifiable as the picture now at the Fitzwilliam Museum, Cambridge, fig. 25), 'A Shower' and 'Hampstead'.[15] In late March, Constable's wife Maria gave birth to their third child, Charles Golding, at a time when their other two children had been ill. Then a few days later, on 1 April, Constable had to arrange to have the window on the stairs at his small house in Keppel Street removed so that *The Hay Wain* could be sent to the Academy – the hall and stairwell presumably being too narrow for the picture to come down the stairs.[16]

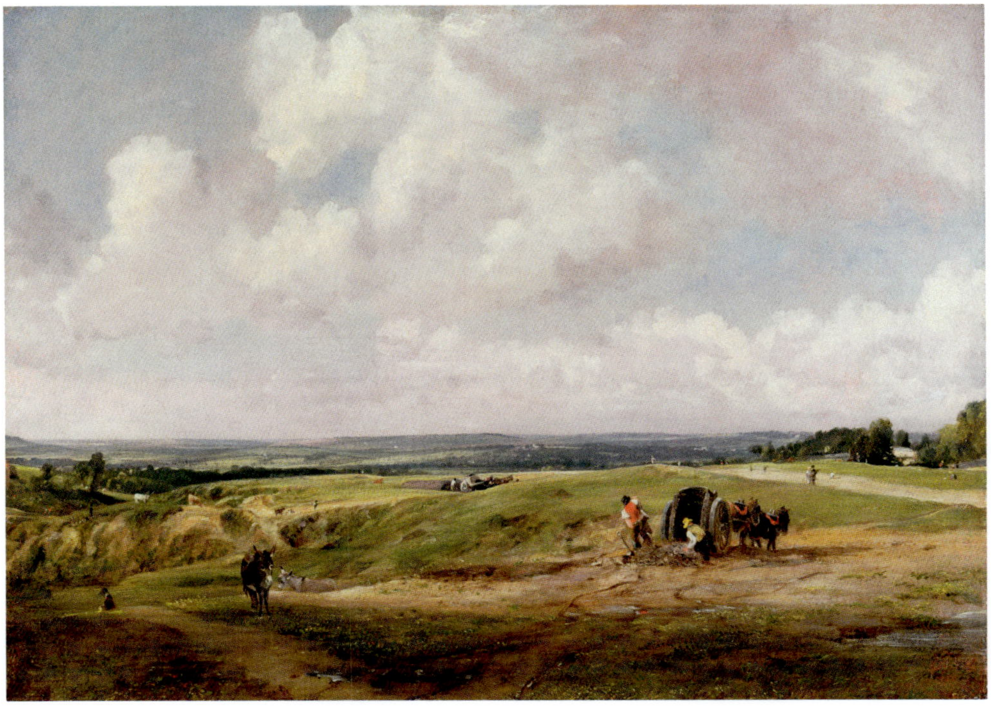

Constable was always anxious when sending in a new large picture for exhibition at the Academy. In 1821, indeed, he may have been more anxious than usual as – by his own admission – *The Hay Wain* had transpired to have 'rather a more novel look than I expected'.[17] However, his worries would surely have been assuaged when, in May, good reviews started to come in. One of the most favourable was penned by the perceptive critic Robert Hunt, writing for *The Examiner*. In his opinion, *The Hay Wain* approached 'nearer to the actual look of rural nature than any modern landscape whatever'.[18] In particular, Hunt singled out the sky in the picture, declaring that 'for noble volume of cloud and clear light we have never at any time seen exceeded except by Nature'.[19]

These comments, highlighting the naturalistic qualities of the picture, would surely have pleased Constable. He had decided to exhibit the painting with the title 'Landscape-Noon' – no doubt with the precise aim of encouraging visitors to appreciate his intention of representing the landscape at a specific time of day ('Hay Wain' was a title first given to the painting by Constable's great friend John Fisher, presumably partly in jest[20]). When we examine the sky in the painting, we notice that dense clusters of cumulus clouds have formed, which indicate a scene consistent with one at noon. Moreover, the clouds are so accurately painted that a modern meteorologist can conclude that, from the depth of their convection, showers will follow later in the afternoon.[21] As it happens, when Constable first painted the sky in *The Hay Wain*, he had not yet embarked on his systematic study of clouds, painted in Hampstead in the summer or autumn of 1821 and 1822 (see figs 84–6). However, as we know that Constable repainted parts of *The Hay Wain* after its return to his studio, he may have retouched the sky having gained fresh knowledge of the movement of clouds on one of his Hampstead 'skying campaigns'.[22]

Robert Hunt ended his review of *The Hay Wain* proposing a 'challenge [to] the Dutch Masters to shew us anything better than this'.[23] Given that Dutch seventeenth-century painters were associated then – as now – with having produced remarkably naturalistic landscapes, Constable would surely have interpreted this comment favourably as well. After all, we know that he greatly admired the Dutch masters not just for their sensitivity to natural detail, but also for their devotion to painting their native scenes; he identified with, and commended, their decision to remain 'stay-at-home' painters.[24] Another reviewer, writing for *The Observer* the following month, commented that Ruisdael had 'evidently been the model' for Constable when painting *The Hay Wain*.[25] Constable would surely have taken this as a compliment, too, Ruisdael being one of the Dutch masters he admired almost beyond any other. Indeed, only a little later that same year, Constable, on seeing a painting by Ruisdael, *Evening Landscape: A Windmill by a Stream* (fig. 26), lent by the Prince Regent to the British Institution (a rival London exhibiting body to the Royal Academy), wrote admiringly of its 'acres of sky expressed' and the fact that he 'could all but see the eels in the pools of water'.[26]

Although it was not uncommon for the critics of the day to draw analogies between contemporary landscape painters and those of the past, the comment made by the writer for *The Observer* in drawing parallels between *The Hay Wain* and the work of the old masters was actually highly perceptive. For despite Constable's determination to paint landscape using a more modern, 'naturalistic' vocabulary and painterly technique, he was nevertheless steeped in admiration for the achievements of earlier landscape painters – not just Ruisdael, or his great hero the French painter Claude, but also the Flemish painter Peter Paul Rubens. Ever since Constable had first come to London as an art student, he had seized every opportunity available to study, or copy, examples of old masters in private collections. Moreover, he continued to study – or collect – examples of works by these masters throughout his life.[27] One of the paintings that had especially impressed Constable in the early years of the century was Rubens's *An Autumn Landscape with a View of Het Steen in the Early Morning* (fig. 27). This had arrived in London with its pair, *The Rainbow Landscape* (about 1636; Wallace Collection, London), from a Genoese collection in 1803, and the two paintings became a major talking point in art circles in the capital at that time.[28] Constable admired both landscapes, but

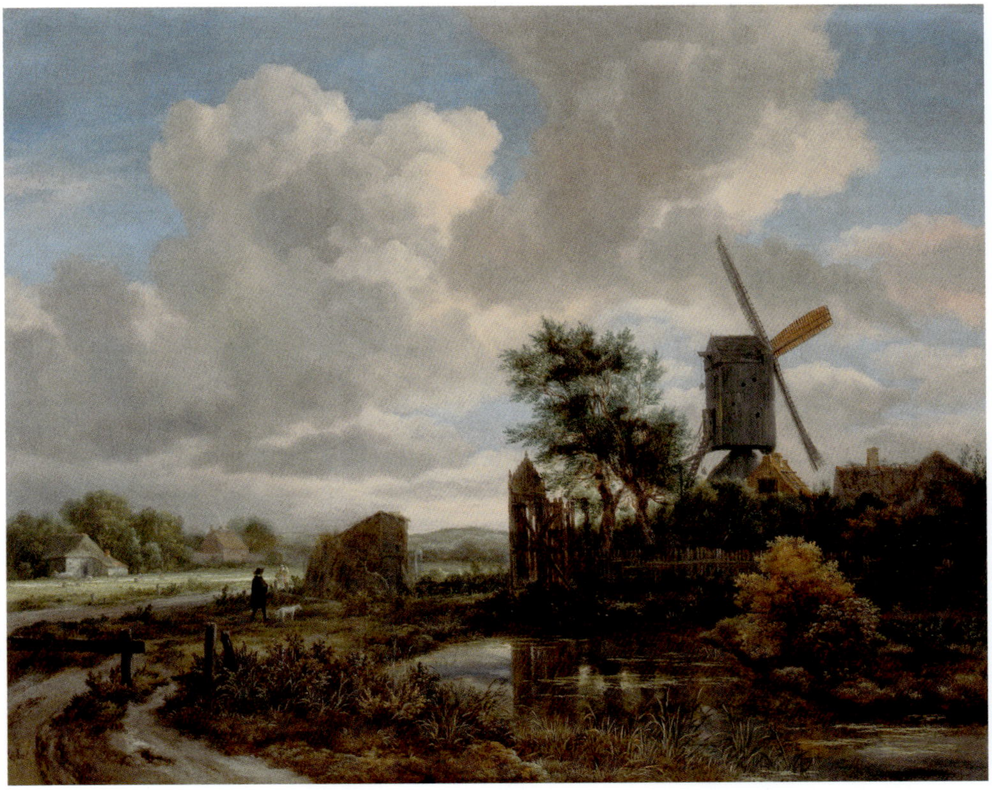

Fig. 26
Jacob van Ruisdael (1628–1682)
Evening Landscape: A Windmill by a Stream, about 1650
Oil on canvas, 79.1 × 102.4 cm
The Royal Collection / HM King Charles III (RCIN 405538)

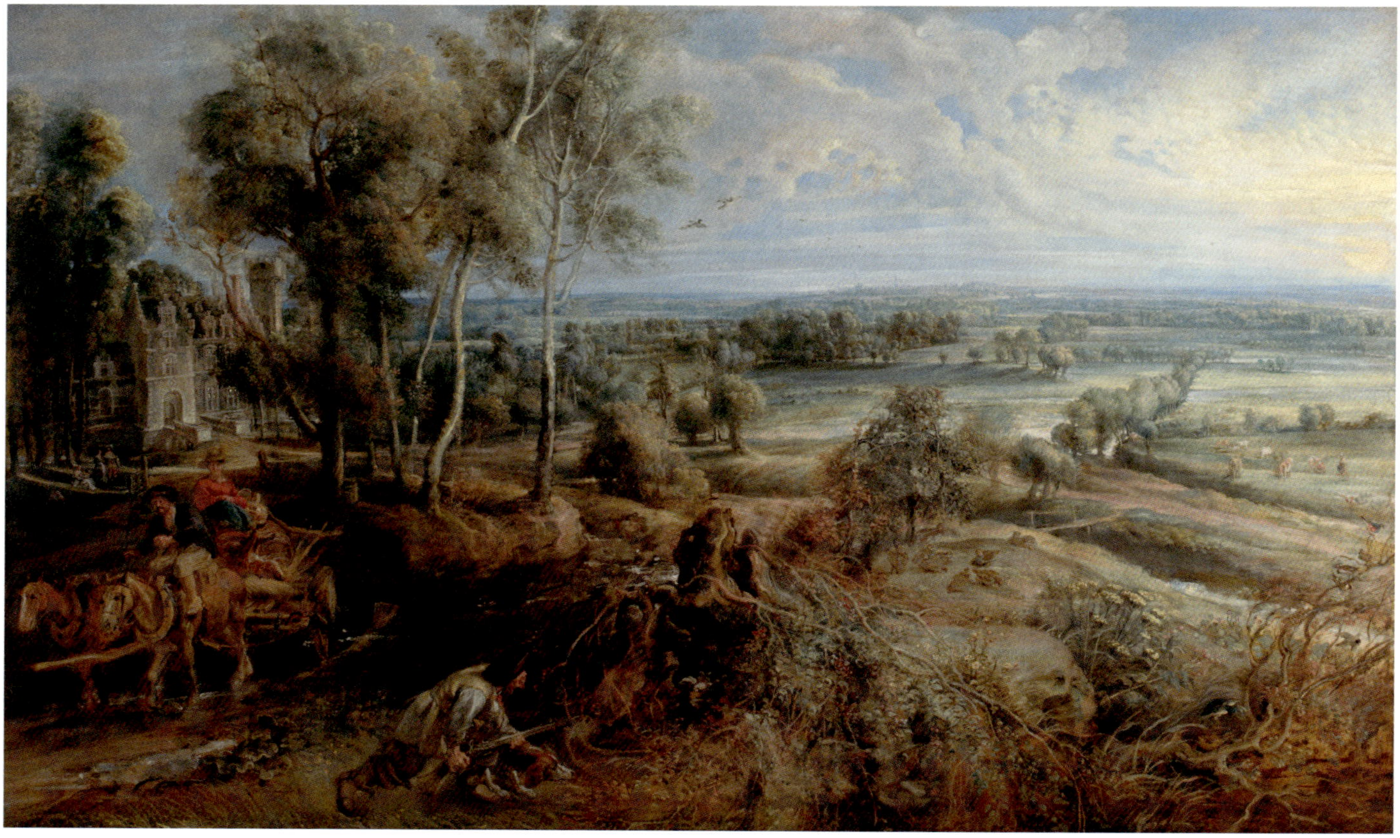

it was *View of Het Steen* that he came to know best. The painting was gifted to his mentor Sir George Beaumont by his wife as a wedding present, and hung for four years in Beaumont's London house before being transferred to his country residence in Coleorton in 1808.

Consciously or unconsciously, Constable clearly modelled the composition of *The Hay Wain* on Rubens's *View of Het Steen*. It can surely be no coincidence – as was pointed out nearly 50 years ago – that the compositions of both paintings share a closed mass of buildings on the left contrasted with the open space of a distant landscape on the right, while in both cases the division between the two is marked by a free-standing tree crossing the horizon.[29] Moreover, while seventeenth-century Dutch and Flemish painters had often included horse-drawn carts carrying rustic figures in their landscapes, the cart in Rubens's *Het Steen* is fording shallow water just like that in *The Hay Wain*. Even Rubens's lurking hunter with his dog in the foreground finds an echo in Constable's fisherman surreptitiously moving forward through the rushes on the right of *The Hay Wain* to reach his moored boat. However, the differences between the two paintings are perhaps as significant as the similarities, and help to emphasise the extent to which, in *The Hay Wain*, Constable departs from some of the conventions of earlier landscape painting. Rubens's painting is set in the early morning so

Fig. 27
Peter Paul Rubens (1577–1640)
An Autumn Landscape with a View of Het Steen in the Early Morning, probably 1636
Oil on wood, 131.2 × 229.2 cm
The National Gallery, London

that – like other seventeenth-century painters such as Claude – he could use the more dramatic 'effect' of long shadows to help weld the composition together.[30] Constable by contrast – as we have seen – rather chooses for *The Hay Wain* the less dramatic moment of noon.

Notably, the painting did not attract universal praise from the critics when exhibited at the Academy in 1821. One critic, for example, objected to what he called Constable's 'excess of piebald scambling [*sic*] in the finishing', another to the brushwork being 'a little too spotty'.[31] Essentially these critics were disapproving of what they saw as Constable's lack of 'finish' in the picture – criticism that would only escalate in the ensuing years as his handling became looser still, especially from the 1830s when he began to use a palette knife in the painting of some of his exhibited works. To a modern audience, familiar with the expressive brushwork used by artists ever since the time of the Impressionists, the handling of *The Hay Wain* looks, if anything, rather restrained (and especially so by comparison with the artist's full-scale composition sketches, which of course remained unseen in his studio to all but a favoured few). However, conventional notions of 'finish' in painting in the early nineteenth century demanded high resolution of detail and smooth, even brushstrokes. Constable, by contrast, was now beginning to use broken brushstrokes in his paintings, and to introduce lightly impastoed highlights and coloured accents.[32]

Something that might be regarded as distasteful to a critic with conservative tastes could, on the other hand, be welcomed as exciting to another artist with an eye on more experimental developments in painting. It was surely in part owing to the novel handling of *The Hay Wain* that the French painter Théodore Géricault declared himself quite stunned ('tout étourdi') by his own experience of viewing the picture at the Royal Academy in 1821.[33] Géricault's enthusiasm helped set up a chain of events whereby in due course the Anglo-French dealer John Arrowsmith was to purchase *The Hay Wain* from Constable early in 1824, and subsequently to send it to the exhibition at the Paris Salon later in the year.[34] The Comte de Forbin (1777–1841), director of the Louvre, tried to buy the painting for the French nation, to join the collection of contemporary art at the Musée du Luxembourg. However, Arrowsmith was unwilling to sell it without the other Suffolk six-footer he had bought with it from Constable, *View on the Stour near Dedham* (see fig. 28).[35] In due course, as explained on p. 65, the painting was repatriated to England and eventually found its way into the collections of the National Gallery.

The Hay Wain has long ago ceased to hold any sense of the radical allure it held in its own day. Nevertheless it will, surely, remain a national icon. For Constable managed to pull off something quite remarkable with his picture. He painted a particular landscape at a specific time of day, yet he also painted an archetypal landscape with timeless and universal appeal.

JENNY GASCHKE

'Landscape not merely as seen, but as experienced': Constable and Europe

In 1824, the same year the National Gallery opened its doors in London, John Constable found – across the English Channel, in France – the popular success that still evaded him at home. In June of that year, the artist's painting *The Hay Wain*, as well as his *View on the Stour near Dedham* (fig. 28) and a view of Yarmouth Jetty, went on display in John Arrowsmith's Parisian gallery in the Rue Grange-aux-Belles. During the ensuing weeks, Eugène Delacroix (1798–1863) visited the Anglo-French art dealer's premises on several occasions. The French painter, already familiar with a small work by Constable in the collection of the artist Jacques Auguste Régnier (1787–1860), was inspired by the Englishman's – to French eyes – revolutionary approach to landscape painting, just as fellow artist Théodore Géricault had been when he encountered *The Hay Wain* in London in 1821 (see p. 51).

In late August 1824, *The Hay Wain* was famously – and to great acclaim – included in the Paris Salon. The gold medal bestowed on Constable by the French king, Charles X, in recognition of his work, is today kept in the National Gallery's archive (see p. 8). Such was the painting's success at the Salon that, by the 1850s, events had been somewhat rewritten and condensed into a story in which Delacroix was so struck by Constable's painting when he encountered it at the Louvre that he supposedly rushed off to re-work the background of his *Massacre at Chios*.[1] Although it entered a private collection rather than being acquired by the French state, *The Hay Wain* was to remain in France until 1838.

The impact Constable's *Hay Wain* had on the course of nineteenth-century French art following its exhibition in Paris in 1824 – manifested in the National Gallery's own collection through paintings by Jules-Louis Dupré (1811–1889;

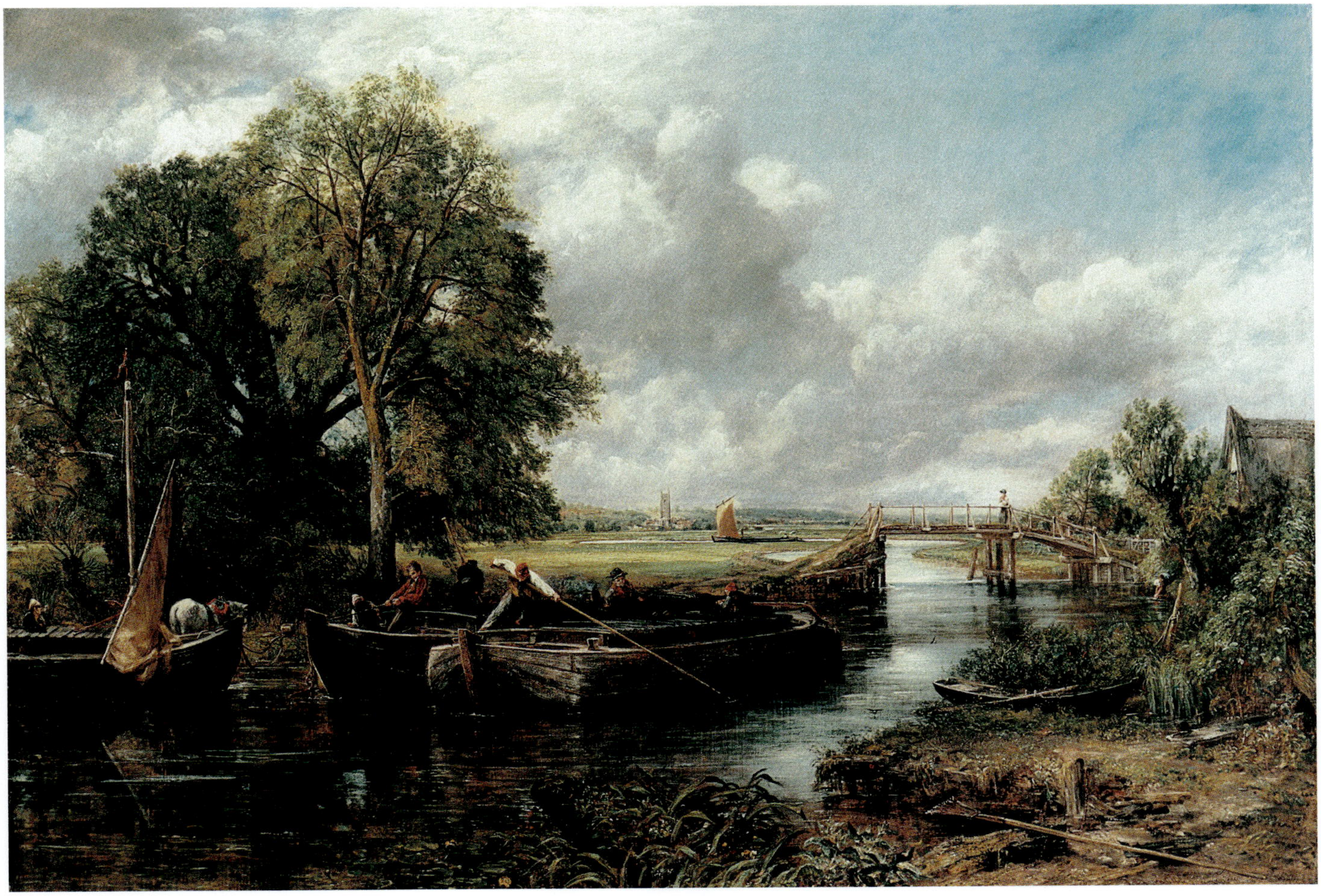

Fig. 28
View on the Stour near Dedham, 1822
Oil on canvas, 129.5 × 188 cm
The Huntington Library, Art Museum, and Botanical Gardens, San Marino

Willows, with a Man Fishing) and Paul Huet (fig. 29) – has long transcended academic writing and instead become a touchstone of popular art history across Europe. This relationship gained new relevance after the end of the Second World War in a climate of cultural renewal.

Only five years after the war, Ernst Gombrich's *Story of Art* reminded readers of Delacroix's enthusiasm for Constable. In his 'Revolution in Permanence' chapter, the Anglo-Austrian art historian elegantly spun his narrative, from *The Hay Wain* via Delacroix and Jean-Baptiste-Camille Corot (fig. 30) to the work of the Barbizon School and eventually Impressionism, along the theme of artistic truth to nature. Importantly, given that the German and French editions of Gombrich's book appeared in 1952 and 1963, he also defined Constable – together with J.M.W. Turner – as a great artist 'among the Romantic painters of *Europe*' [my italics].[2]

Throughout the latter half of the twentieth century and into the twenty-first, exhibitions, too, organised both from within Britain and by European museums, played a key role in shaping the perception of Constable and his work for audiences across mainland Europe. Not only had *The Hay Wain* itself already returned to Paris

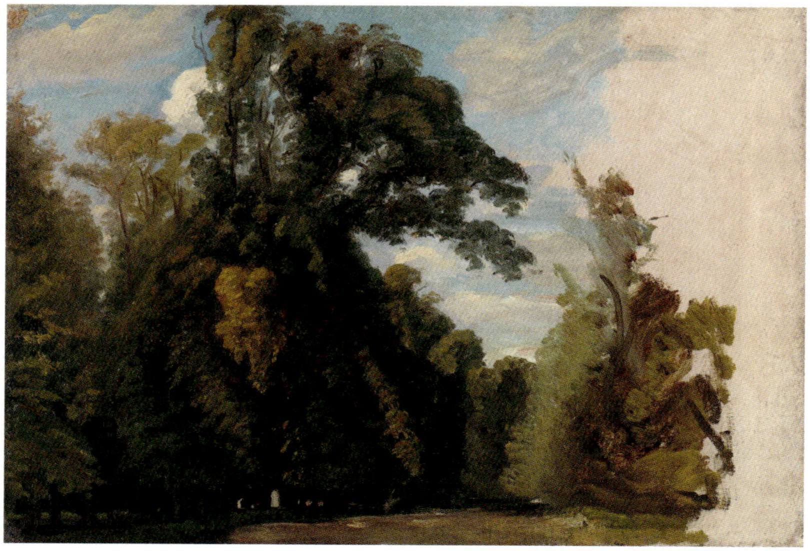

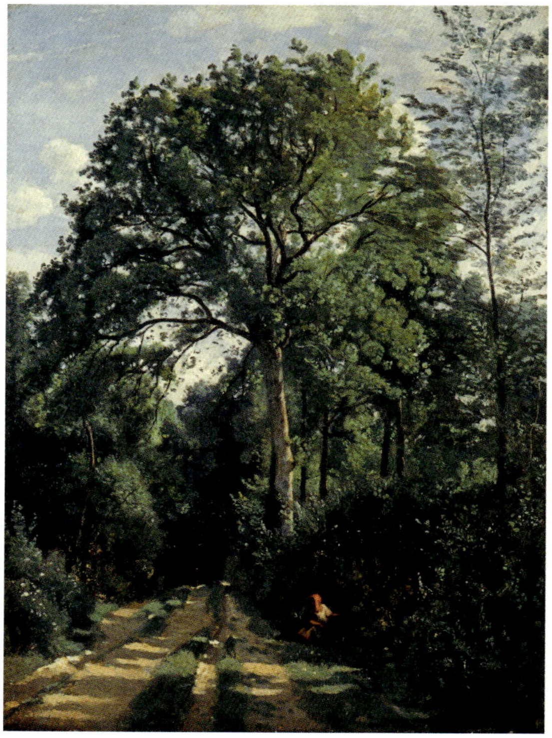

in 1938 and 1948, but in 1950 (the same year Gombrich's *Story of Art* was published) the British Council also presented its *Exhibition of Works by John Constable, Matthew Smith, Barbara Hepworth* at the Venice Biennale. In the accompanying catalogue, the Victoria and Albert Museum's director Eric Maclagan argued that the display in Venice would finally allow a wider public to appreciate Constable and Turner as equal 'masters in the art of landscape painting'.[3] But notably, and while referencing Constable's success in France, Maclagan included the verdict: 'It is impossible to imagine a painter more characteristically and completely English.'[4]

This dualism and occasional tension of Constable's 'Englishness' and his status as a European figure were to remain issues to consider when exhibiting his work 'on the Continent' in the post-war era. Whether this could be seen as a metaphor of the relationship between Britain and its neighbours cannot be answered here, but displaying Constable in Europe has provided vehicles for new cultural narratives ever since.

During his lifetime, despite choosing not to travel abroad himself, Constable regarded his own work as rooted within a European landscape tradition. This much is obvious not only from his study of the 'Angerstein' Claudes now in the National Gallery, but also from his lecture series on the origins and development of landscape painting covering the Northern, Venetian, Bolognese, and later Dutch and Flemish schools.[5] Furthermore, his paintings and drawings *did* leave Britain, thanks to an internationally active network of art dealers. This is particularly well documented for *The Hay Wain* in Paris in 1824; *The White Horse*, which won

Fig. 29
Paul Huet (1803–1869)
Trees in the Park at Saint-Cloud, probably 1850s
Oil on canvas, 37.6 × 55.5 cm
The National Gallery, London

Fig. 30
Jean-Baptiste-Camille Corot (1796–1875)
Ville d'Avray: Entrance to the Wood, about 1823–5, with later reworking, probably early 1850s
Oil on canvas, 46 × 35 cm
Scottish National Gallery, Edinburgh

the artist a second gold medal, in Lille in 1825; and *The Cornfield* (see fig. 87), which was submitted to the Paris Salon in 1827. In fact, it is estimated that at least 22 of Constable's paintings had travelled to France by 1827.[6]

But Constable's work was not only shown in France. The German Realist painter Adolph Menzel enthusiastically recalled seeing two of Constable's paintings at the Hôtel de Russie in Berlin in 1839, one of which has been identified as *Child's Hill*, 1824/5; and Menzel's own painting *Palaisgarten des Prinzen Albrecht* (fig. 31) has subsequently been linked to this experience.[7]

Even so, unlike in France, Constable's contribution to continental European landscape painting was not universally recognised across the German art scene until the end of the nineteenth century. For example, while influential writer and art critic Theodor Fontane (1819–1898) must have been aware of Constable's work when he visited the 1857 *Art Treasures Exhibition* in Manchester during his extensive travels across England and Scotland, he did not single him out to his readers.[8]

Towards the end of the nineteenth century and at the beginning of the twentieth, prominent museums across continental Europe nevertheless began to acquire Constable's work, following on a smaller scale the step change in

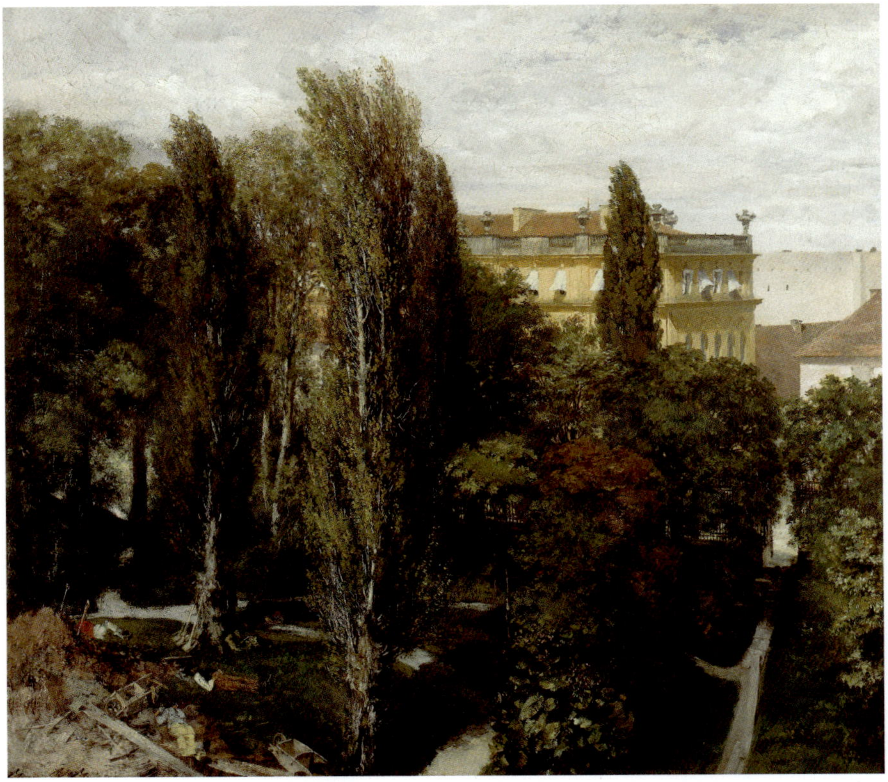

Fig. 31
Adolph Menzel (1815–1905)
Palaisgarten des Prinzen Albrecht (Palace Garden of Prince Albrecht), 1846/1876
Oil on canvas, 68 × 86 cm
Nationalgalerie, Staatliche Museen zu Berlin

public access to the artist's paintings and drawings in Britain. Engagement with Constable's work in London's National Gallery, Tate Gallery and the South Kensington Museum (now Victoria and Albert Museum) had revolutionised not only the British but also the international perception of his art. The German art critic and historian Julius Meier-Graefe (1867–1935), for example, particularly highlighted the public display of Constable's oil sketches in his book *Modern Art*, praising their status above mere preparations for finished paintings and linking them to the work of both Claude Monet and Adolph Menzel.[9] Museum directors across Europe clearly agreed.

A year after *The Hay Wain* entered the National Gallery collection, the Statens Museum for Kunst in Copenhagen acquired its first Constable drawing, *Landscape with a View of Dedham Vale seen from Langham*, and in 1896 Berlin's Nationalgalerie accepted the gift of *Higham Village on the River Stour*. The National Gallery of Ireland in Dublin acquired several drawings and watercolours in 1892/3, and the Museum of Fine Arts in Budapest purchased its oil sketch of *The Celebration in East Bergholt of the Peace of 1814 Concluded in Paris between France and the Allied Powers* in 1913.[10] The Louvre's acquisition history eclipses these early examples. It had acquired several oil sketches in the early 1870s (although the majority were, in fact, wrongly attributed to Constable). His portrait sketches entered the collection in 1924 – exactly a hundred years after the artist's triumph at the Salon.[11]

Both the nature of the private collections from which these acquisitions were sourced and the question of whether the institutional interest in Constable was driven in all instances by a Post-impressionist curatorial taste – as was the case in Germany – will require a more comprehensive and geographically nuanced investigation in the future, but the artist's work was now certainly desirable enough that several museums accidentally acquired forgeries and copies.[12]

Ian Fleming-Williams and Leslie Parris highlighted the relevance of the 1937 centenary of Constable's death in the developing appreciation of his art,[13] and collecting continued throughout the twentieth century on a small scale. Another significant change in European access to Constable's work occurred when Britain began to 'use' Constable as an instrument of diplomatic soft power after 1945.

The exhibition at the Venice Biennale was not the first British Council effort to (re-)introduce Britain's European neighbours to Constable's art. In 1949, the exhibition *British Painting from Hogarth to Turner* had been sent to Hamburg, Oslo, Stockholm and Copenhagen. Presenting key eighteenth- and nineteenth-century British artists to its German and Scandinavian audiences, this exhibition took Meier-Graefe's and Gombrich's line of 'Constable, the European': it included seven works by the artist, notably *Flatford Mill* (see fig. 16), at that time in the National Gallery, and explained the legacy of Dutch seventeenth-century art in Constable's work. The introduction to the catalogue, written by Ellis Waterhouse, director of the National Gallery of Scotland, emphasised the close relationship between continental (particularly Northern European) and British artists, while reinforcing Constable's status as an ancestor of Impressionism.[14]

Unlike the display in Venice the following year, which highlighted his 'Englishness', this portrayal of Constable as a painter in dialogue with European art was to become a dominant theme of exhibitions initiated and curated on the Continent. Indeed, it has been central to a number of high-profile shows organised since the beginning of the twenty-first century. Several largely non-monographic exhibitions shifted the lens from Constable's place in an assumed linear stylistic development of European art to new areas of interest. Particular attention was paid to the nature of the 'Northern European' Romantic movement as an intellectual and cultural phenomenon in itself.

In 2002–3, the Hamburger Kunsthalle staged *Expedition Kunst: Die Entdeckung der Natur von C.D. Friedrich bis Humboldt* (*Expedition Art: The Discovery of Nature from C.D. Friedrich to Humboldt*). In this exhibition, dedicated to artists' travels in Europe and South America, Constable's cloud studies (see figs 84–6) featured as images at the intersection of landscape art and science. The rise of meteorology since the eighteenth century as a scientific and artistic collaboration resulted in a presentation of his oil sketches alongside images by his contemporaries such as Carl Gustav Carus (1789–1869) and Johan Christian Dahl (1788–1857). Here, Constable was presented as subsumed into a larger Northern European art movement, not on stylistic but on intellectual grounds.[15]

In 2007, *The Abstraction of Landscape: From Northern Romanticism to Abstract Expressionism* at the Fundación Juan March in Madrid was to include Constable's oil sketches in the visual manifestation of Robert Rosenblum's thesis on the 'abstract sublime'. The Spanish exhibition, too, severed the link between Constable and Impressionism, and instead drew an arc from Northern Romantic portrayals of nature to North American Abstract Expressionism of the post-war period as an alternative route from nineteenth-century art to modernity. As Rosenblum stated: 'No French Impressionist picnics or strolls could take place in these sanctified Northern landscapes; they are, rather, the shrines where Nature's ultimate mysteries are contemplated.'[16]

Ten years later, the Groninger Museum again pushed the narrative of Constable's impact on French art to one side, in order to contextualise the artist within the art scene of the Netherlands, Germany, Scandinavia and Britain of his own lifetime. *Romanticism in the North: From Friedrich to Turner* included five small works by the artist. The exhibition's aim was to portray Romanticism as an avant-garde, revolutionary movement, with artists approaching 'landscape not merely as seen, but as experienced, as *felt*'.[17] Consequently, the catalogue, which included essays by the German Constable specialist Werner Busch, focused on the interplay of Constable's biography with his art and his deep engagement with meteorological phenomena, while mentioning *The Hay Wain* and the artist's success in France merely in passing.

Some museums in the Netherlands returned to a key theme of the 1949 *British Painting* exhibition, using the occasion of a Constable display as an opportunity to highlight the importance of Dutch seventeenth-century painting in the story of European art. The 2020–1 exhibition *John Constable* at the Teylers Museum in Haarlem, the first retrospective of Constable's work in the Netherlands, portrayed the artist as the link between Dutch old masters and modernity. The display was not only assembled from museum loans but also included a significant number of artworks from the holdings of the Canadian collector David Thomson, a throwback to nineteenth-century exhibitions of the artist's work. Furthermore, with this exhibition the Teylers Museum celebrated the first acquisition of seven Constable drawings by a Dutch museum (fig. 32) and also introduced a new superlative in the language employed to describe Constable to European audiences: in the catalogue's foreword, Marjan Scharloo called Constable 'one of the greatest landscape painters of all time'.[18]

In 2021, the Dordrechts Museum hosted *In the Light of Cuyp: Aelbert Cuyp & Gainsborough – Constable – Turner*. Here, the influence of Dutch seventeenth-century art on British art took centre stage. The analysis of Constable's debt to the Italianate Dutch painter again focused on his drawings and sketches. The catalogue also reminded its readers of the nineteenth-century collections of European 'old masters' in Britain available to artists, not least at the newly opened National Gallery.[19]

These exhibitions – beyond the loans from collections in Britain – frequently relied on the contribution of British art historians and curators, such as Anne Lyles and Mark Evans, thereby replicating the integrated European approach under discussion in Constable's work itself. A similar example was the 2014 exhibition *Hogarth, Reynolds, Turner: British Painting and the Rise of Modernity* at the Fondazione Roma, which collaborated with an academic committee of largely British scholars. The Fondazione's aim was to investigate the legacy of ancient Rome in European art and its role in defining cultural identity. As Turner's counterpart, Constable was here presented as standing 'at the culmination of a long-drawn-out development of sensibility towards landscape in England' on another path to modernity.[20]

But placing Constable into a wider European picture was also enabled by the research of Constable specialists born and working in countries other than the UK. Alongside Werner Busch, the Belgian art historian and museum director Robert Hoozee belonged to a group of European colleagues who championed the academic study of British art – thereby adding a different, 'continental' perspective on Constable, too. The 2007–8 exhibition *British Vision: Observation and Imagination in British Art 1750–1950* at the Museum of Fine Arts in Ghent introduced audiences to the great arc of British art from the mid-eighteenth century to the twentieth century through the subjects of 'Society', 'Landscape' and '"The Visionary"' – thereby investigating the complex notion of Britishness in art itself. Hoozee centred his catalogue essay on Constable around *Flatford Mill* (see fig. 16), an example of 'Everyday Landscape' formed by the power of observation.[21]

One of the many sponsors of the exhibition in Ghent was the British Council. Of course, British institutions including the British Council have never ceased to help with, if not organise entirely, the 'export' of Constable exhibitions to continental Europe. While frequently income-generating, these projects have

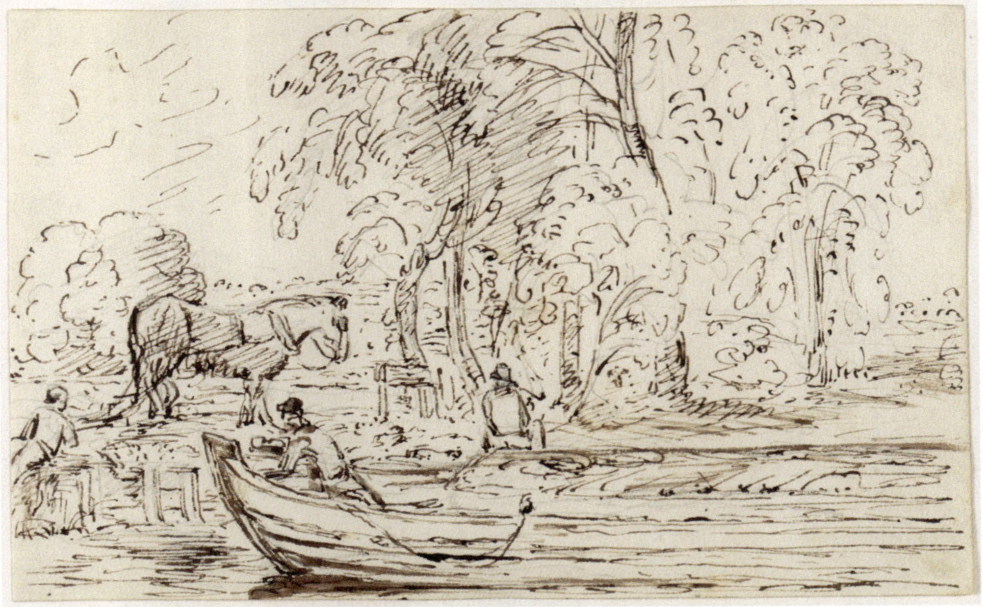

Fig. 32
On the Stour, about 1832
Pencil, pen and brown wash on paper, 11.4 × 18.8 cm
Teylers Museum, Haarlem
(KT 2018 034)

generally been seen as examples of cultural and diplomatic soft power, and not only since the British exit from the European Union. National museums in the UK, for example, have regularly been their own agents of international touring exhibitions, including of Constable's work.

In 2022, the first ever Romanian exhibition of Constable's art opened in Bucharest. It was curated by the Victoria and Albert Museum with a brief to address an audience that was both aged under 40 and not yet familiar with Constable's life and work. In the view of its Romanian hosts, the exhibition brought prestige to their new cultural venture, 'Art Safari', by displaying, again, 'one of the greatest landscape painters of all time, John Constable'.[22] Reviews of the show used the occasion to link Constable's work not only with the display of Romanian painter Ștefan Popescu (1872–1948) in an adjacent pavilion, but also with the work of the country's most famous nineteenth-century landscape painter, Nicolae Grigorescu (1838–1907), who had studied with the Constable-inspired Barbizon artists.[23] *Seeking Truth: The Art of John Constable* provided an opportunity to write previously overlooked Romanian artists back into a wider narrative of European art history.

But results of touring Constable exhibitions curated in Britain to the European mainland could be mixed. Eleven years earlier, in 2011, an exhibition of the artist's oil sketches went on a continental tour. Before travelling to Ghent, where Robert Hoozee was already director, the exhibition opened at the Staatsgalerie Stuttgart. This gallery, the main art venue in the federal state of Baden-Württemberg, had previously not engaged deeply with its own limited British collections, celebrating French art instead – an understandable focus, given the geographical proximity and political effort of post-war West Germany to overcome historical adversities between the two countries. In 2005 Sean

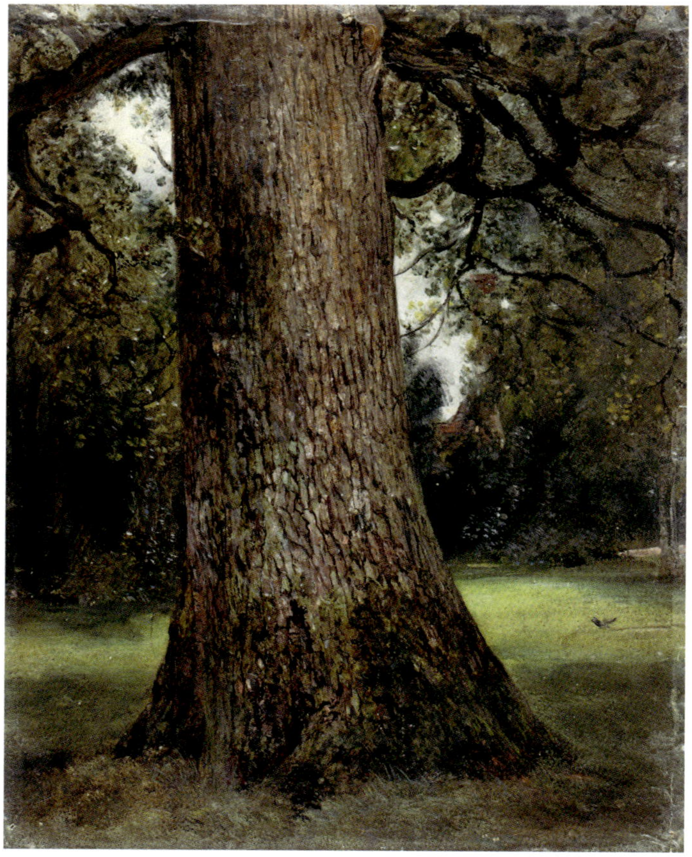

Fig. 33
Study of the Trunk of an Elm Tree, about 1821
Oil on paper, 30.6 × 24.8 cm
Victoria and Albert Museum, London

Fig. 34
Installation shot of *The Atlantic Ocean* exhibition (26 April–15 September 2024), showing John Constable's work *Hove Beach with Fishing Boats* (1824) on the left.
Henie Onstad Kunstsenter, Høvikodden, Norway

Rainbird had joined the Staatsgalerie from Tate, and his directorship had brought opportunities for a change in perspective. The commissioned German introduction of the exhibition catalogue, written by the gallery's curator for nineteenth-century art, Christofer Conrad, nevertheless still reflected a significant degree of uneasiness at engaging with Constable, if not with British art in general. Constable was here introduced as a virtually unknown painter (compared to popular Turner), and the previous study of his work in mainland Europe was described half-heartedly as 'niche'.[24] It seemed as though the author had taken his cue from the 1950 Venice exhibition, rather than the 1949 *British Painting* show.

But to return once more to *The Hay Wain*, France and the British Council: given *The Hay Wain*'s original success in Paris in 1824, it may not be surprising that the only place across the English Channel that the painting (as opposed to the more easily transportable oil sketches) repeatedly returned to was Paris. After the work's inclusion in the 1972 British Council show *La Peinture romantique anglaise et les préraphaélites* (*English Romantic Painting and the Pre-Raphaelites*) at the Petit Palais, the Grand Palais took an altogether different, artist-led approach in 2002, again with the help of the British Council – and under the patronage of President Jacques Chirac and Queen Elizabeth II. The artist Lucian Freud (1922–2011) was asked to select the works for the exhibition. After Freud had emigrated from Germany

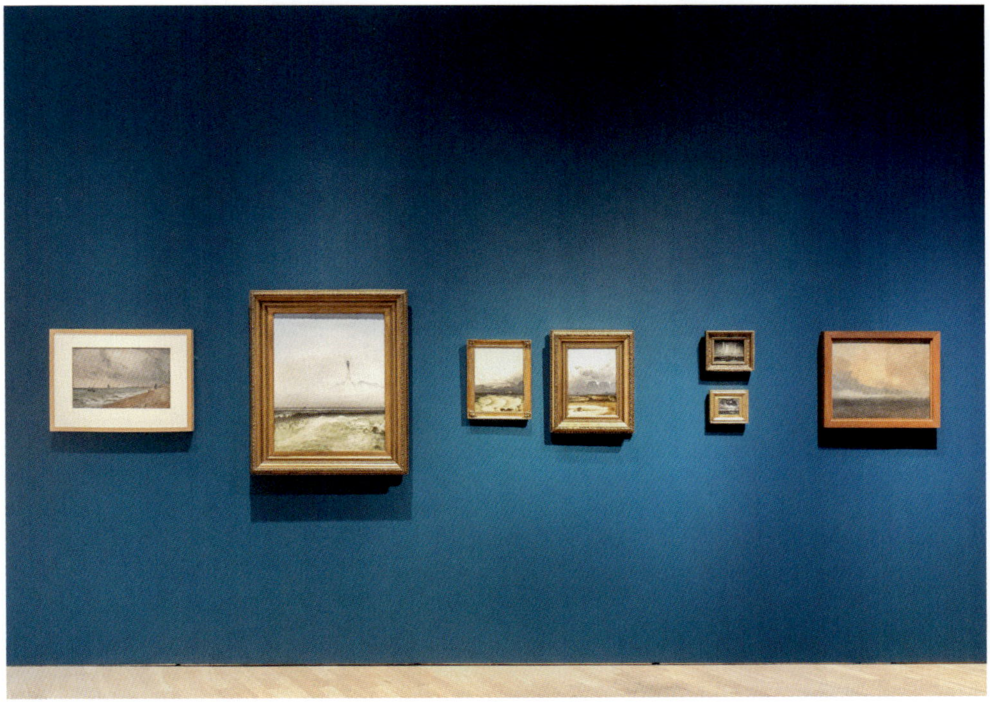

to Britain in 1933, the omnipresence of *The Hay Wain* in popular British culture originally tainted his opinion on Constable. But in a conversation with William Feaver, the exhibition curator, Freud described his personal discovery of Constable as a modern, emotional and 'English' painter. Unsurprisingly, and unlike the majority of the art historians and curators before him, Freud was particularly interested in Constable portraits, but also his *Study of the Trunk of an Elm Tree* (fig. 33), which Freud had attempted to copy as a student. At the opening of the exhibition, visitors found this work paired with Freud's own *Naked Portrait Standing*, 1999/2000. Furthermore, the following year Freud produced the etching *After Constable's Elm*.[25] As in Delacroix's case 200 years earlier, taking *The Hay Wain* back to the city of Constable's original triumph had resulted in another painter's work moving forward.

The examination of Constable's work for today's audiences, who are more conscious of global issues and are asking new questions of canonical art, continues in Britain and continental Europe. In April 2024, for example, Henie Onstad Kunstsenter in Norway opened an exhibition dedicated to the Atlantic Ocean from a global cultural, historical and eco-critical perspective (fig. 34). Here, Constable's beach scenes stand in as images that have shaped collective imaginations of the sea. In this global context, the question of whether the great landscape painter is English, British or European has – after 200 years of Constable in Europe – become irrelevant.

MARY MCMAHON

From 'dull replica' to 'national treasure': The Afterlife of *The Hay Wain*

Upon his death in 1837 it was far from apparent that John Constable would come to be considered a central figure in early nineteenth-century British art, or that *The Hay Wain* would reach its current status as a masterpiece of the English landscape. The fortunes of this artist's reputation, and that of his most famous painting, tie into both the history and development of the National Gallery. Constable's work acquired greater acclaim after his death, though for the first few decades this was not forthcoming in his home country. Harsh criticism of his style and process from prominent figures, such as John Ruskin (1819–1900), would result in an initial decline in the critical appreciation of his work in Britain, before it began its persistent rise spurred by the acknowledgement of his influence on the work of French artists, including Delacroix (see p. 52), Huet (see fig. 29) and Constant Troyon, who were excited by his approach to representing nature and a national landscape. Constable's work came to hold significance for later generations of British artists, from Sir John Everett Millais and Sir David Murray to Lucian Freud (see p. 61) and Peter Kennard (see fig. 42).

Constable's attachment to his 'own dear England' is well documented and was most publicly expressed in his published print series of 1833, referenced in shorthand as 'English Scenery', though interestingly *The Hay Wain* was not engraved during the artist's lifetime.[1] The subsequent association of his art with a distinctive Englishness has seen *The Hay Wain* often co-opted into visions of a British landscape now lost, or at least under threat. Furthermore, the regular reproduction of this painting in print and on household items throughout the twentieth century caused it to become part of public visual memory. By the twenty-first century it was often repeated that Constable's

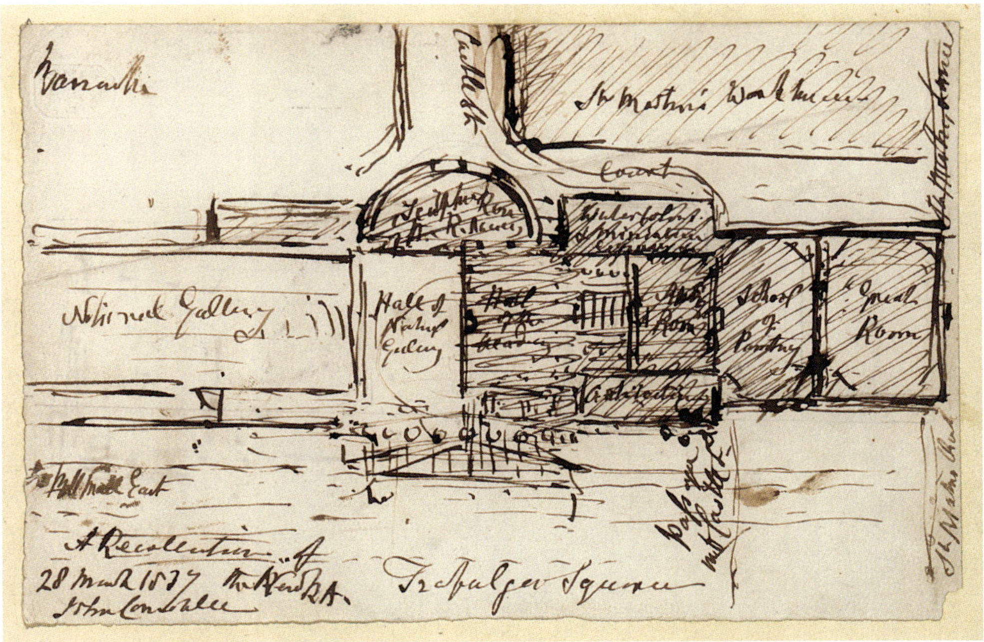

Fig. 35
A Recollection of the New RA (detail), 1837
Pen and brown ink on medium, smooth, cream wove paper, 34 × 25.4 cm
Yale Center for British Art, Paul Mellon Collection, New Haven

representation of the English landscape had 'become bound up with the identity of the nation itself'.[2]

After receiving great acclaim at the Paris Salon of 1824 and a gold medal from King Charles X (see p. 8), *The Hay Wain* remained in France for around 14 years.[3] At the time of Constable's death on 31 March 1837 it was in the collection of Jean-François Boursault, a successful theatre manager. Shortly thereafter, around 1838, the painting returned to Britain when 80 pictures from Boursault's collection were purchased by Henry Artaria for Edmund Higginson of Saltmarsh Castle in Herefordshire.[4] Eight years later, at the Higginson sale at Christie's on 4 June 1846 and then titled 'A wagon passing through a river', it was bought for £378 by the dealer Thomas Rought, after which it passed to another dealer, D.T. White, from whom George Young 'of Ryde' had purchased the picture by 1853.[5] Young was a surgeon and a friend of Constable, and assisted at the artist's post-mortem.[6] While in his collection, *The Hay Wain* was displayed in the winter exhibition of 1853 at the British Institution, a private society founded in 1805 that mounted annual exhibitions in Pall Mall until 1869.[7]

Over the nineteenth century, the National Gallery would become the best place in the UK for the public to see work by British and foreign artists. Constable himself was initially critical of the idea of a national gallery, concerned that '[t]he manufacturers of pictures are then made the criterion of perfection & not nature'.[8] Over time he appears to have begrudgingly accepted this new institution. On 28 March 1837, three days before he died, the artist drew *A Recollection of the New RA* (fig. 35): the Royal Academy was to be housed in the same building as the Gallery from 1838 until 1869. As a tribute to Constable, friends selected a work from his studio that they wished to give to the national collection to ensure he was represented. For this they sought subscriptions, and ultimately received money from 113 subscribers, including the artists Sir William Beechey, Sir Charles Eastlake (later to become the first director of the National Gallery), William Etty, Clarkson Stanfield and Sir David Wilkie, among others. Scientist Michael Faraday, poet William Wordsworth, collector John Sheepshanks, the artist's brother Golding Constable and the previously mentioned surgeon George Young also subscribed. *The Cornfield* (see fig. 87) became the first work by Constable to enter the collection in December 1837.[9] As the first publicly owned example of a work by the artist, it was therefore influential on the public's view of him. Also significant was C.R. Leslie's 1843 publication entitled *Memoirs of the Life of John Constable*. A friend of the artist, he gave a positive, albeit selective, representation of the man himself and his desire for 'truth to nature'.

In his 1854 publication *Treasures of Art in Great Britain*, art historian Gustav Friedrich Waagen described the then burgeoning collection of the National Gallery. Drawing a comparison with a five-month visit made in 1835, he remarked on the 'decided progress in the school of English painting'. Waagen recorded the pictures of the English school from 1730 to the present as having been moved to Marlborough House and now on display in a 'suite of rooms granted for that purpose'. This was the result of limited space in the building in Trafalgar Square.[10] Making particular note of landscape painting as the second best-served department, next to subject painting, Waagen touches on works by J.M.W. Turner ('the greatest landscape-painter of all times') and Richard Parkes Bonington, before lauding Constable's 'realistic tendency', depicting rural English scenes in the 'most unpretending and attractive form', and noting the inclusion of both *The Cornfield* and *The Valley Farm* in the Gallery's collection.[11] The range of gifts and bequests to the British collection in the nineteenth century caused it to grow 'haphazardly and far more rapidly than those of the foreign schools'.[12]

From the mid-nineteenth century, with the establishment of new public institutions and a higher number of regular exhibitions, the visibility of Constable's work was growing. In 1857, five paintings and a drawing by the artist were included in the section on 'Modern Masters' at the highly influential Manchester *Art Treasures* exhibition at Old Trafford.[13] With more than 1.25 million visitors, this exhibition was significant for being the first of its scale to represent works from the collections of rich northern industrialists, rather than the historically dominant collections of the aristocracy and landed gentry. In *The Art-Treasures Examiner*, Peregrine Sketchly described Constable as an artist drawn to subject matter with no poetry or beauty but made attractive through a 'peculiar elemental effect'. He admired Constable's defence of his own style throughout his career, exclaiming 'all honour to thy honest noble heart!'[14] In this same year, Constable's *Salisbury Cathedral from the Bishop's Ground* (see fig. 89) along with other works by the artist, was given to the South Kensington Museum (from 1899 the Victoria and Albert Museum) by the notable collector Sheepshanks, whose donations and bequests would have a big influence on public collections of British art.[15]

The full-scale sketches Constable produced to assist with the creation of his 'six-footer' series of scenes on the river Stour are significant when tracing the development of his reputation, as they played a role in making his practice visible to the public and would be read increasingly positively by audiences conditioned by the looser stylistic movements of the late nineteenth and early twentieth centuries. Several large, full-size sketches are mentioned in the auction catalogue for the executors' sale of Constable's studio contents in London on 16 May 1838. The lot appears to have been bought on behalf of Constable's family. The sketches can be traced after this point in C.R. Leslie's house, where he was looking after them 'for want of room elsewhere'.[16] The dealer D.T. White, previously mentioned as holding the finished version of *The Hay Wain*, is described showing the sketches of *The Hay Wain* and *The Leaping Horse* to viewers around 1853, before selling them both to the antiquarian Henry Vaughan by 1862.[17]

It was in that year that George Young lent the finished *Hay Wain* to the International Exhibition, which was held at the South Kensington Museum and included works by artists influenced by Constable, such as Paul Huet's *The Flood at Saint-Cloud* (Louvre). In the exhibition handbook, Constable is described as 'the first painter to reinstate pure English rural landscape ... since Gainsborough and Crome ceased to paint it'.[18] In the same year, Henry Vaughan presented the full-scale sketches as long-term loans to the Sheepshanks Gallery adjoining the same museum (which at this point was known as the National Gallery of British Art).[19] It was therefore possible for the first time for the public to compare the full-size sketch of *The Hay Wain* with the completed work hung in the neighbouring gallery.[20]

At George Young's sale at Christie's on 19 May 1866, the finished version of *The Hay Wain* was bought by William Cox, buying agent for Joseph Gillott, a collector and dealer with an interest in British landscape painting. Gillott resold the work later that year to Henry Vaughan.[21] While in this collection, the painting was finally etched and printed by 'De Baines' from a Goupil photograph supplied by Vaughan, making it possible for the image to be more widely reproduced and circulated.[22] He also lent the painting to the Burlington Fine Arts Club *Old Masters* exhibition in 1871, and to the Royal Academy's winter exhibition of the same year, and again to the Academy in the winter of 1885–6.[23] In 1886 an exhibition in Edinburgh was organised by Mr Hamilton Bruce, which in part sought to demonstrate the influence of Constable on the French and Dutch schools of landscape painting.[24]

Constable was now readily included in significant books that traced the history of art in Britain. In 1866 Richard and Samuel Redgrave published their influential *Century of Painters of the English School*, in which they described a growth of public interest in works of art from Britain. In this influential volume, Constable is presented as the first artist 'who wholly emancipated himself from the schools' to produce pure and thoroughly 'English' landscape art. The Redgraves saw no references to Italian, French or Dutch artists in his work, rather identifying nature as his primary teacher and his approach as 'thoroughly original'. The authors note the 'glitter and sparkle of white lights on his foliage'

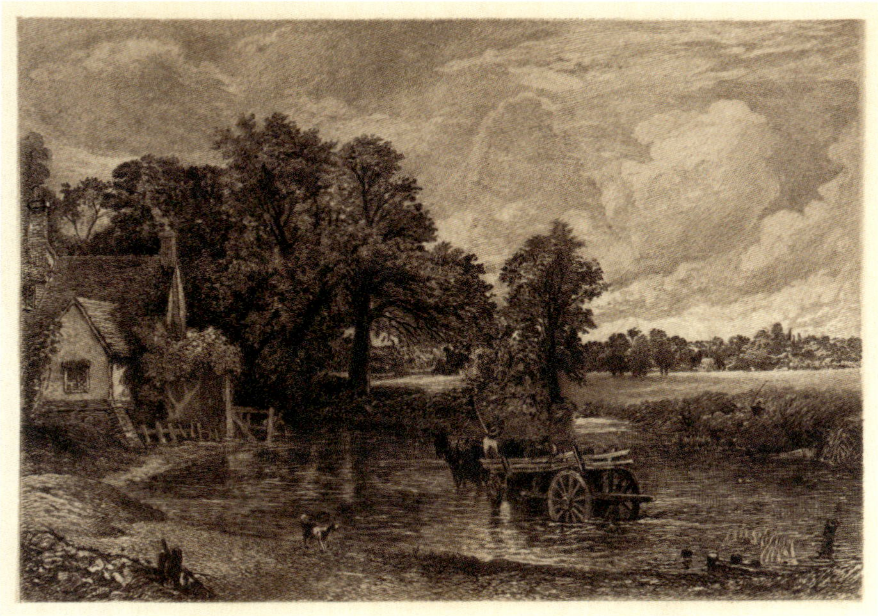

Fig. 36
Edward Paxman Brandard
(1819–1898)
The Hay Wain, 1887
Etching, 16.3 × 23.6 cm (image);
23.4 × 30.7 cm (sheet)
The National Gallery, London
(NG72/49)

in their argument against Constable's contemporary critics of this effect, writing that one only needed to look at nature to see these characteristic flashes of sunlight. While addressing Constable's lack of popularity and fame in his own time, they repeated from Leslie that the artist himself sought not to flatter or court these, but rather was confident that he would come to be appreciated. They singled out the purchase of *The Cornfield* for the National Gallery as having created a 'better feeling for his art', leading to his works being 'treasured in all collections'.[25] In 1880 Mrs Charles Heaton revised and expanded on the seminal work by Allan Cunningham, *The Lives of the Most Eminent British Painters*, which had been published from 1829 to 1831 and was credited with fixing the idea that Britain had its own national school of art. Heaton's expansion, some 50 years later, demonstrated that this had firmly taken root. In the original version, the only landscape painters included were Richard Wilson and Thomas Gainsborough, but in the revised version this was greatly extended, and included Constable. Heaton drew upon the Redgraves' biography and highlighted the severity of Ruskin and Fuseli's critiques earlier in the century, the latter calling for his 'great coat and umbrella' when looking at Constable's paintings. She described his work as 'genuinely English, locally English even', and his primary achievement 'as a painter of our English skies', bringing a 'scientific knowledge of the anatomy ... of the clouds'.[26] Both the Redgraves and Heaton referenced Constable's success at the 1824 Paris Salon and his influence on French landscape art, by then a commonly acknowledged point made by British artists and critics of the late nineteenth century.[27]

In 1880 Mrs Charles Heaton was still recording *The Cornfield* and *The Valley Farm* as the only works by Constable in the National Gallery Collection, though by then six were held at the South Kensington Museum. The late 1880s were key years for the entry of works by Constable into public collections. In 1886 Henry Vaughan donated *The Hay Wain* to the National Gallery. It was included in the Royal Academy's winter exhibition of 1886 and engraved by E.P. Brandard for reproduction in *The Portfolio* in 1887 (vol. XVIII; fig. 36). The accompanying text by Cosmo Monkhouse records the picture hanging alongside the two other works by the same artist. The writer draws out the effect of this particular work on the modern school of French landscape and Constable's own reference that those responding at the Paris Salon recognised 'the richness of texture and the surface of things'. Terms such as 'vitality' and 'freshness' henceforth became frequently used in discussion of Constable's work.

In 1886 Isabel Constable, the artist's second daughter and his last surviving child of seven, donated one of her father's palettes to the Royal Academy (see fig. 68). Two years later she bequeathed a large group of his work to various institutions on behalf of her late siblings Maria Louisa and Lionel Bicknell Constable, and herself. Where works were donated is a good indication of how the collections of different institutions were viewed at this juncture. For the National Gallery, she included the *Cenotaph* (see fig. 88), which honoured the memory of the British artist Sir Joshua Reynolds, placing him in the history of 'Western' art through the inclusion of busts of Raphael and Michelangelo.[28] Constable's small-scale sketches and studies were given to the South Kensington Museum, to join the full-size sketches along with other significant finished works by the artist. In the 1888 and 1889 summer exhibitions at the Grosvenor Gallery, which explored 'A Century of British Art from 1737 to 1837', Constable was well represented, with 33 paintings on display in 1888 (including a number of studies), and eight named paintings in 1889, along with a room filled with sketches by Constable. These sketches were lent by various members of the artist's family and had never before been exhibited to the public.[29] They depicted nature recorded 'en plein air', further revealing Constable's knowledge and processes, and they would lead to the development of his reputation as an innovator. Through their entry to the public collection at South Kensington, this visual revelation about the artist's process would not be fleeting.

An album put together by Henry Vaughan between 1886 and 1893, now in the archive at the National Gallery, includes correspondence and published excerpts relating to the painting's exhibition, photography, engraving and art historical importance.[30] Together they demonstrate the late nineteenth-century focus on Constable's influence on the French school and the need for the British school to 'catch up'. Vaughan included a woodcut print of *The Hay Wain* that appeared as the frontispiece of *The Magazine of Art* in June 1886. The accompanying text described it as 'in some sort the most memorable picture of the century' and linked it to the evolution of the great school of landscape painting in France, referencing Charles-François Daubigny and Corot, and presenting the British art school as misled by Ruskin (or the 'Oxford Graduate', as he is called). The author suggests the proper place for the picture to be the Louvre, rather than the National Gallery, since the British nation has had to understand Constable 'through a series of French translations'. Alexandre-Gabriel Decamps (1803–1860) is quoted as saying: 'We, French Artists, look upon Constable as the Father of French Landscape Art.'

In 1897 the National Gallery of British Art, later Tate Gallery, opened at Millbank. At this point a division was made of the British collection, with works deemed 'masterpieces' remaining at Trafalgar Square. Six paintings by Constable were transferred at this point (there were 16 in total in the collection by this date). In 1915 this justification was expanded upon in the Curzon Report: 'the supreme glories of British painting' were to remain in the Square, while those who wished to see the 'history and evolution of indigenous art' could find this at Millbank. Portraiture, in particular, predominated at Trafalgar Square, but a few landscapes were retained, and they included *The Hay Wain*.

The growth of the representation of Constable in public collections towards the end of the nineteenth century increased public knowledge of his work, but events of the twentieth century strengthened the identification of his landscapes with an idealised, even nostalgic, 'vision of England' and 'Englishness'. The First and particularly the Second World War would see a proliferation of material centring the British landscape as the worthy subject of protection. In this, *The Hay Wain* emerged as a focus for nostalgia. As part of the George Salting Bequest of 1910 the National Gallery received *Weymouth Bay: Bowleaze Cove and Jordon Hill* (1816–17) and *Salisbury Cathedral and Leadenhall from the River Avon* (1820). In 1936 Kenneth Clark, director of the National Gallery from 1934 to 1946, referenced the full-size sketches of *The Hay Wain* and *The Leaping Horse* at the V&A as the greatest thing in British art, placing them in opposition to the finished works, which he described as 'dull replicas, finished for exhibition according to the timid taste of the day'.[31]

The anniversary of the death of the artist was marked in 1937 by the *Centenary Exhibition of Paintings and Water-Colours by John Constable, R.A.* at the Tate Gallery, and the following year by the republication of Leslie's *Memoirs* by the Hon. Andrew Shirley and the Medici Society. Also in 1938, *The Hay Wain* was included in an exhibition in Paris of *La Peinture anglaise: XVIIIe et XIXe siècles* (*English Painting: XVIIIth and XIXth Centuries*). The increased patronage of British artists during the war, amid displays and concerts at the gallery, indicated the patriotism of the period. In 1944 Clark wrote an introductory book focused on *The Hay Wain* for the National Gallery, and in 1949 he would describe the finished work as 'an eternally moving expression of serenity and optimism', despite the 'destructive popularity' of its mass reproduction.[32] Following the end of the Second World War, *The Hay Wain* was included in the grand exhibition sent to Chicago, New York and Toronto in the years 1946 to 1947: *Masterpieces of English Painting: William Hogarth, John Constable, J.M.W. Turner*.[33] In the accompanying publication, Clark repeated his assertion that the full-size sketches were 'Constable's most successful works ... perhaps the greatest pictures ever painted in England'.[34] Naming Constable in the title confirms his increased status, and the inclusion of *The Hay Wain* extended knowledge

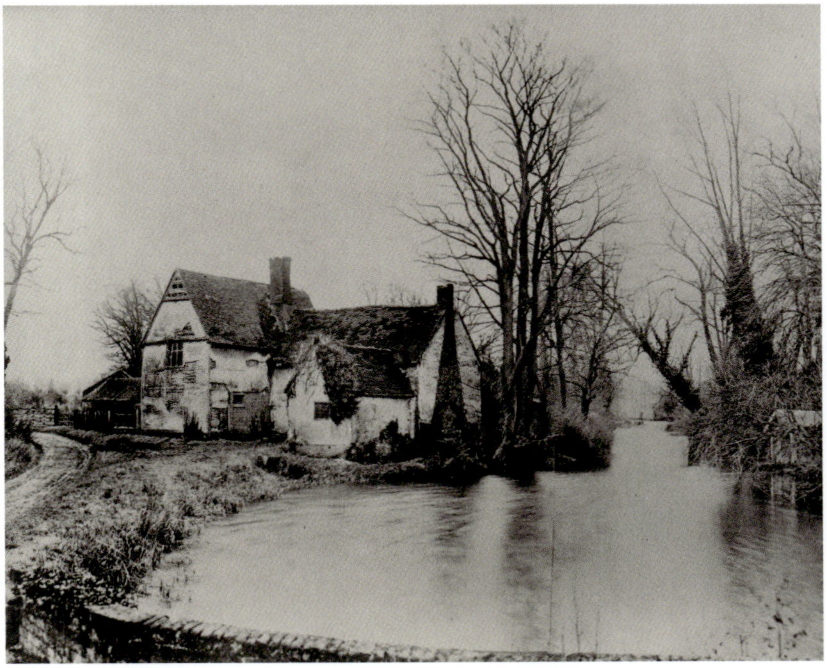

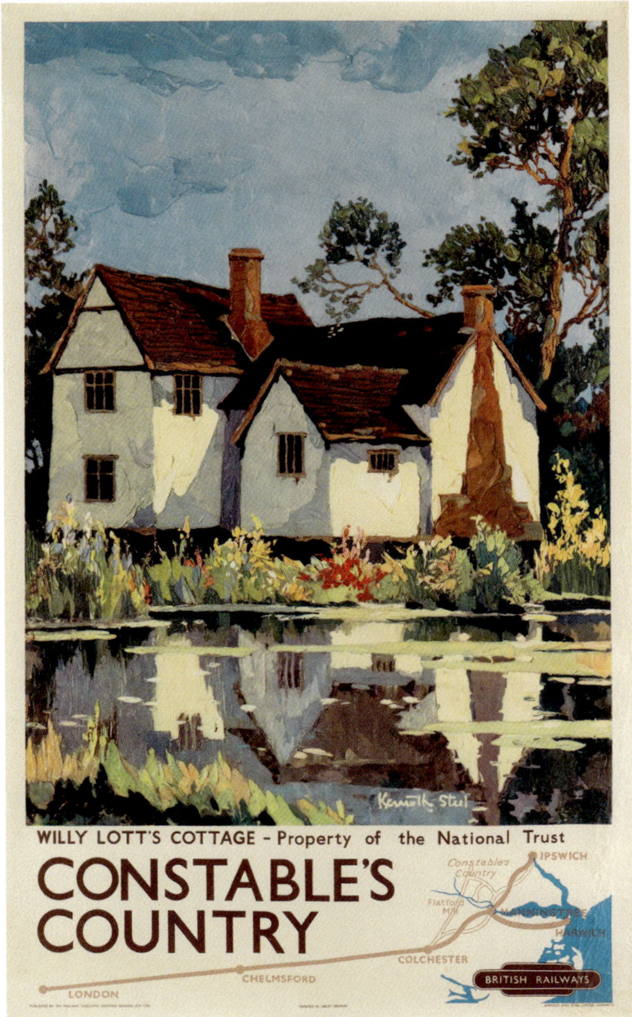

Fig. 37
Historical photograph of Willy Lott's House, Flatford, before restoration.
The National Gallery, London

Fig. 38
Kenneth Steel (1906–1970)
'Constable's Country', about 1950
British Railways poster showing Willy Lott's House.
Private collection

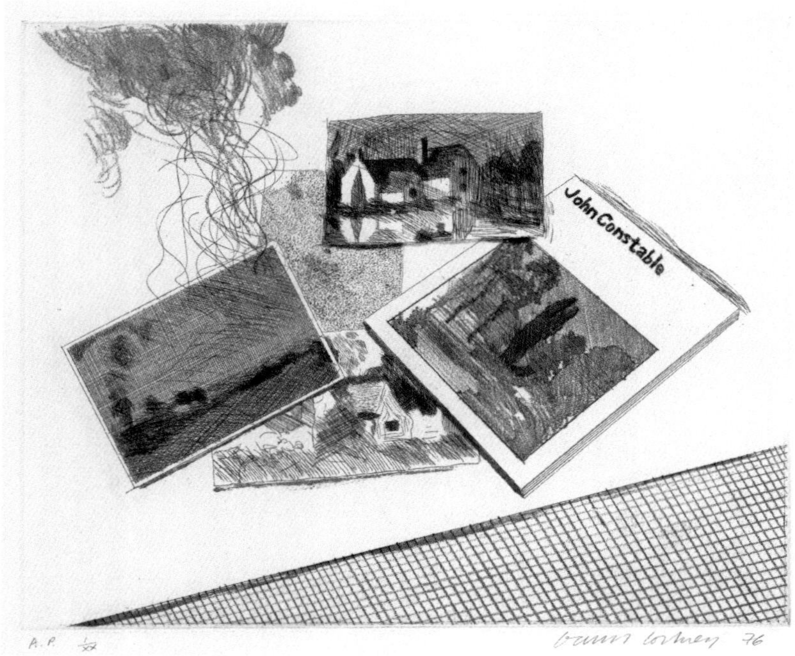

Fig. 39
David Hockney (born 1937)
'For John Constable', 1976
Etching, 38.1 × 44.5 cm
Edition of 100

Fig. 40
Stratford Mill, 1820
Oil on canvas, 127 × 182.9 cm
The National Gallery, London

of this work internationally. Shortly thereafter, in 1948, the painting was included in a display in Paris. It featured in the Royal Academy's exhibition on 'The first hundred years of the Royal Academy 1769–1868' in 1951–2, and in 1972 at the Petit Palais in *English Romantic Painting and the Pre-Raphaelites* (British Council).

Suffolk's identification with 'Constable Country' was long established, even within the artist's own lifetime, but this link grew over the century following his death. Thomas Cook & Son were listing 'A visit to Constable's Country' on their tour options by 1893. The increased fame of *The Hay Wain* in the first half of the twentieth century was demonstrated by the fortunes of Willy Lott's House (see p. 32). By 1925 the house had fallen into disrepair, and was taken on as a project by Thomas Parkington, who had purchased the Flatford Mill Estate (fig. 37). Over two years he completed the restoration of the house; when he died in 1943, the National Trust agreed to buy Flatford Mill from his Trustees (fig. 38). Since 1995 it has been a Grade I listed building.[35]

The cataloguing of works by Constable would be a feature of the second half of the twentieth century and established the extent and variety of his production, and worthiness for study. In regard to this, Graham Reynolds (1914–2013), former Keeper of Paintings at the Victoria and Albert Museum, would be the most influential figure in Constable studies in the twentieth century. In 1960 he first published a catalogue of the paintings and drawings by Constable in the Victoria and Albert Museum, but his defining publications would be his catalogue raisonné of Constable's work: first the later paintings and drawings in 1984, followed by the early paintings and drawings in 1996.[36]

R.B. Beckett's publication of Constable's correspondence in the 1960s and 1970s greatly expanded the representation of the artist given by C.R. Leslie in his *Memoirs*. By publishing Constable's writing in full, Beckett allowed the artist to emerge as a more interesting if complex figure. This series included casual remarks by the artist in his private letters, as well as his more thoughtful professional presentations, thereby giving greater insight into his beliefs around art and nature. The correspondence also revealed the acerbic tone the artist could adopt when discussing contemporaries with his close friends, and his at times combative nature in communications with David Lucas, the engraver of his prints.

The bicentenary of Constable's birth in 1976 saw the culmination of a number of projects celebrating the artist. At the Tate Gallery, *Constable: Paintings, Watercolours & Drawings*, accompanied by a catalogue, was the first comprehensive exhibition of Constable's work.[37] The art dealer and publisher Bernard Jacobson commissioned 19 contemporary artists to respond with a print to include in the portfolio *For John Constable*, including David Hockney (fig. 39).[38] In 1981 curator

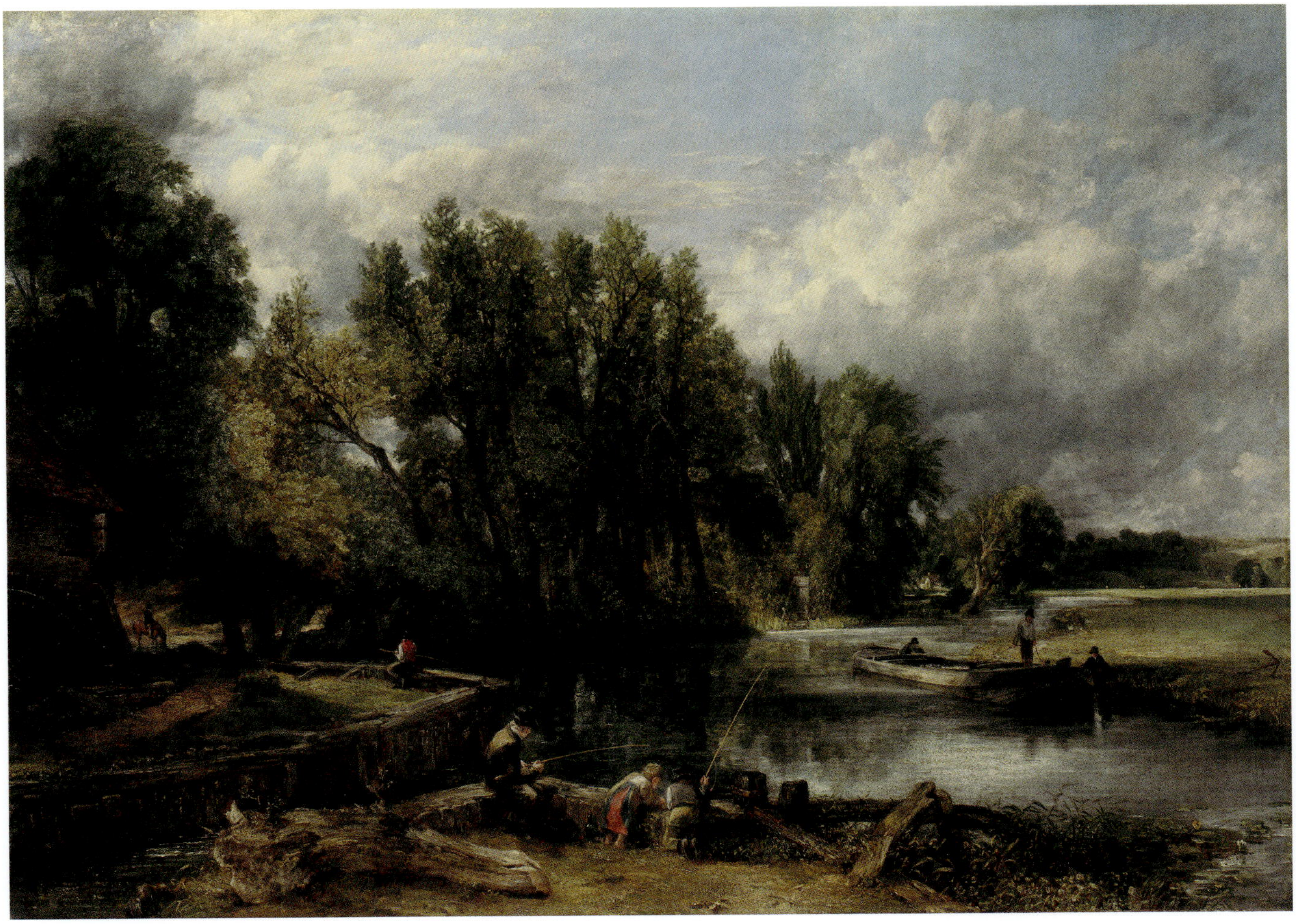

Leslie Parris published the catalogue of the Constable collection held at Tate. Three years later he collaborated with Ian Fleming-Williams for the 1984 publication *The Discovery of Constable*, and in 1991 for the *Constable* exhibition also at Tate.[39]

Meanwhile, at the National Gallery, two casts of the gold medal awarded to Constable at the Paris Salon, which had been fixed to the frame in the National Gallery for historical interest, were stolen in 1963 during opening hours.[40] The number of works by the artist grew in 1987 when *Stratford Mill*, an earlier work from the artist's six-foot scenes on the river Stour (fig. 40), was presented to the gallery through the Acceptance-in-Lieu procedure. In 1996 the only Constable exhibition ever held at the National Gallery, *At Home with Constable's Cornfield*, looked at how the artist's images had entered people's homes on a range of objects from wallpaper to biscuit tins. In the accompanying publication, retired art dealer Ian Nicholson wrote: 'Constable, for me, encapsulates an England that doesn't exist anymore. It's a bit of history. I love this country and the natural beauty of it and I think there's something there that, perhaps, is lost and he has recorded.'[41]

Constable has continued to be the subject of significant exhibitions in the twenty-first century, in both large and small displays, and in national and regional institutions. To name a select few that relate to the current exhibition: in 2002–3 artist Lucian Freud curated an exhibition on Constable at the Grand Palais in Paris (see p. 61). In 2006, at Tate Britain, Anne Lyles curated *Constable: The Great Landscapes*, which brought together Constable's seminal 'six-footer' series for the first time. In 2014 Mark Evans curated *Constable: The Making of a Master* at the Victoria and Albert Museum, which examined the artist's knowledge of and interest in the work of the 'old masters', countering the commonly held assertion that he was a purely 'natural painter'.[42] In 2021–2 Emma Roodhouse curated the exhibition *Creating Constable* at Christchurch Mansion, Ipswich, looking at influential figures on the artist and his early works. Also in 2021–2, Lyles curated *Late Constable* at the Royal Academy, with Per Rumberg, focusing on the free and expressive brushstrokes of the artist's later work.

The recognisability of *The Hay Wain* and its association with the English landscape have resulted in it often being adopted for protests against change. As early as 1929 the image was the basis for a cartoon for the Campaign to Protect Rural England published in *The Daily Express*, which depicted the scene reimagined 'had John Constable lived to-day' and used it to advertise a 'Save-the-Countryside' exhibition then on show at Westminster Hall in London (fig. 41). In 1980, as part of a Campaign for Nuclear Disarmament campaign, and in protest against American cruise missiles being deployed in the UK, artist Peter Kennard would add weaponry to the image, in *Haywain with Cruise Missiles* (fig. 42). Ken Livingstone, then leader of the Greater London Council, commissioned Kennard to give visual expression to his declaration that London was a 'nuclear-free zone', based on the strength of this image. The resulting series was described by art critic Richard Cork as the 'most hard-hitting attack on government imbecility',

Fig. 41
'Had John Constable Lived To-Day', *The Daily Express*, 2 March 1929

Fig. 42
Peter Kennard (born 1949)
Haywain with Cruise Missiles, 1980
Chromolithograph on paper and photographs on paper, 26 × 37.5 cm
Tate, London

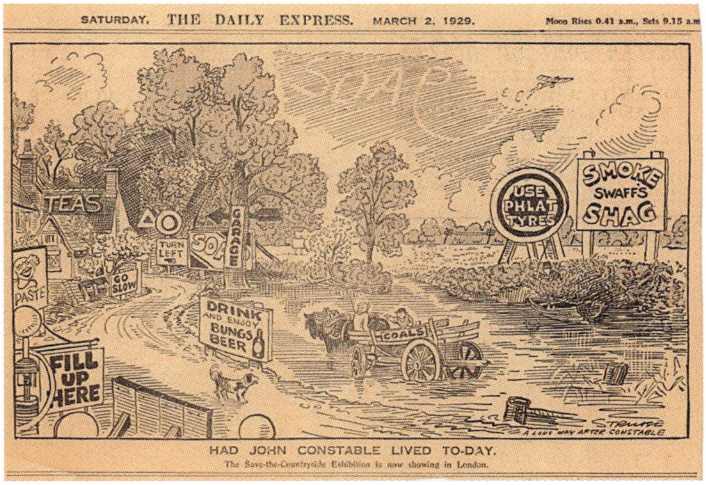
SATURDAY. THE DAILY EXPRESS. MARCH 2, 1929. Moon Rises 0.41 a.m., Sets 9.15 a.m.

HAD JOHN CONSTABLE LIVED TO-DAY.
The Save-the-Countryside Exhibition is now showing in London.

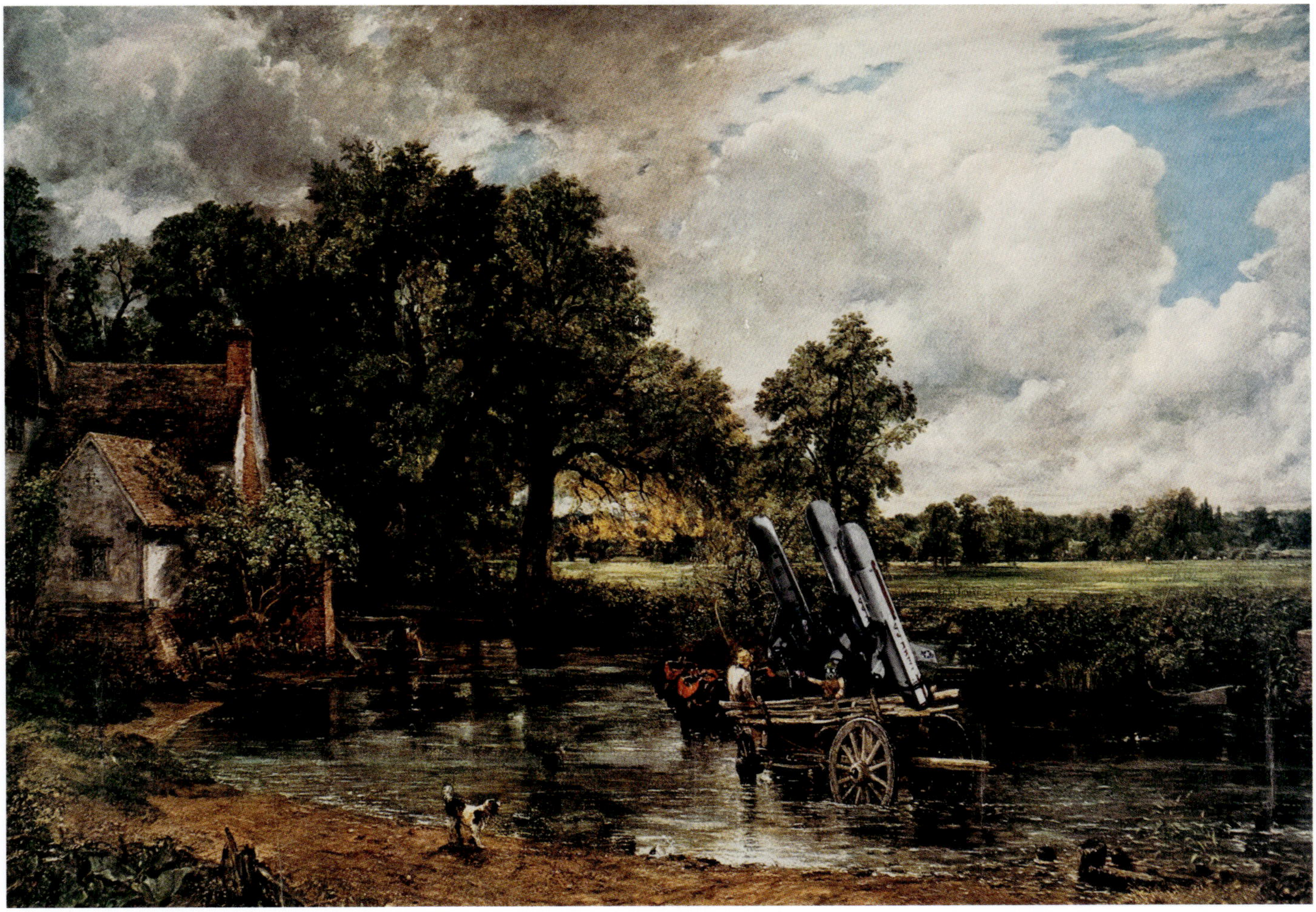

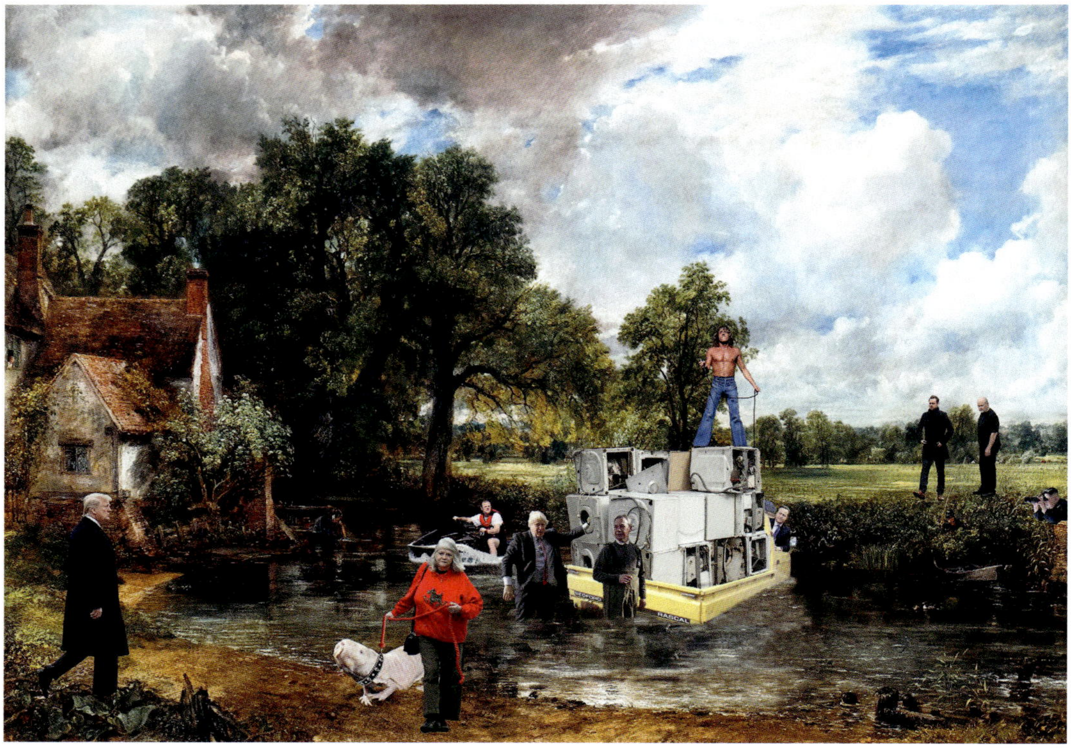

Fig. 43
Cold War Steve (born 1975)
Hey Wayne, 2019
Giclée print, 59.4 × 42 cm
Collection of the artist

Fig. 44
Frank Auerbach (born 1931)
Drawing after Constable's
The Hay Wain, 1989
Felt tip pen and oil pastel
on paper, 28.5 × 41.4 cm
The National Gallery, London

Fig. 45
Chris Shaw (born 1967)
The Haywain by Constable,
2007–12
Photograph, gelatin silver print
on paper, 40.4 × 30.4 cm
Tate, London

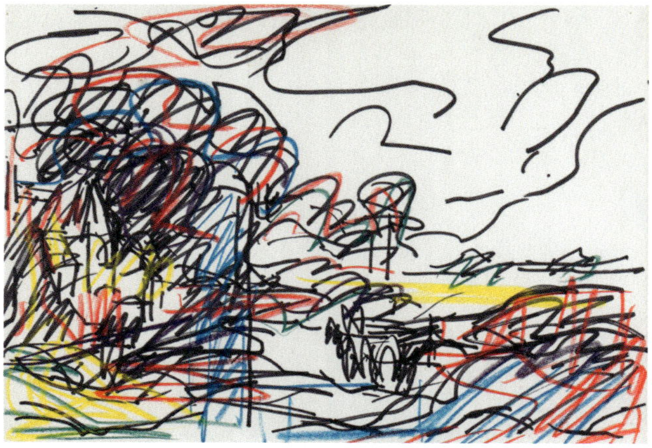

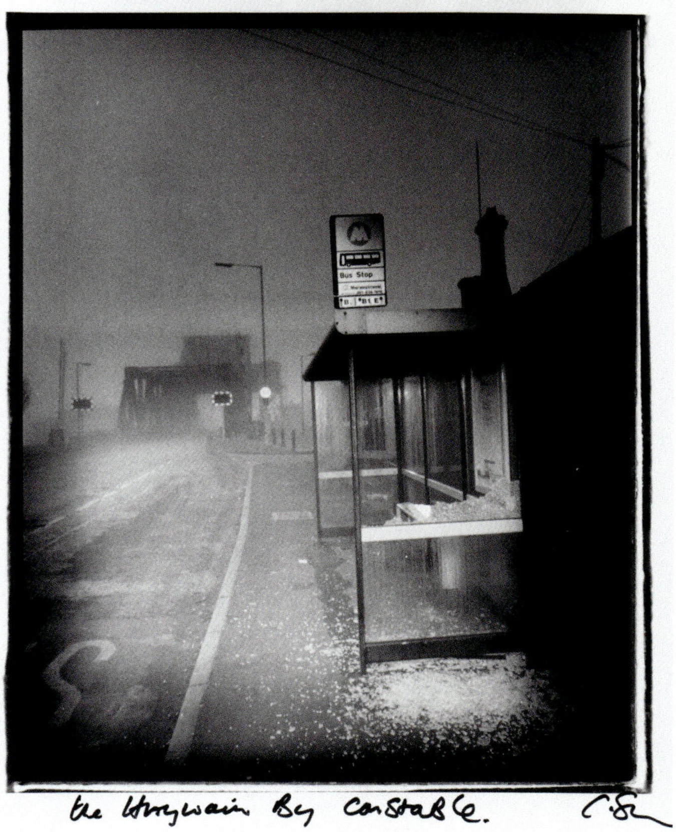

and curator Richard Slocombe referred to Kennard as 'Britain's most important political artist'.[43] *Haywain with Cruise Missiles* was reproduced as posters and smaller leaflet-sized images, and their dissemination furthered the awareness and contemporary relevance of the original.[44] In July 2019, the British artist and satirist Cold War Steve used *The Hay Wain* as the setting for one of his distinctive collages, recording recent events in politics and popular culture (fig. 43).

Constable's painting itself has also been the subject of protest action. In 2013 a protester for Fathers4Justice stuck a photograph of a young boy to the painting. In 2022 Just Stop Oil protesters attached a print of a manufactured landscape over the painting at the National Gallery. The amended image included jumbo jets, tower blocks, dead trees, fire and a burnt-out car, the river now covered by asphalt, and a washing machine visible in the wain. One of the protesters released a statement saying that when crop failures result from further oil extraction, '[y]ou can forget our "green and pleasant land"'. The use of this quotation from William Blake, now commonly associated with the hymn 'Jerusalem', confirms the perceived association of *The Hay Wain* with a nostalgic vision of England. These constructed scenes of protest rely upon public familiarity with the original painting, held in the collective memory.

There is also a strong thread of contemporary artists responding to Constable's work. In 1989 Frank Auerbach produced drawings of *The Hay Wain* in his series 'working after the masters', in which he sought to understand their compositional secrets (fig. 44). Reflecting that the artist meant more to him over time, Auerbach showed admiration for Constable's care and detailing of his landscapes: 'Everything has been worked for and made personal so you sometimes feel that Constable's own body is somehow inside the landscapes there.'[45] Photographer Chris Shaw responded to the idyllic English scene with *The Haywain by Constable* (2007–12). By adopting Constable's title, he presents a shattered bus stop as a contrasting representation of the British landscape today (fig. 45). In a broader work relating to the artist, in 2019 Bridget Riley (born 1931) produced the commission *Messengers* as a large-scale wall painting in the National Gallery, referencing a phrase Constable used in relation to clouds. In 2022 Riley wrote on the influence of Constable's work upon Delacroix, and in turn – through his processes – upon 'succeeding generations of aspiring colorists', herself included.[46]

In 2024, as part of the National Gallery's Bicentenary celebrations, *The Hay Wain* was included in the 'National Treasures Tour': 12 masterpieces from the collection were loaned to 12 partner venues in the UK for them to curate displays or exhibitions. Constable's masterpiece went to Bristol Museum & Art Gallery to be included in their May–September 2024 exhibition *National Treasures: Constable in Bristol 'Truth to Nature'*. After its return, the *Discover Constable & The Hay Wain* exhibition at the National Gallery is the first to mark the significance of this work in the collection to which it was given for the nation.

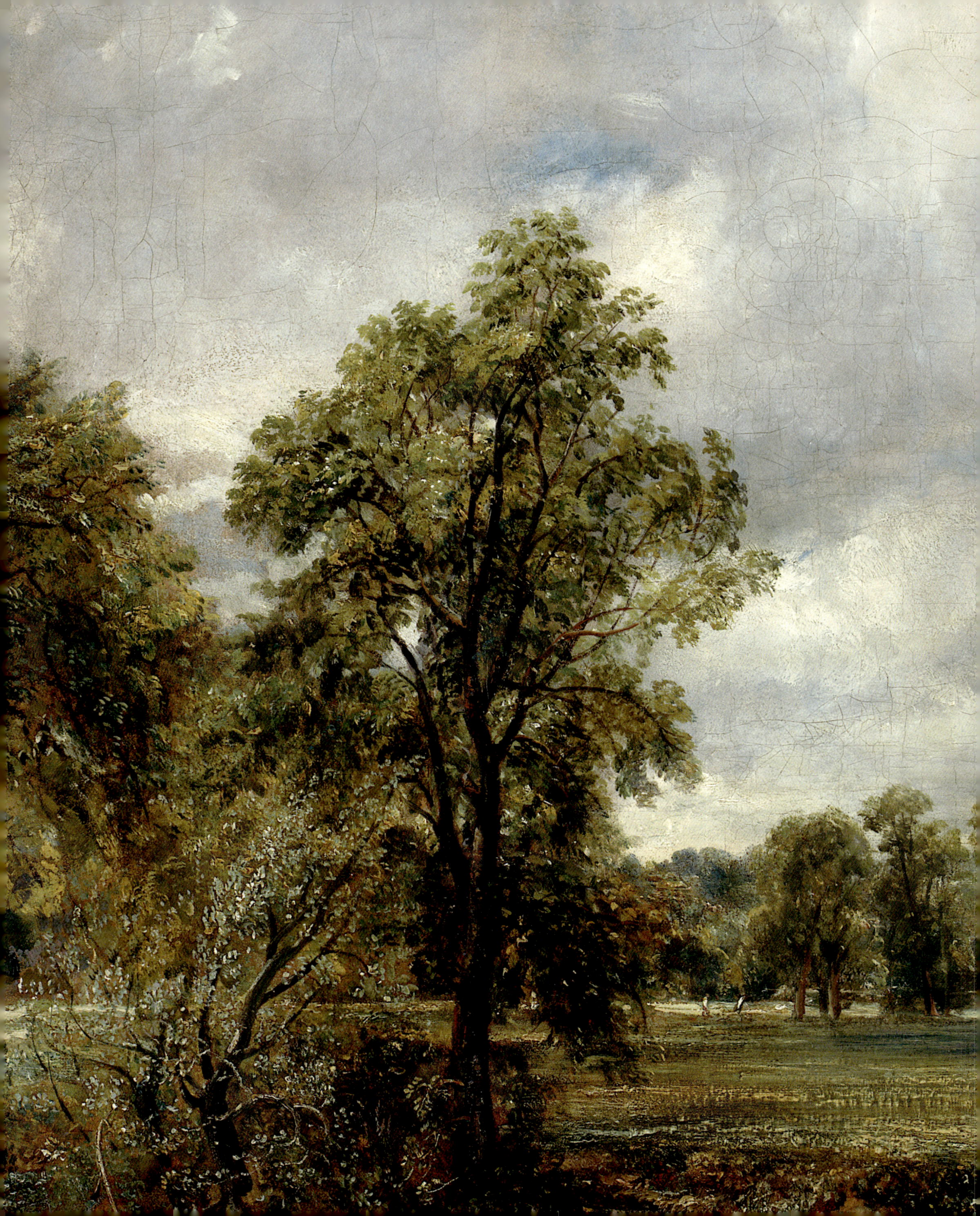

PLATES

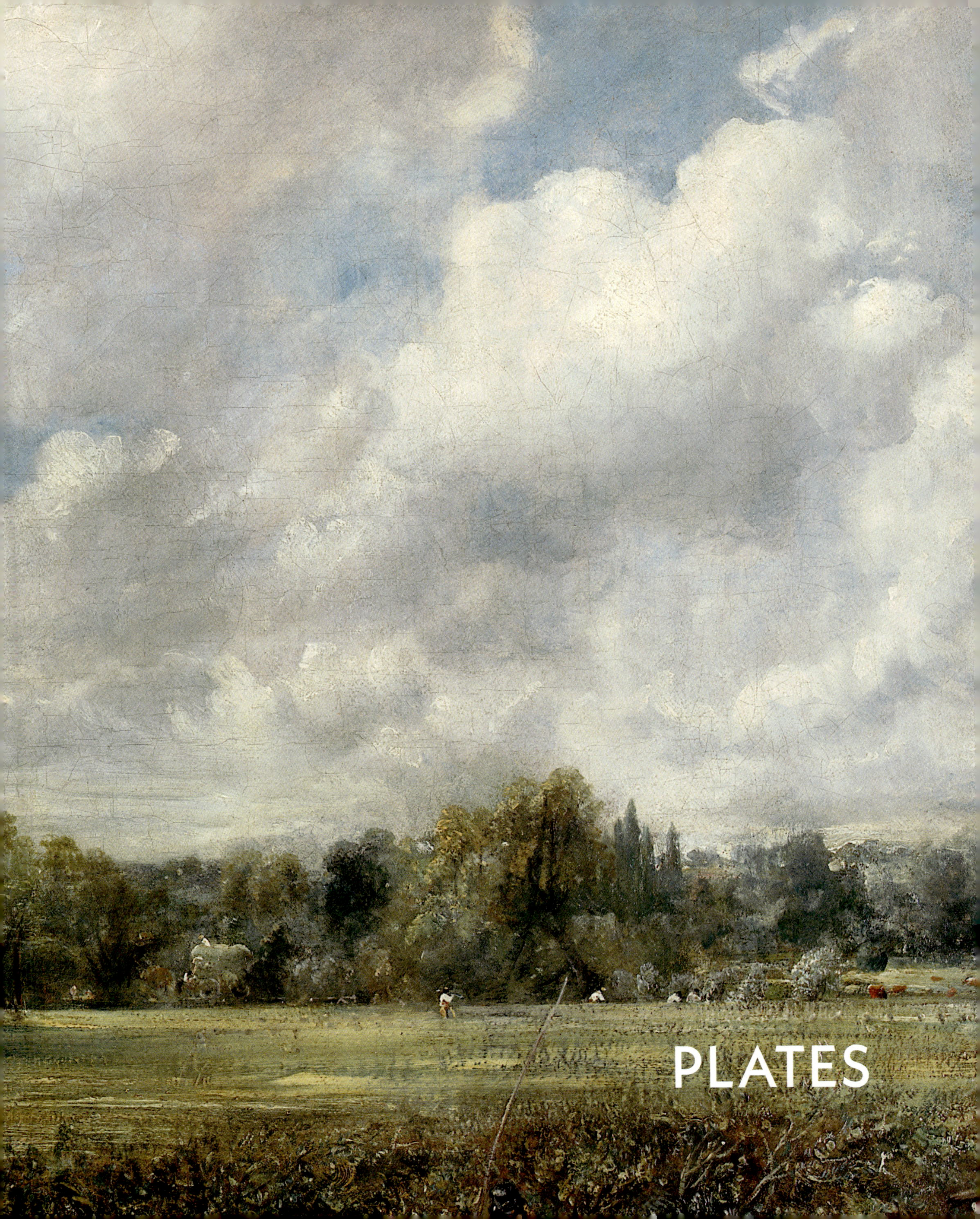

Landscapes of Tradition and Innovation

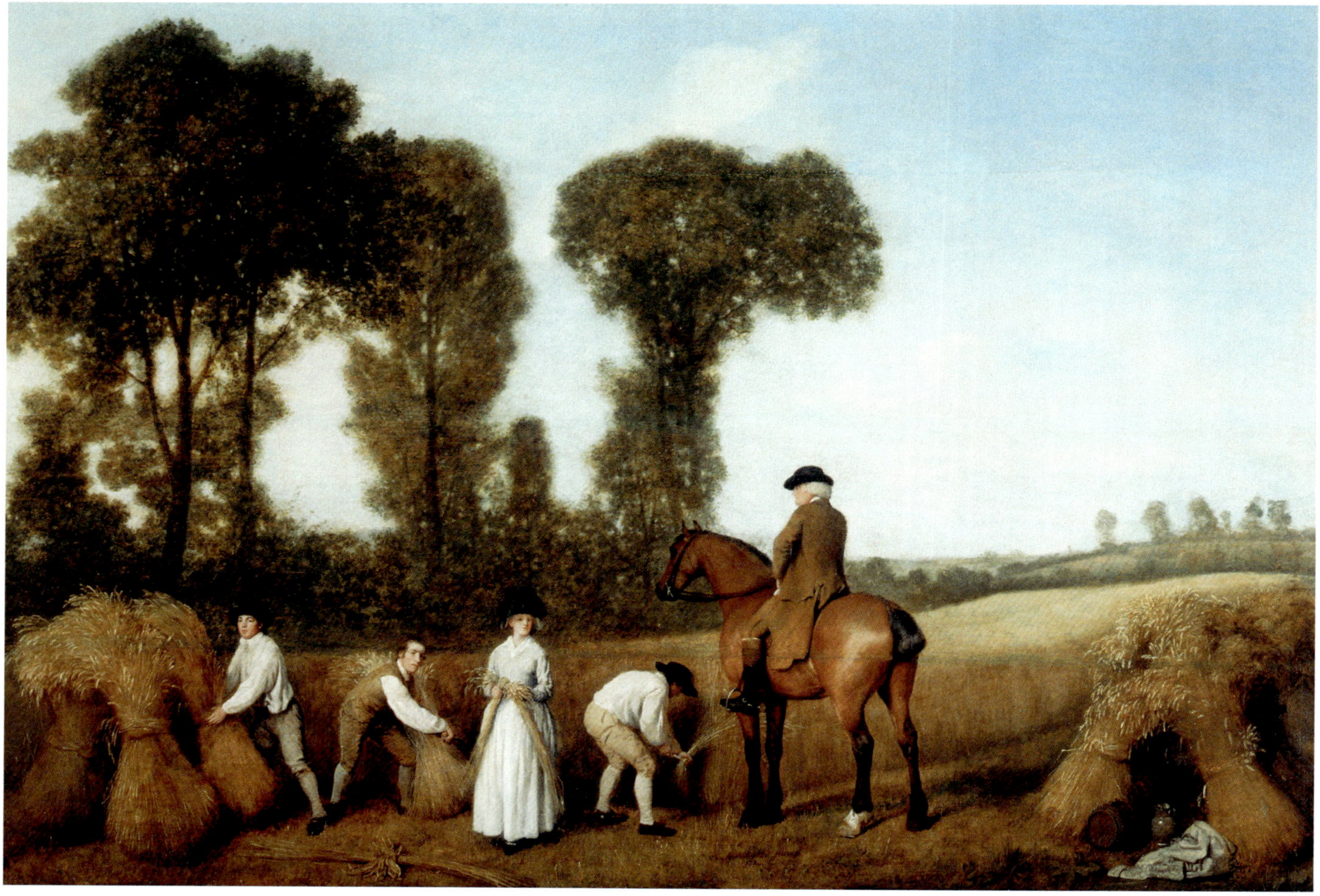

Fig. 46
George Stubbs (1724–1806)
The Reapers, 1783
Oil and enamel on panel (oak), 91.4 × 137.3 cm
National Trust Collections, Upton House (The Bearsted Collection)

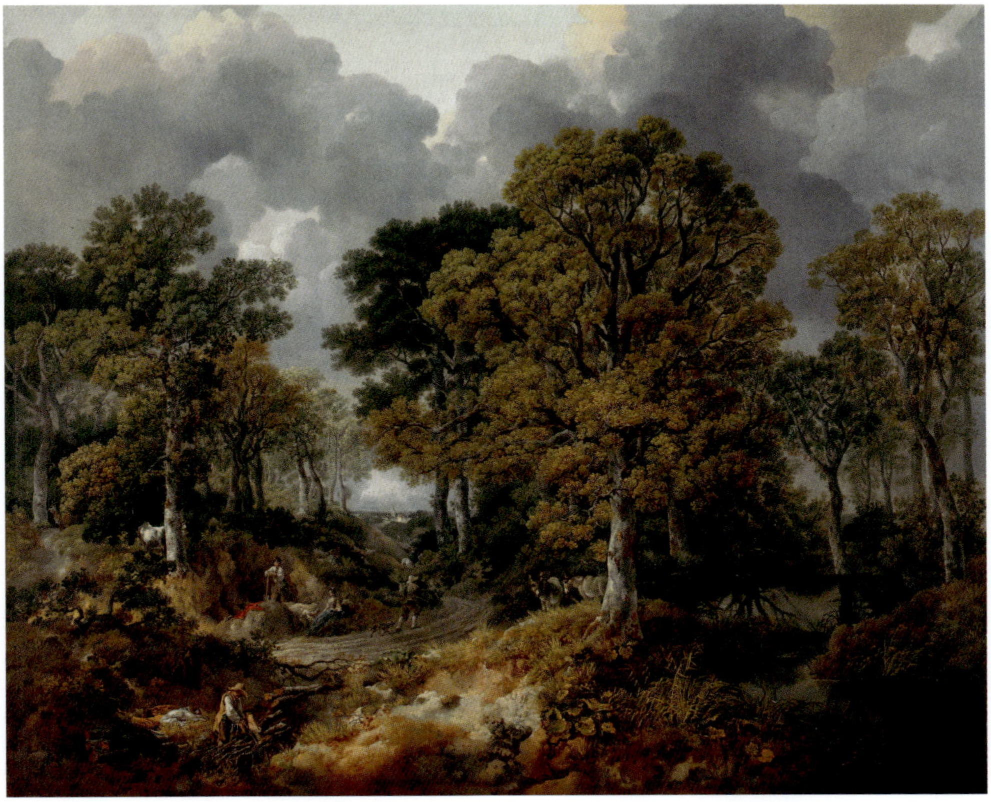

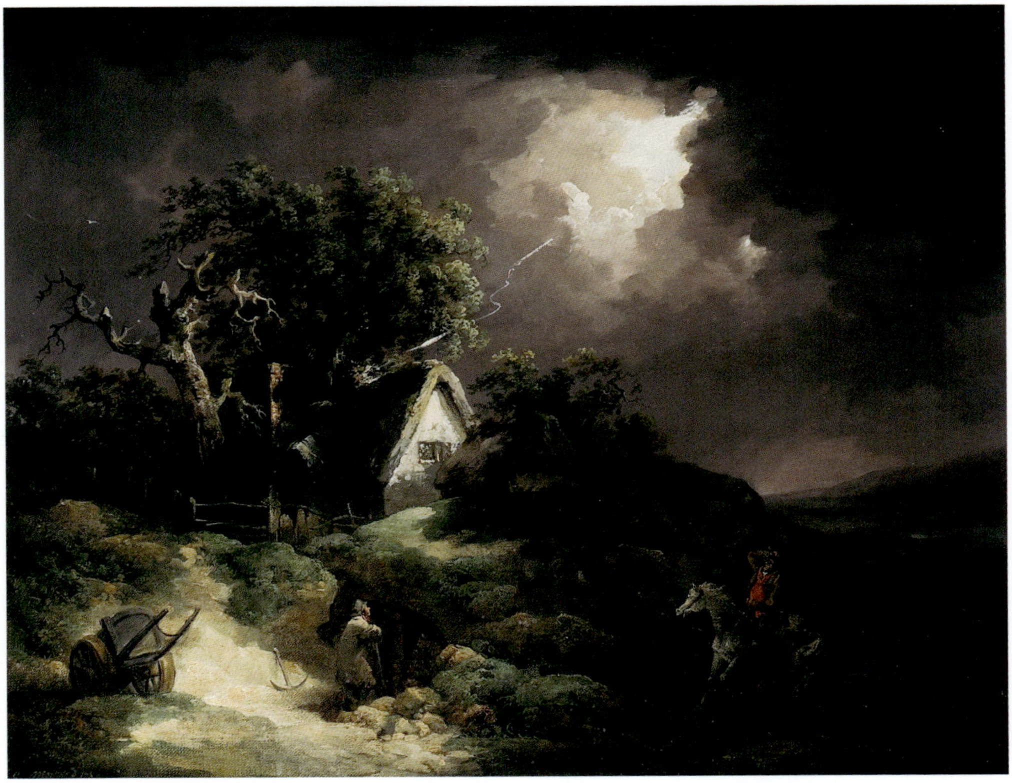

Fig. 47
Thomas Gainsborough
(1727–1788)
Cornard Wood, near Sudbury, Suffolk, 1748
Oil on canvas, 122 × 155 cm
The National Gallery, London

Fig. 48
George Morland (1763–1804)
The Coming Storm, Isle of Wight, 1789
Oil on canvas, 51.5 × 64.6 cm
Wolverhampton Art Gallery

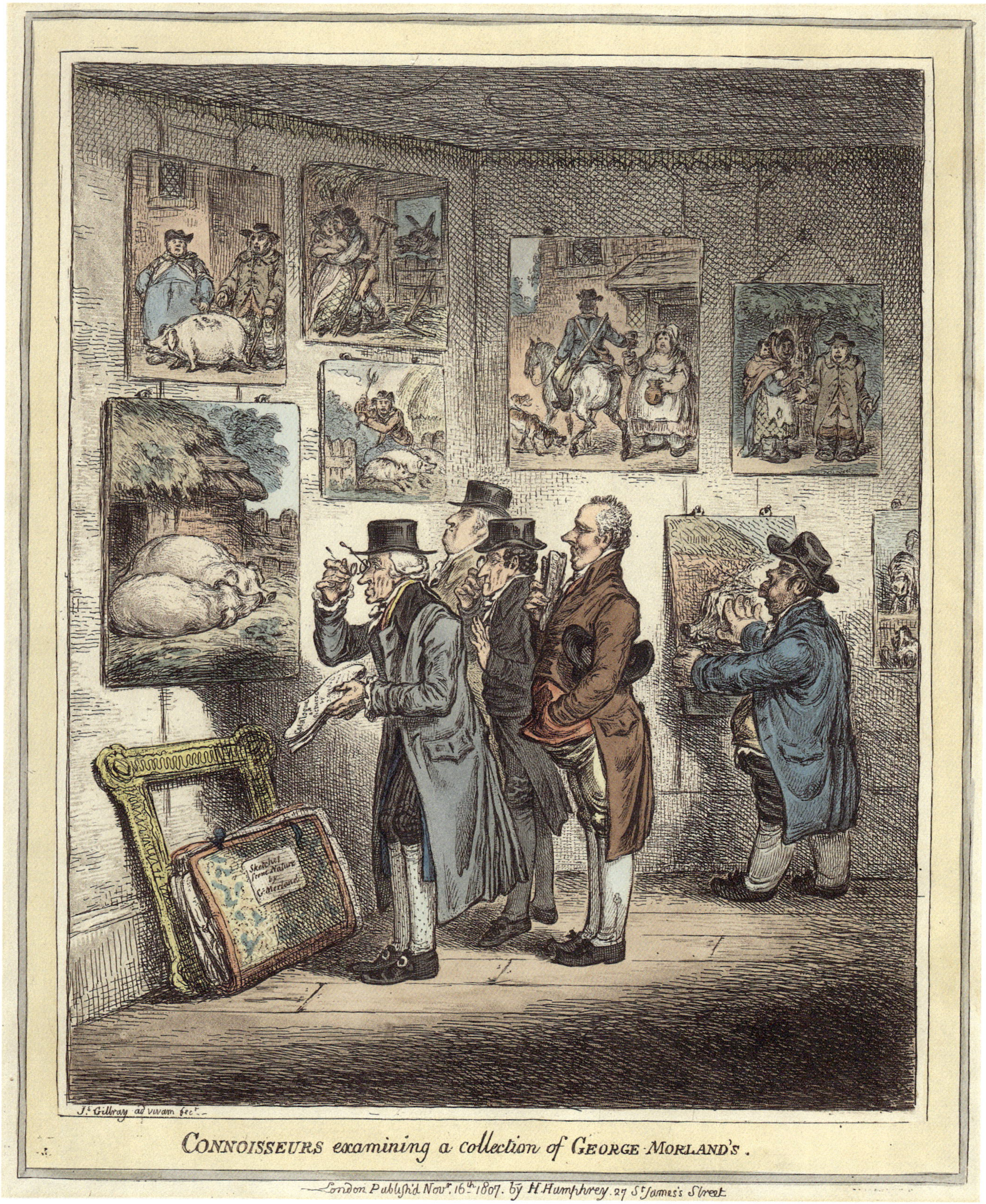
Sketches from Nature by G. Morland
Js. Gillray ad vivam fect.
CONNOISSEURS examining a collection of GEORGE MORLAND's.
London Publish'd Novr. 16th 1807. by H. Humphrey 27 St. James's Street

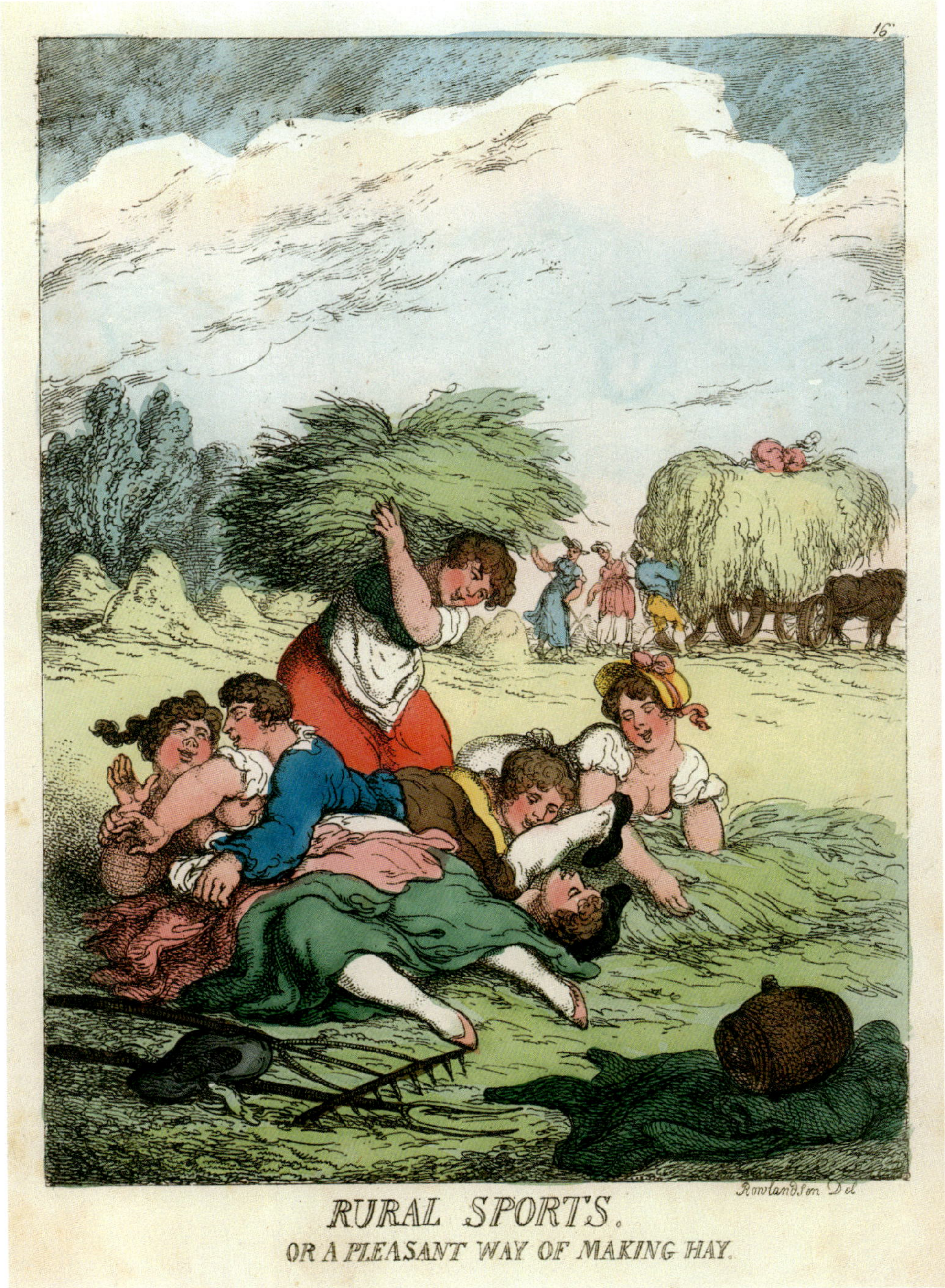

Fig. 49
James Gillray (1756–1815)
'Connoisseurs examining a collection of George Morland's', 1807
Hand-coloured etching and aquatint on paper, 43 × 33 cm
Omek and Linda Marks Family Collection

Fig. 50
Thomas Rowlandson (1756–1827)
'Rural sports. Or a pleasant way of making hay', 1814
Etching with contemporary hand colouring on wove paper, 38.8 × 26.2 cm
Nicholas J.S. Knowles

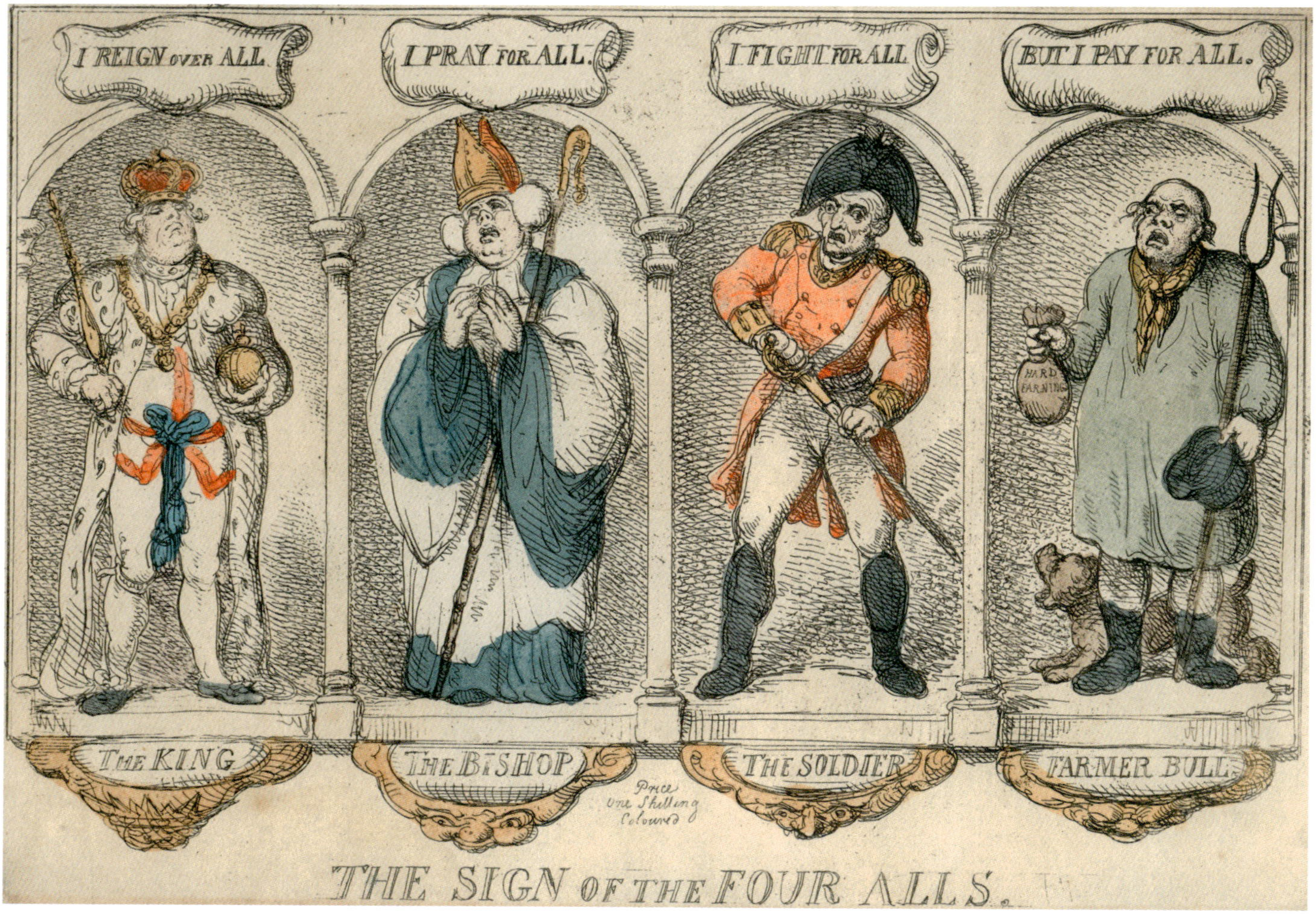

Fig. 51
Thomas Rowlandson (1756–1827)
'The Sign of the Four Alls', 1810
Etching with contemporary hand colouring on wove paper,
24.5 × 34.5 cm
Nicholas J.S. Knowles

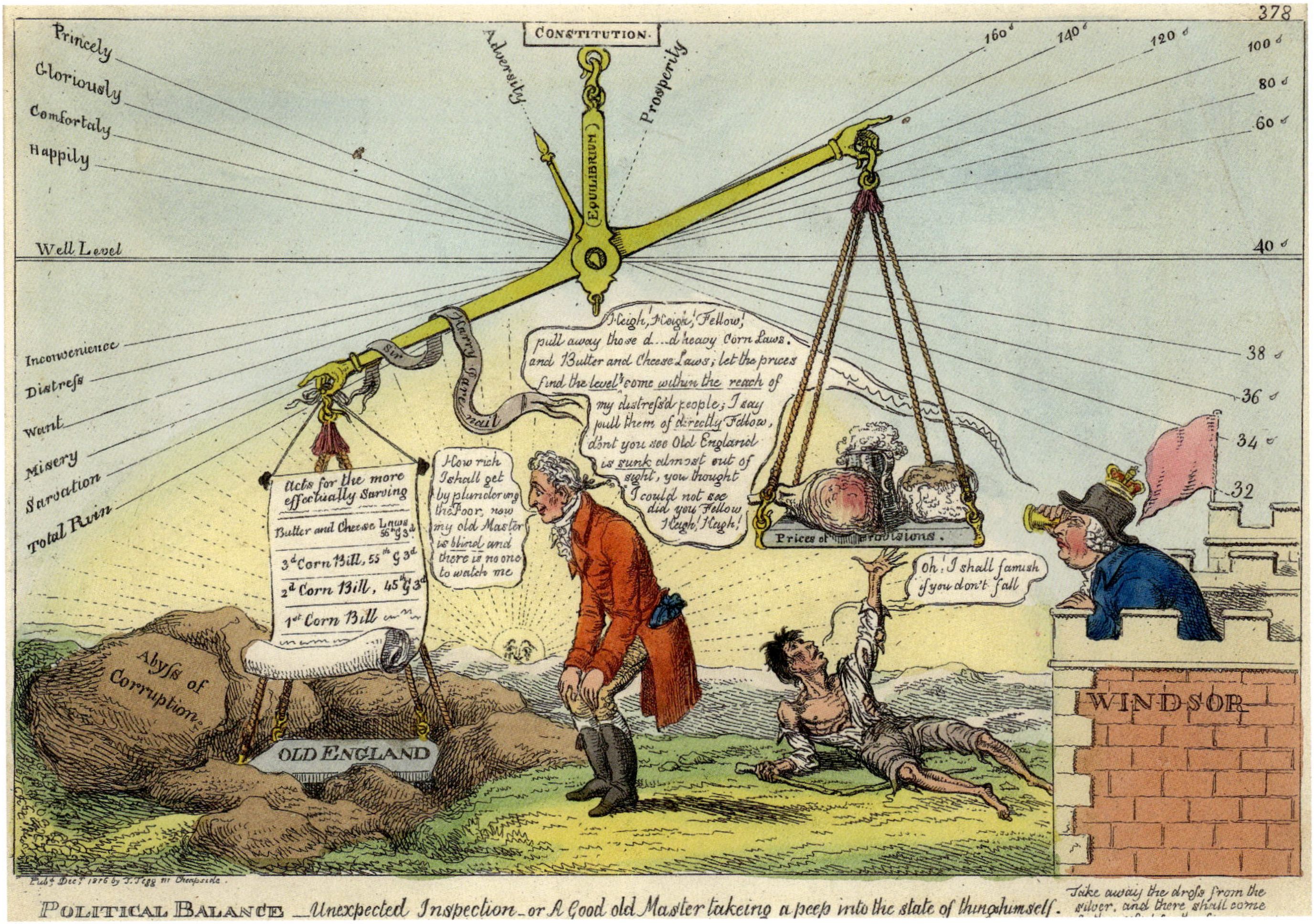

Fig. 52
Charles Williams (active 1796–1830)
'Political Balance', 1816
Hand-coloured etching on paper, 23.7 × 34 cm
Fagan Collection of Political Prints and Caricatures, Pol P 25. University of Nottingham Manuscripts and Special Collections

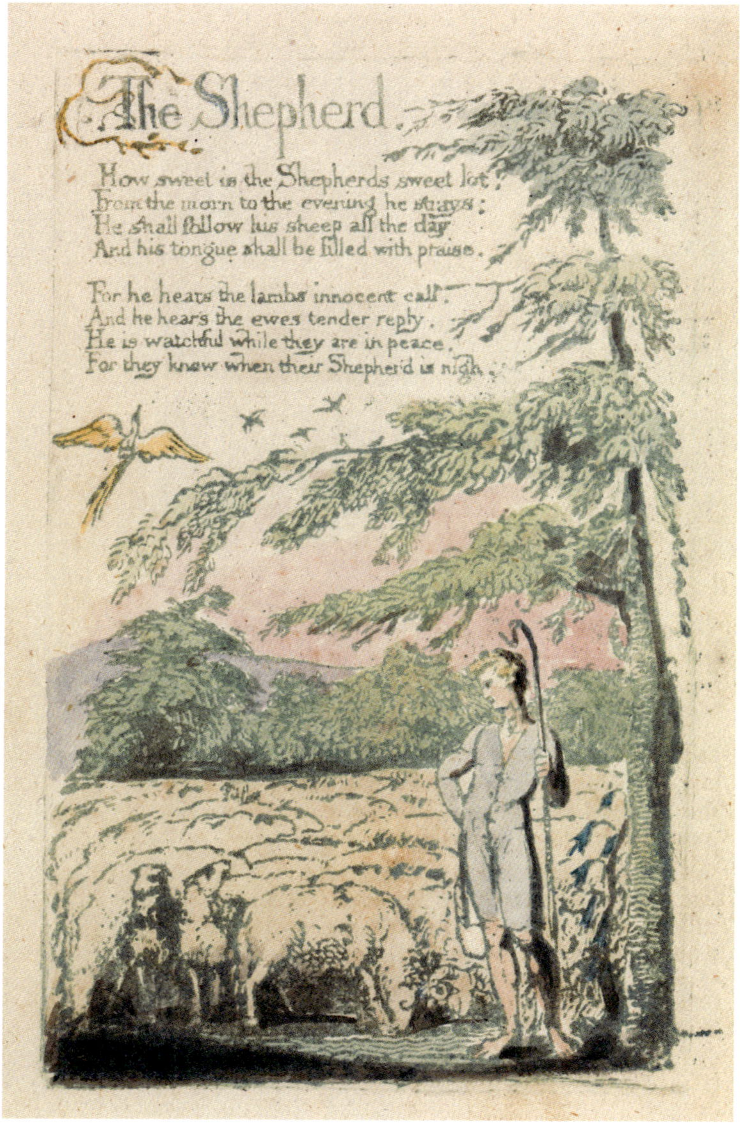

Fig. 53
Print made by William Blake (1757–1827)
Songs of Innocence and of Experience, Plate 4, 'The Shepherd' (Bentley 5), 1789
Relief etching printed in green ink, with watercolour, pen and black ink on wove paper, 11.1 × 7 cm
Yale Center for British Art, Paul Mellon Collection, New Haven

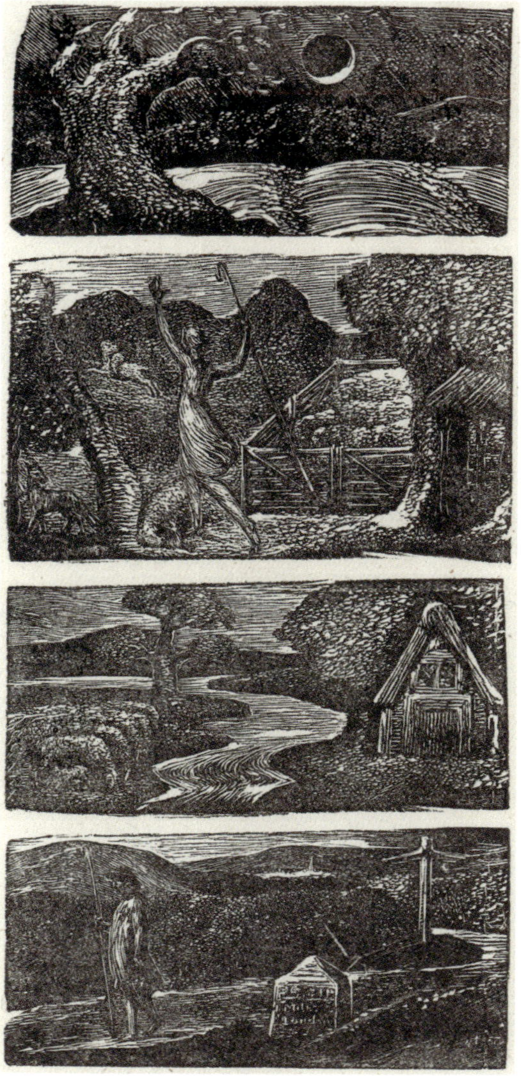

Fig. 54
William Blake (1757–1827)
From top: The Blighted Corn; 'Nor Fox, nor Wolf, nor Rat among our Sheep'; Sabrina's Silvery Flood; and Colinet's 'Fond Desire Strange Lands to Know', 1821
Wood-engraving and letterpress printed on laid paper, 3.3 × 7.4 cm (each image)
From R.J. Thornton, *The Pastorals of Virgil*, 3rd edn, London 1821: vol. 1, p. 15
Royal Academy of Arts, London

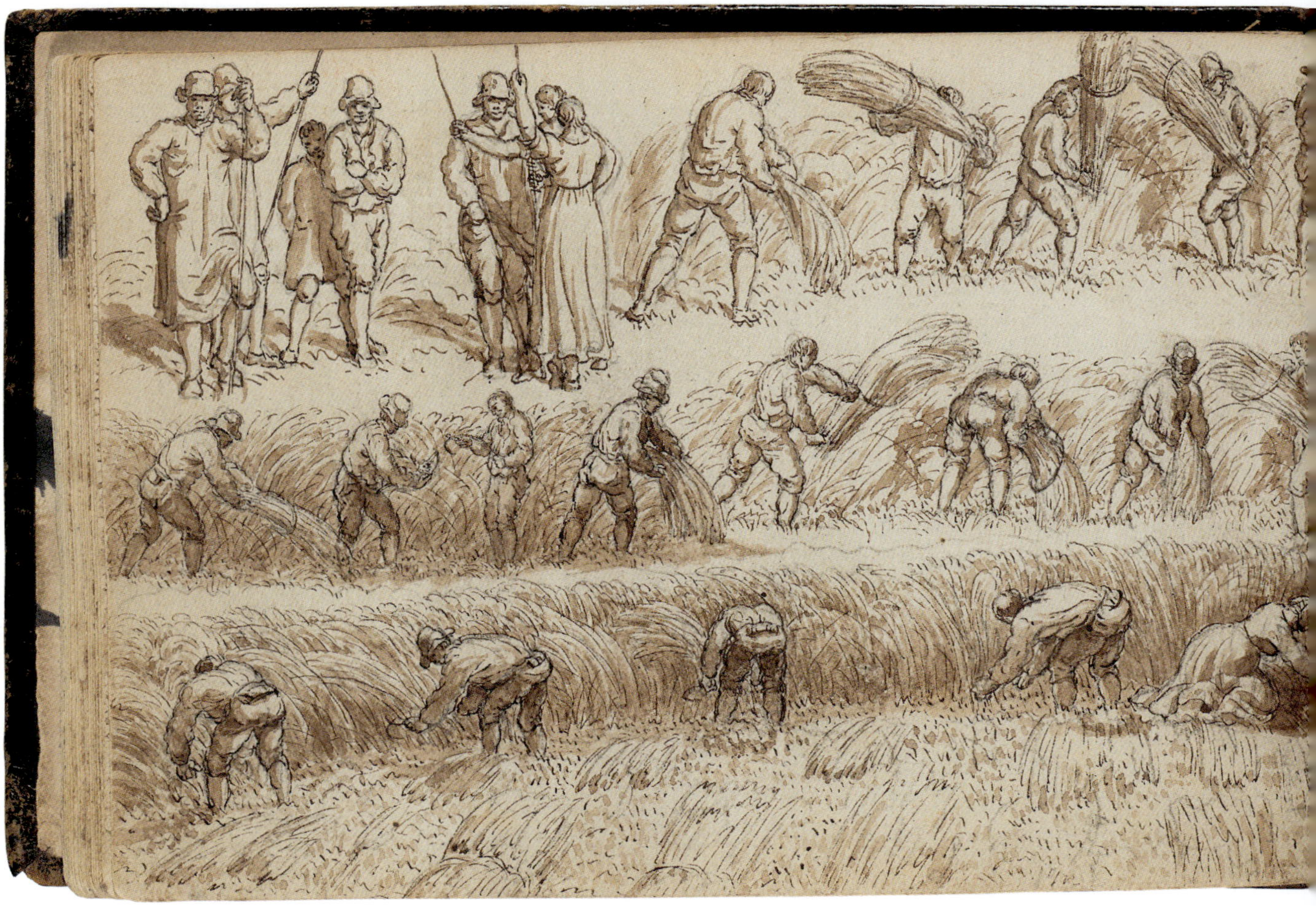

Fig. 55
George Robert Lewis (1782–1871)
Sketchbook, about 1815
Pen and wash drawing, with pencil sketch underneath, on paper
Victoria and Albert Museum, London

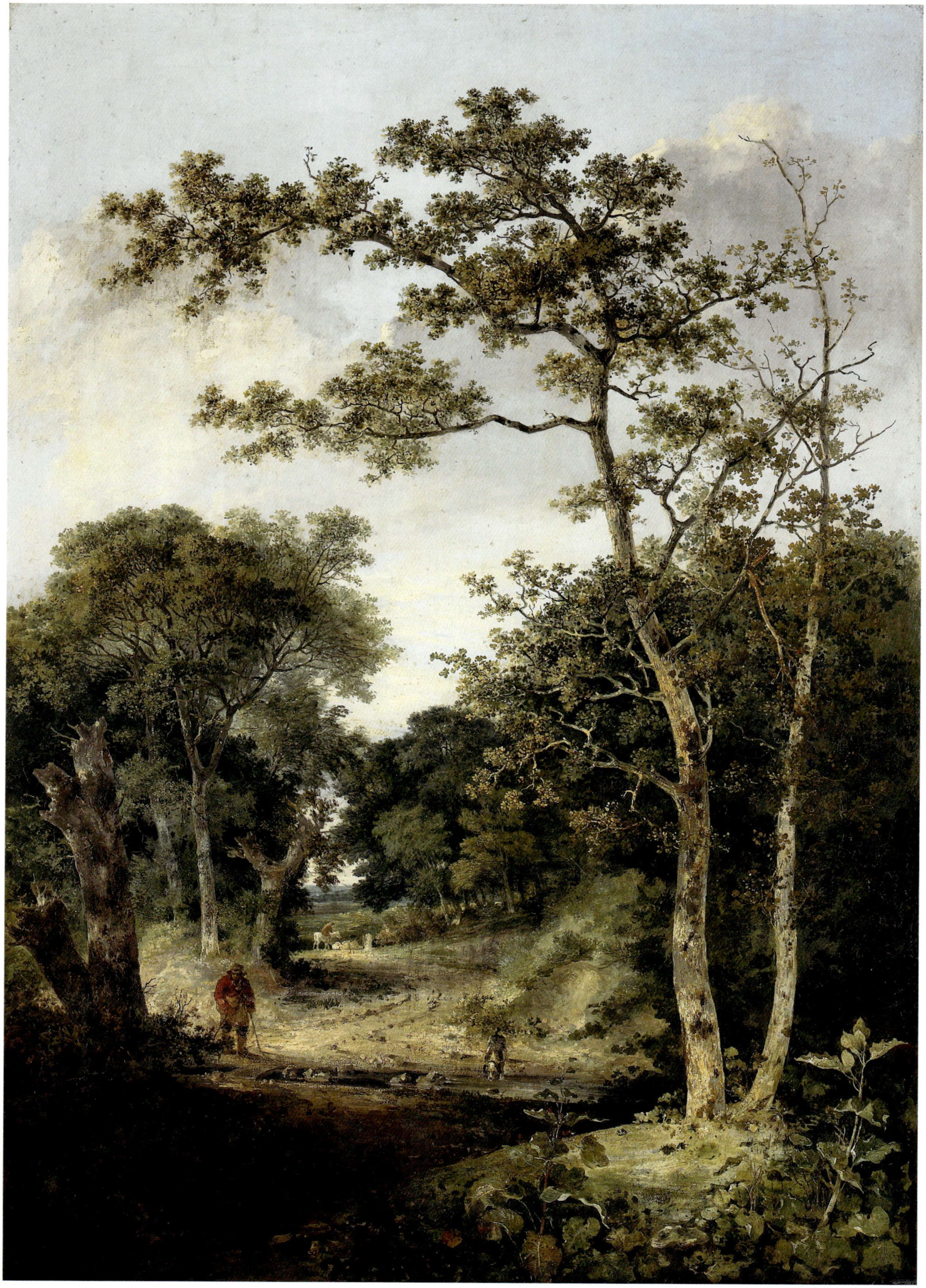

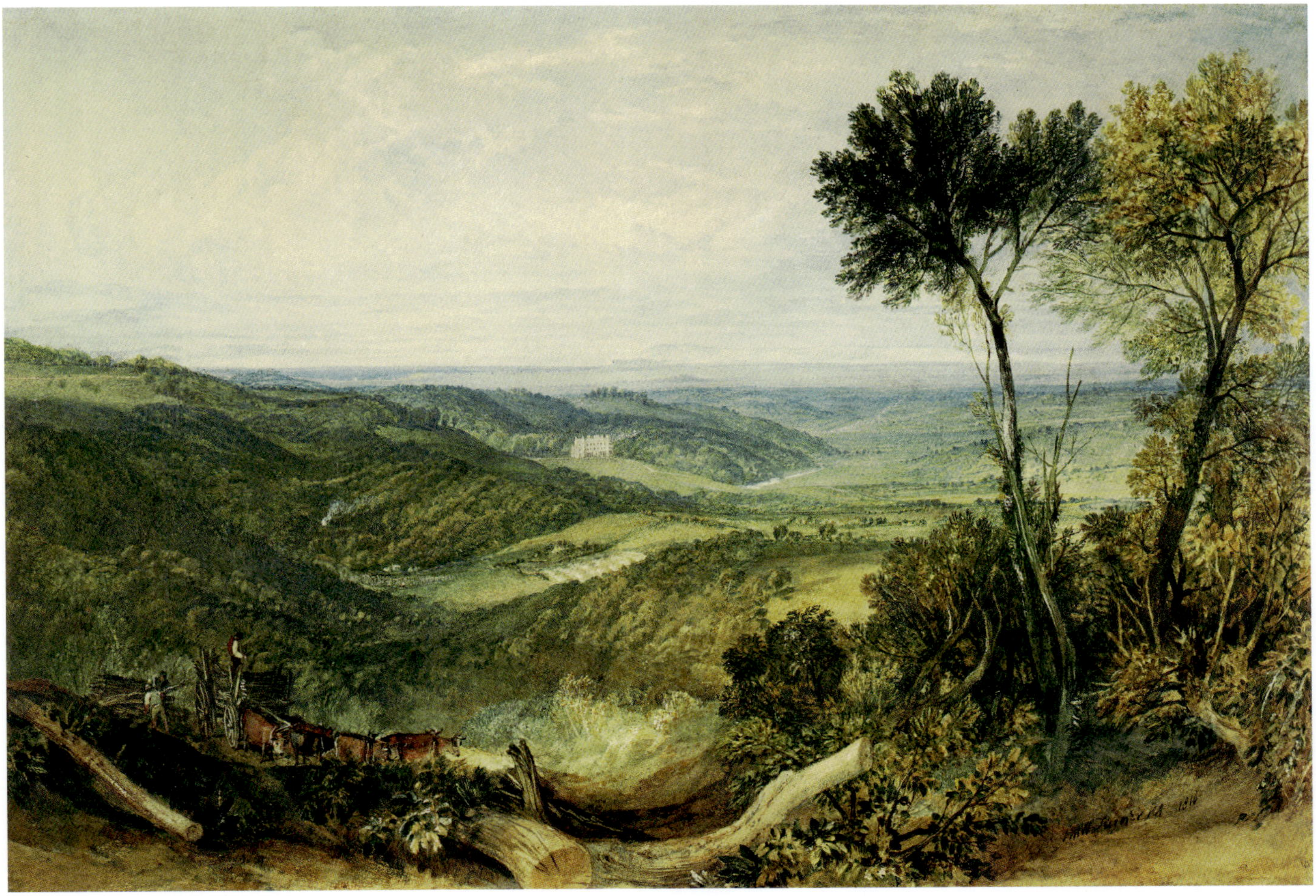

Fig. 56
John Crome (1768–1821)
Marlingford Grove, about 1815
Oil on canvas, 136.5 × 100.5 cm
National Museums Liverpool,
Lady Lever Art Gallery

Fig. 57
Joseph Mallord William Turner
(1775–1851)
The Vale of Ashburnham, 1816
Watercolour on paper, 38 × 56.4 cm
British Museum, London

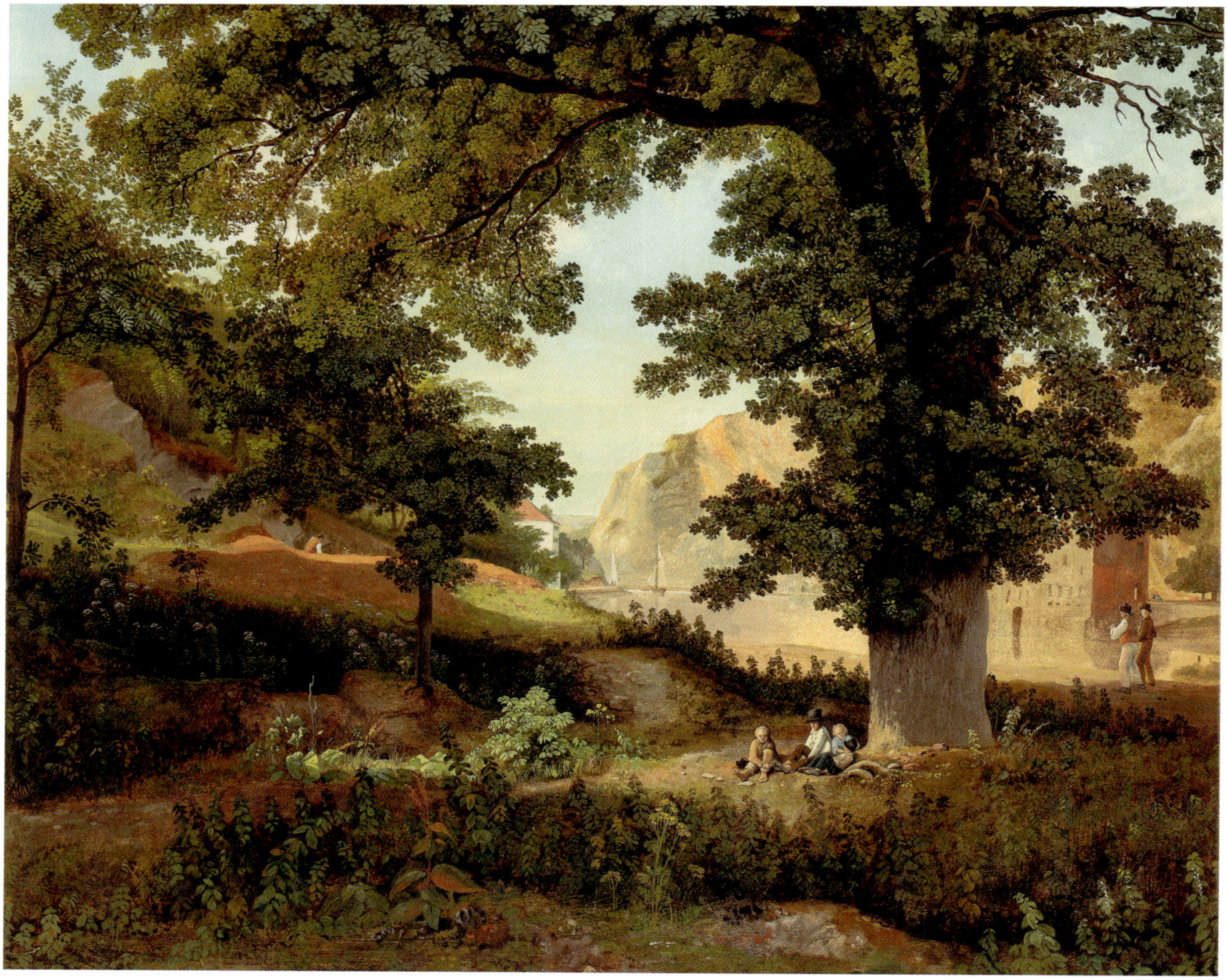

Fig. 58
Francis Danby (1793–1861)
Clifton Rocks from Rownham Fields, about 1821
Oil on panel, 40 × 50.8 cm
Bristol Museums: Bristol Museum & Art Gallery

Fig. 59
Francis Danby (1793–1861)
A Scene in Leigh Woods, 1822
Oil on panel, 35.2 × 50.4 cm
Bristol Museums: Bristol Museum & Art Gallery

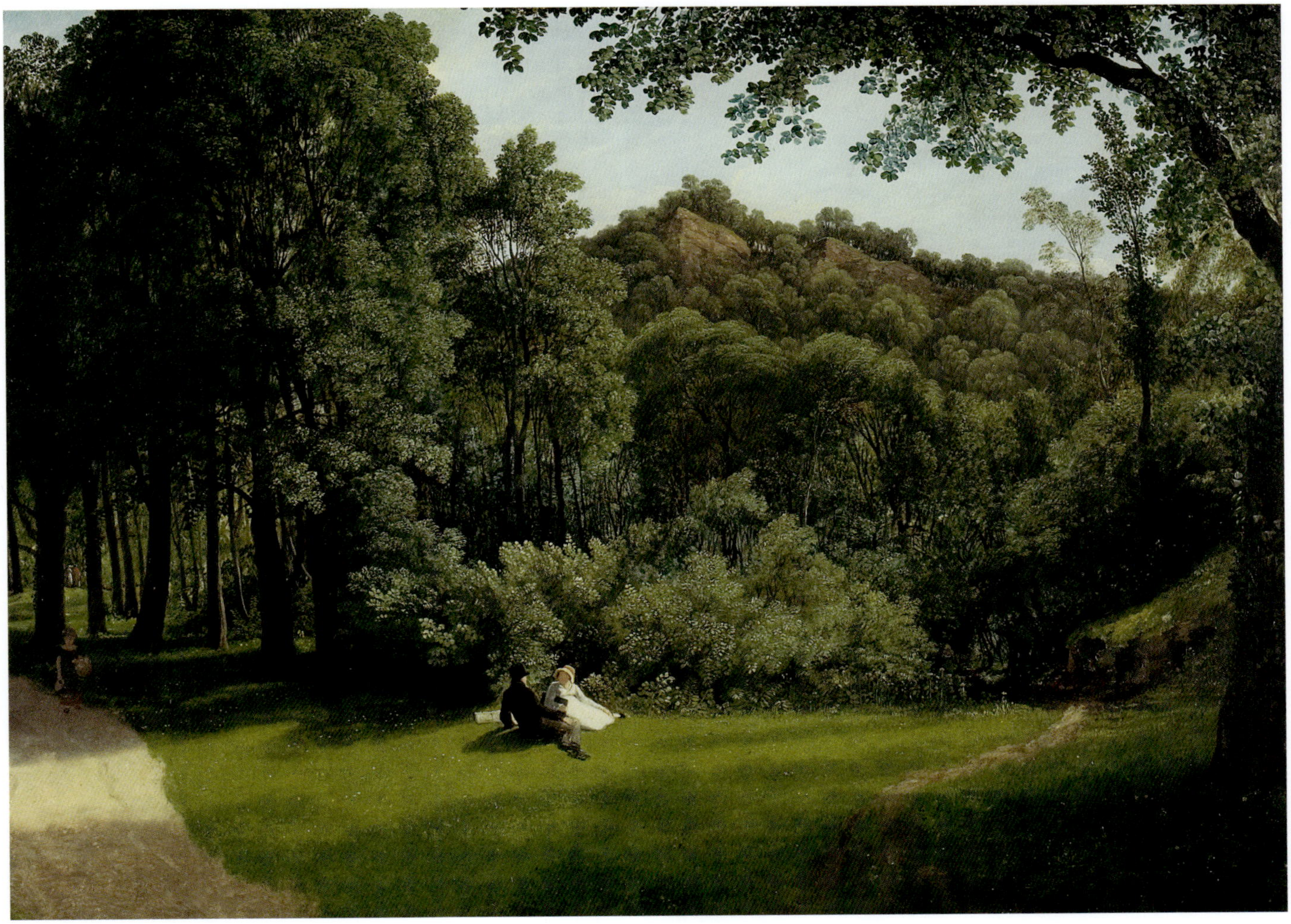

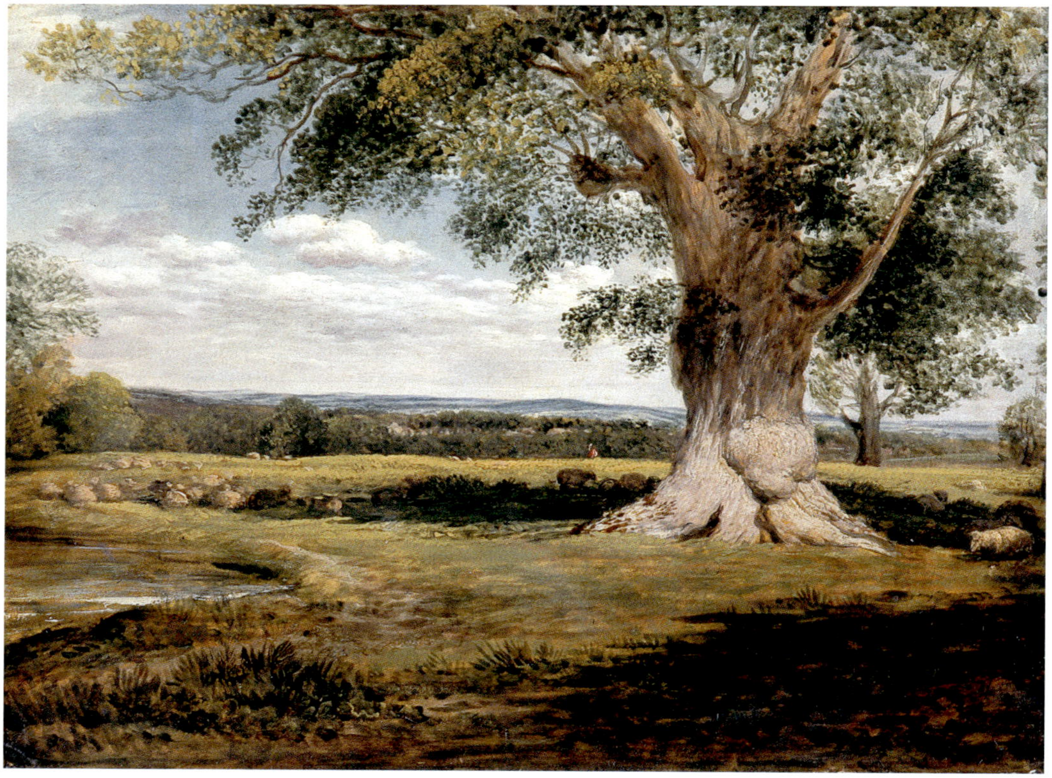

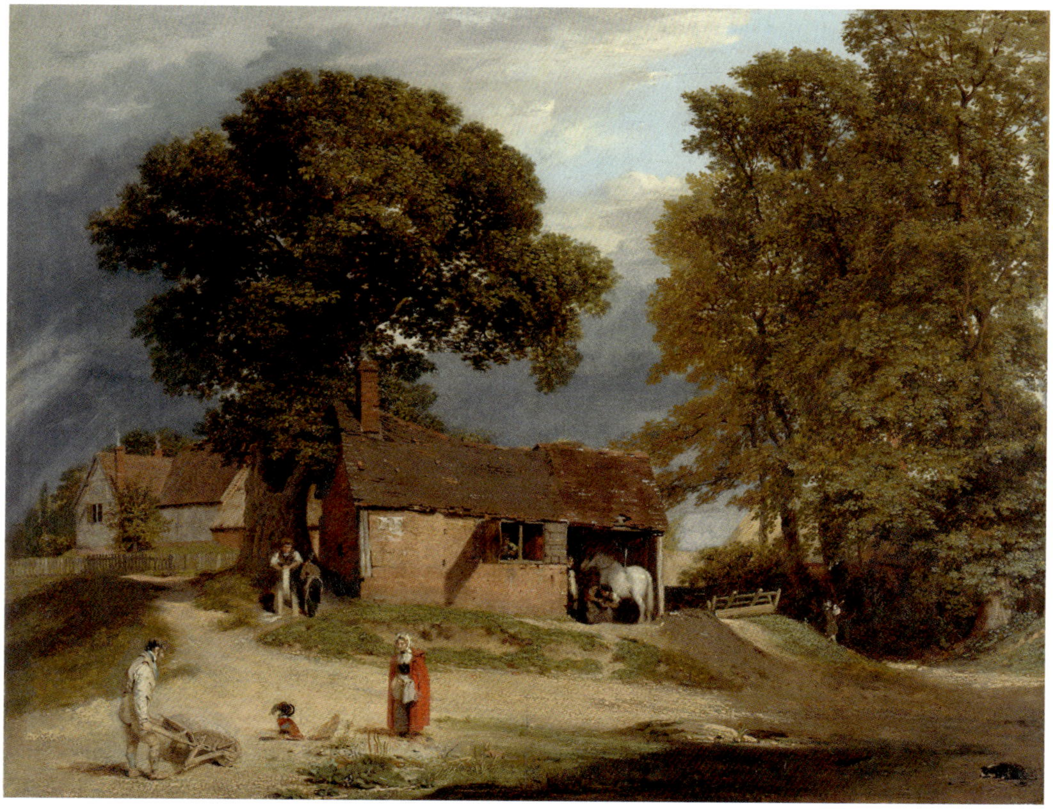

Fig. 60
John Linnell (1792–1882)
Woody Landscape, 1824
Oil on panel, 24.7 × 32.2 cm
Brighton & Hove Museums

Fig. 61
William Mulready (1786–1863)
The Farrier's Shop, after 1820
Oil on canvas, 40.9 × 52.1 cm
The Syndics of the Fitzwilliam Museum, University of Cambridge

Fig. 62
Richard Parkes Bonington (1802–1828)
A Wooded Lane, about 1825
Oil on millboard, 27.9 × 22.9 cm
Yale Center for British Art, Paul Mellon Collection, New Haven

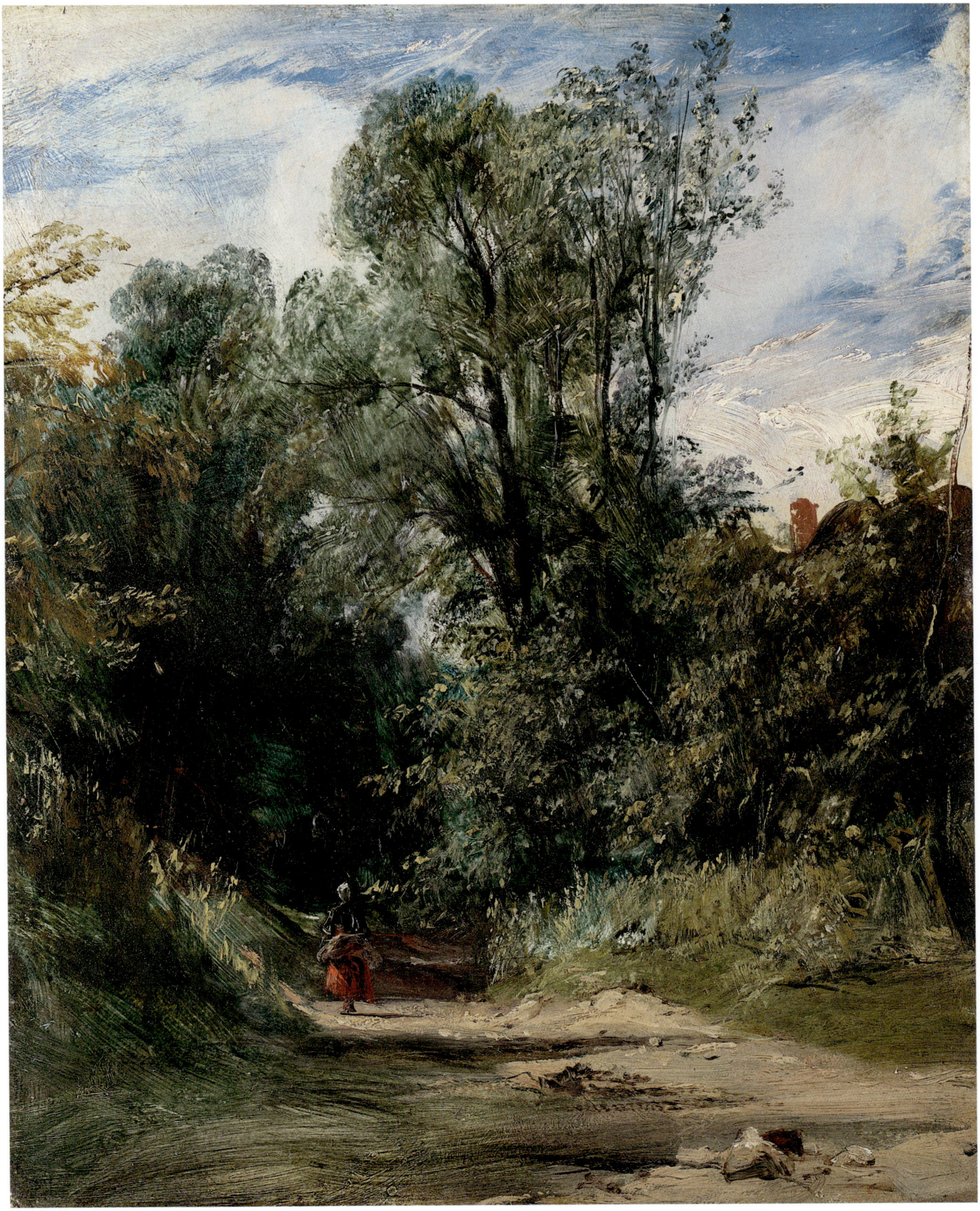

Constable before *The Hay Wain*

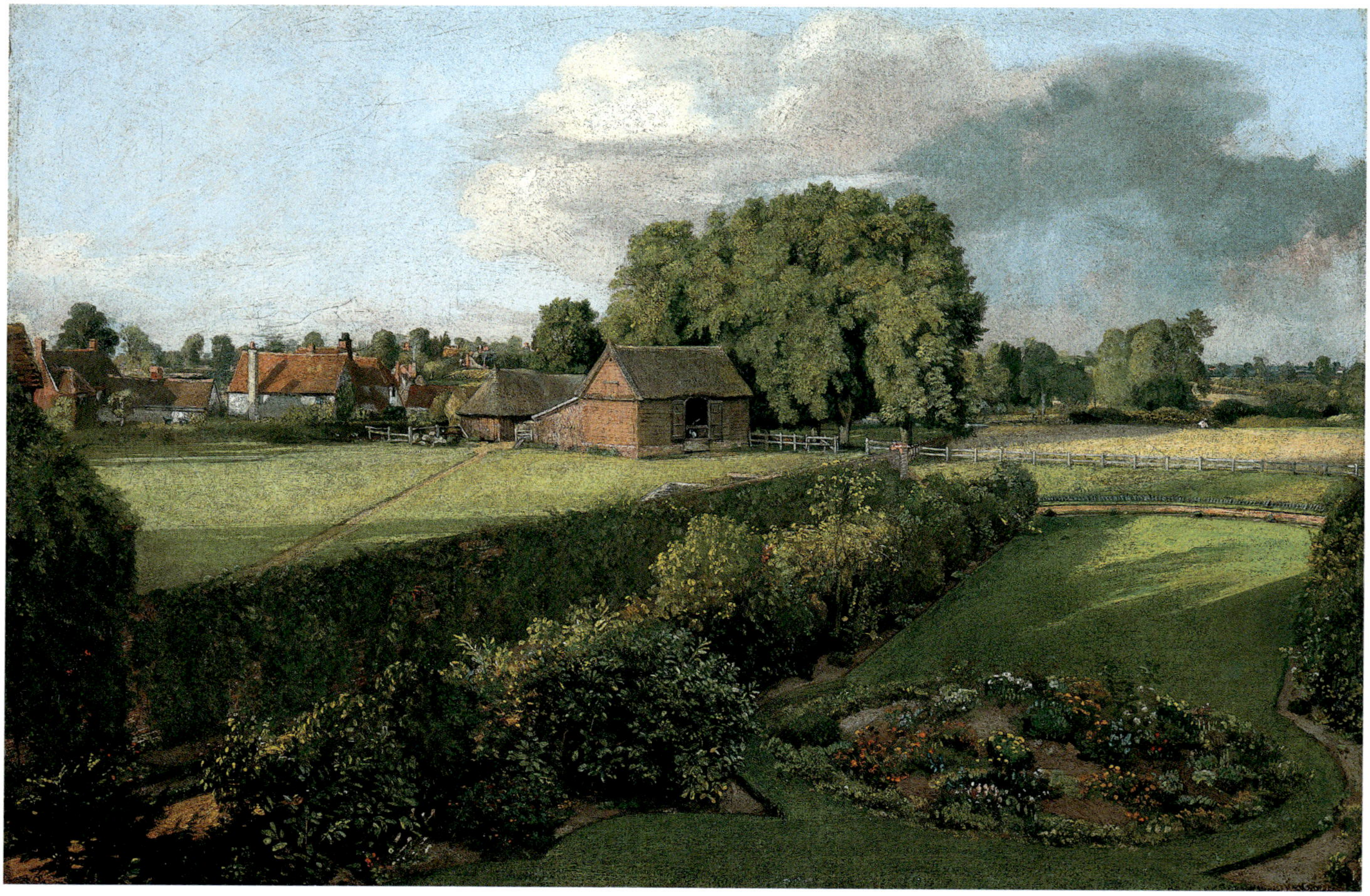

Fig. 63
Golding Constable's Flower Garden, 1815
Oil on canvas, 33.1 × 50.7 cm
Ipswich Borough Council Collections: Colchester and Ipswich Museum Service

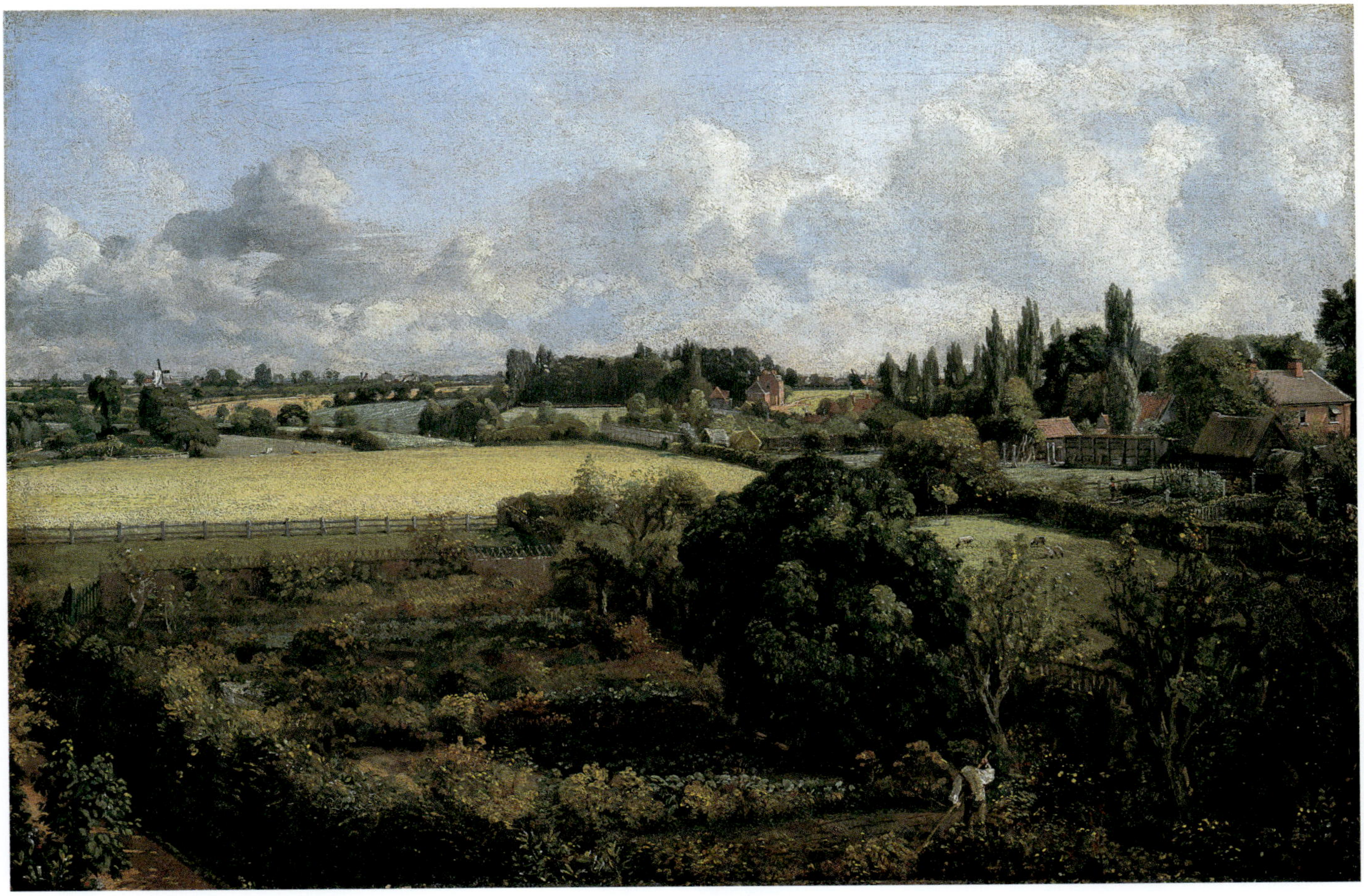

Fig. 64
Golding Constable's Kitchen Garden, 1815
Oil on canvas, 33.4 × 51.1 cm
Ipswich Borough Council Collections: Colchester and Ipswich Museum Service

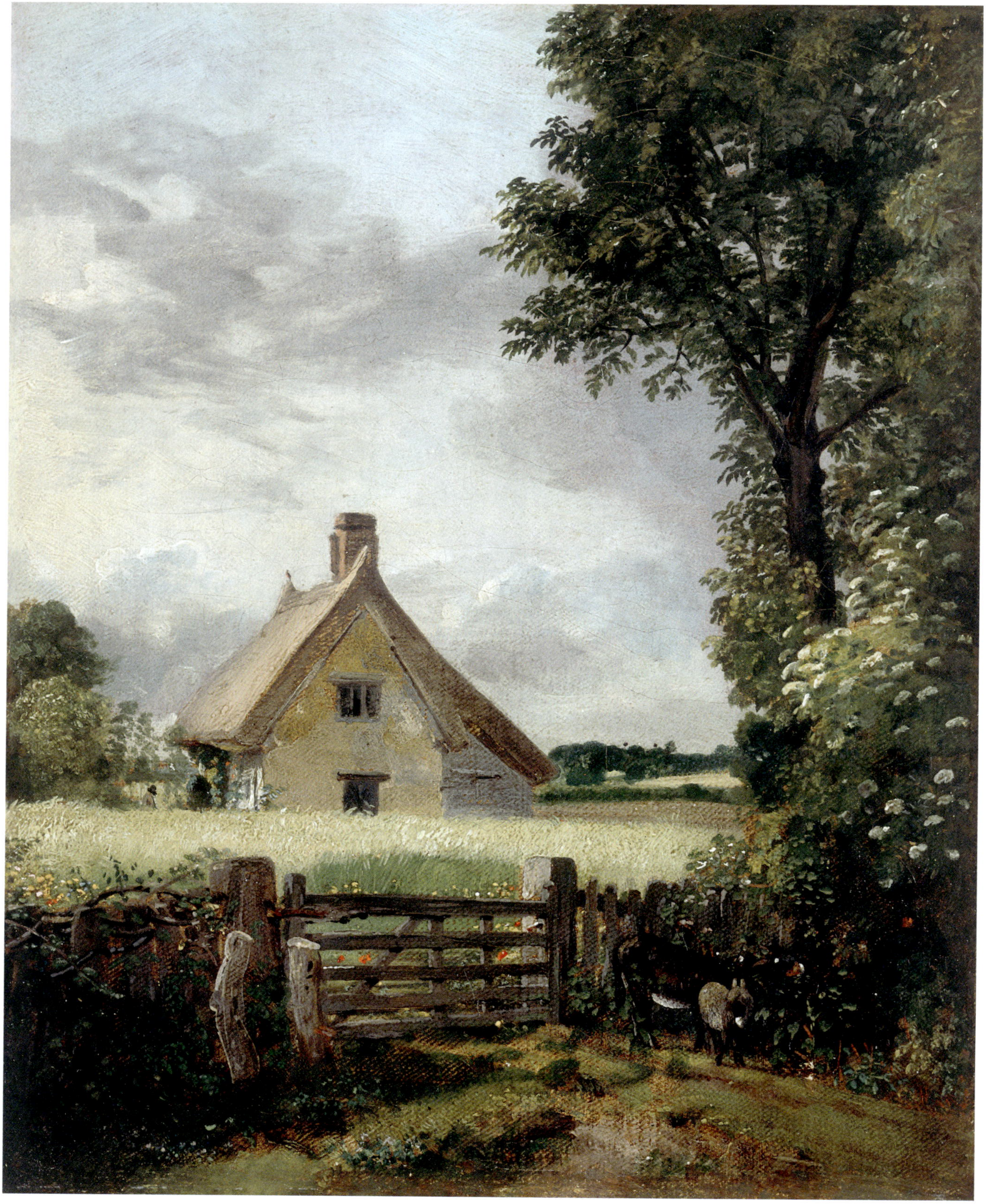

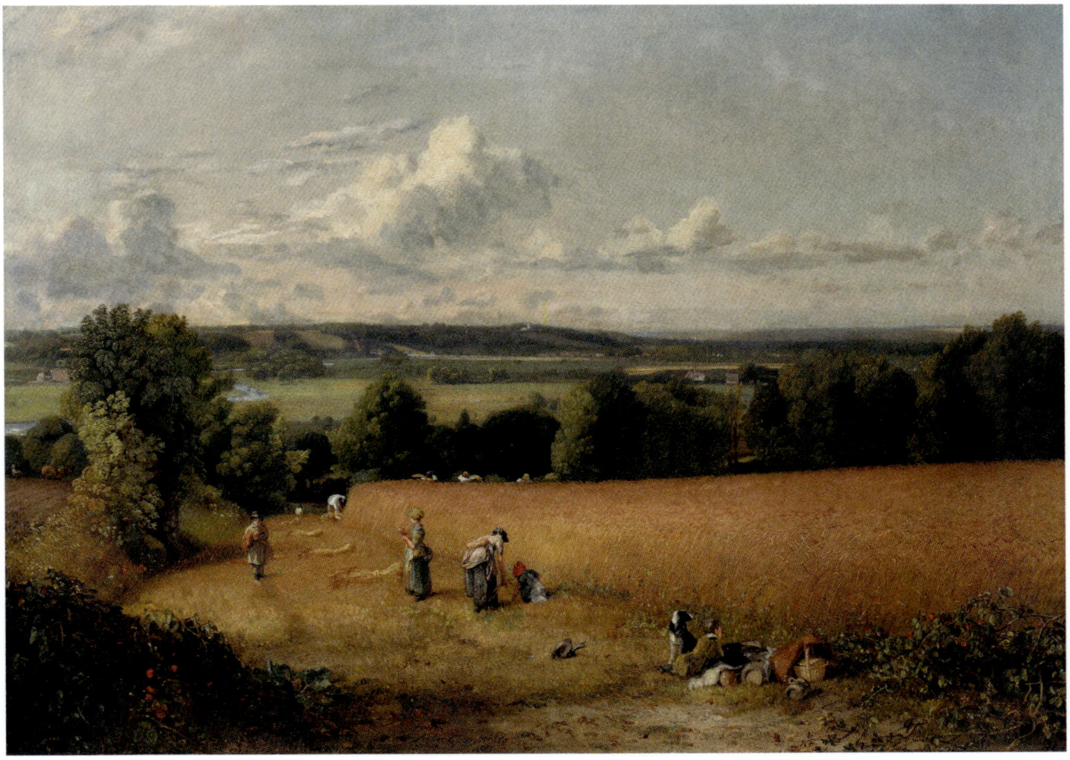

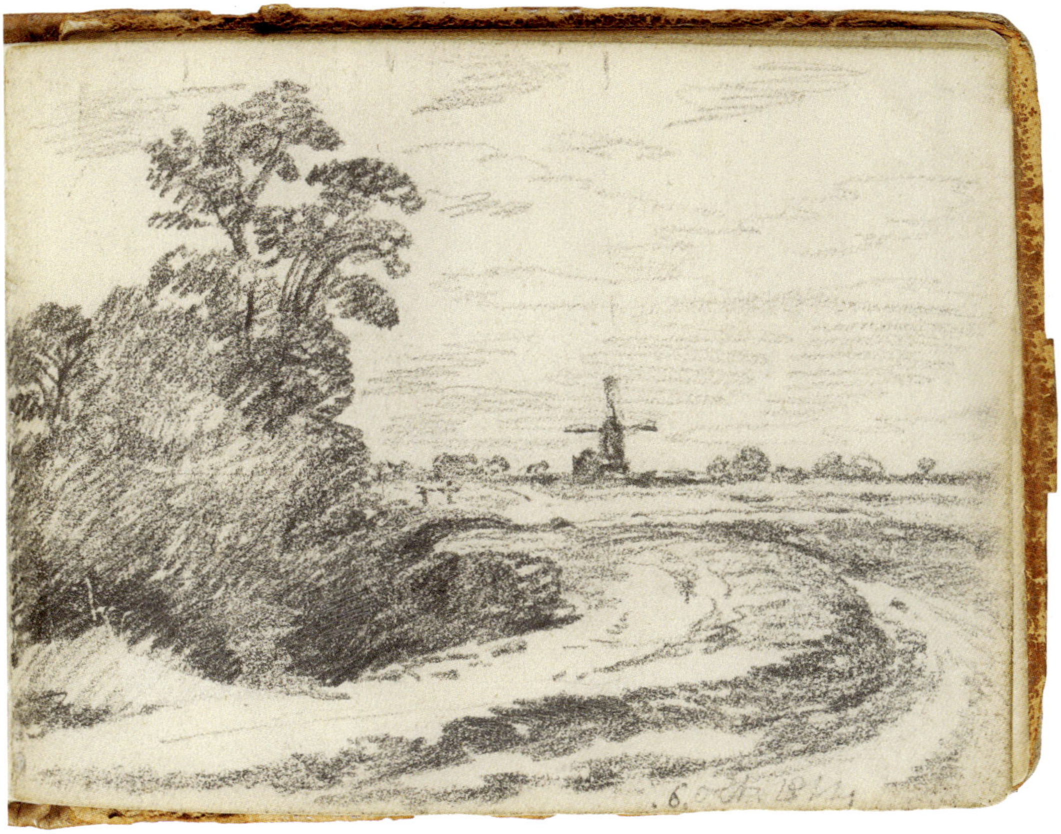

Fig. 65
A Cottage in a Cornfield, 1817
Oil on canvas, 31.5 × 26.3 cm
Amgueddfa Cymru – Museum Wales

Fig. 66
The Wheat Field, 1816
Oil on canvas, 54.6 × 78.1 cm
Clark Art Institute, Williamstown, Massachusetts

Fig. 67
Sketchbook owned by John Constable, 1814
Pencil and watercolour on paper
Victoria and Albert Museum, London

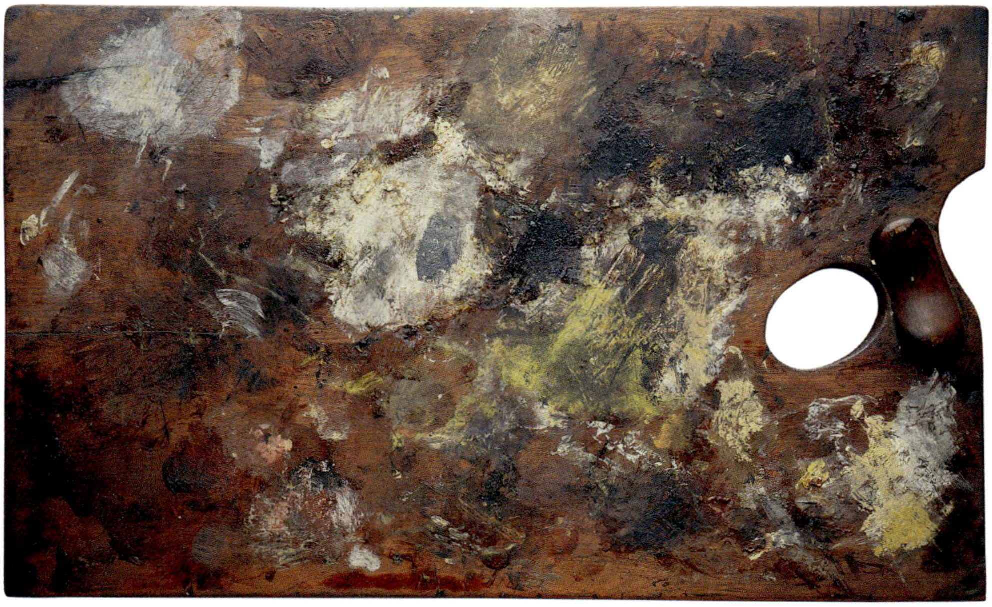

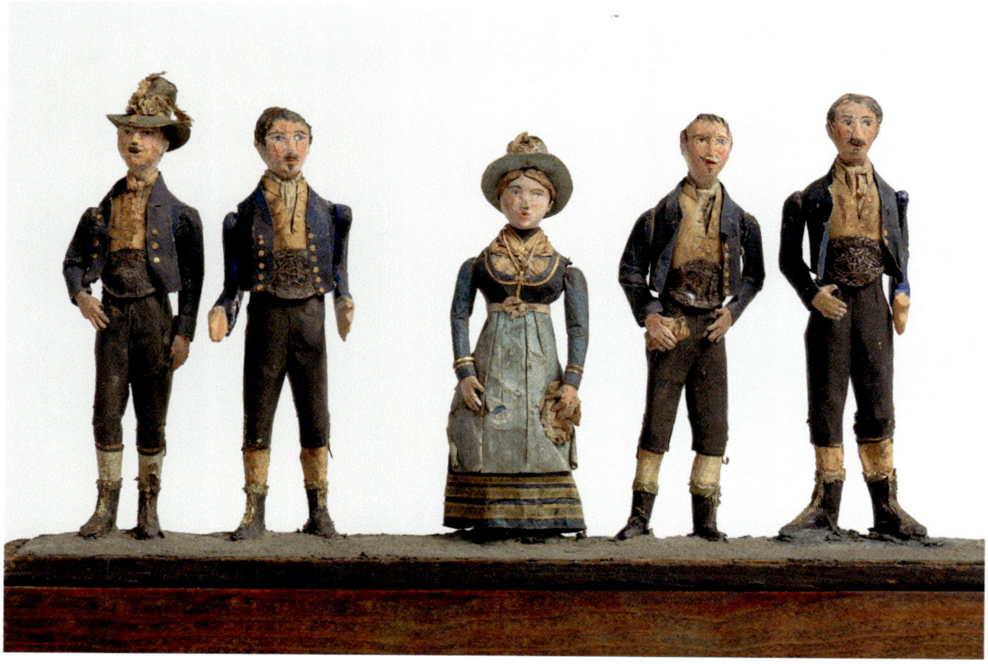

Fig. 68
Palette owned by John Constable, RA, date unknown
23 × 40 cm
Royal Academy of Arts, London

Fig. 69
Attributed to John Constable
East Bergholt Singers, about 1800
Carved and painted wood with textile, 15.5 × 28.5 × 12.6 cm
Ipswich Borough Council Collections: Colchester and Ipswich Museum Service

Fig. 70
Willy Lott's House, East Bergholt, about 1812–13
Graphite on three sheets of wove paper joined together, 20.1 × 28.4 cm
The Courtauld, London (Samuel Courtauld Trust)

Fig. 71
Rowing Boat moored beneath a Bank, around 1809
Graphite on blue-grey laid paper, 9 × 12.5 cm
The Courtauld, London (Samuel Courtauld Trust)

Making *The Hay Wain*

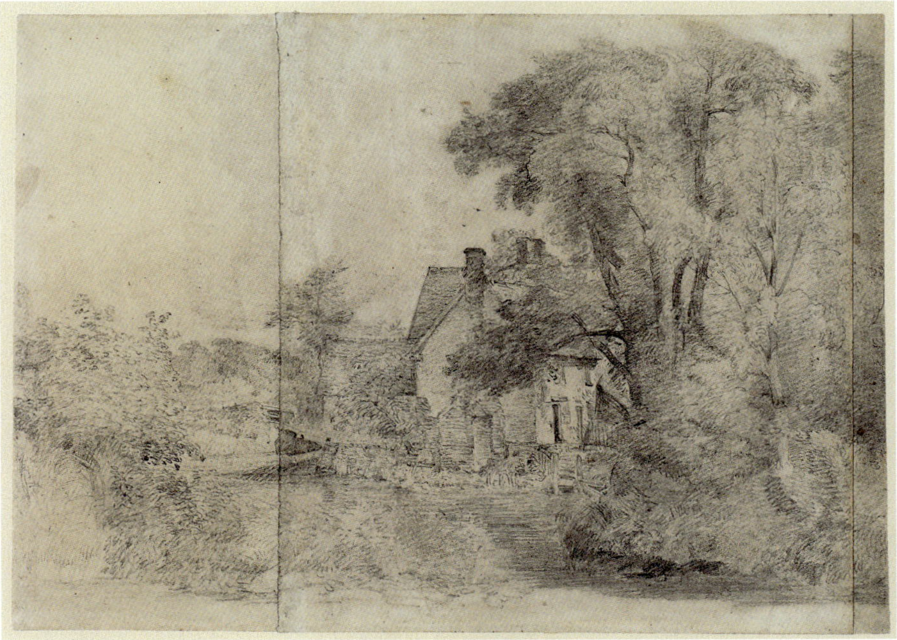

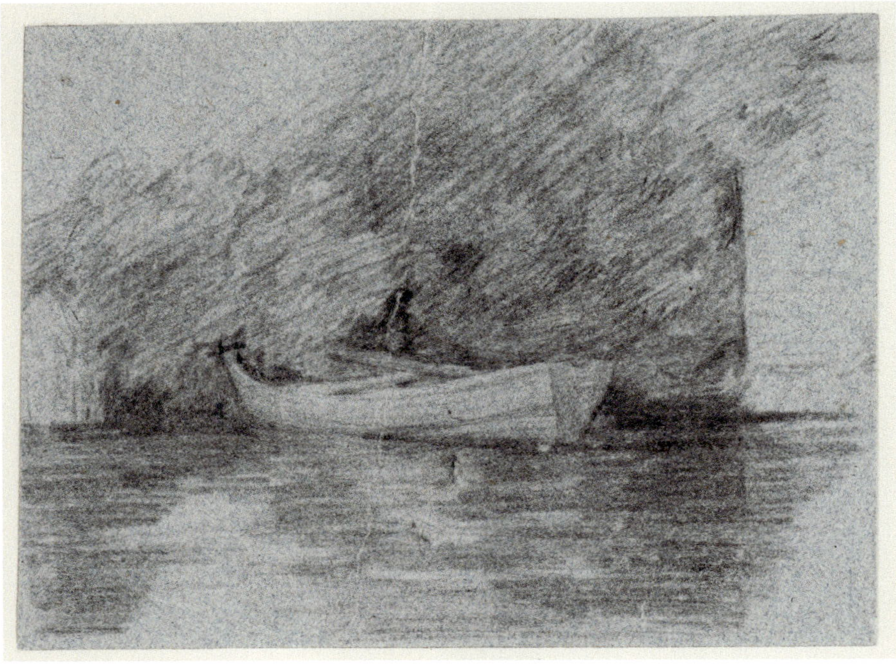

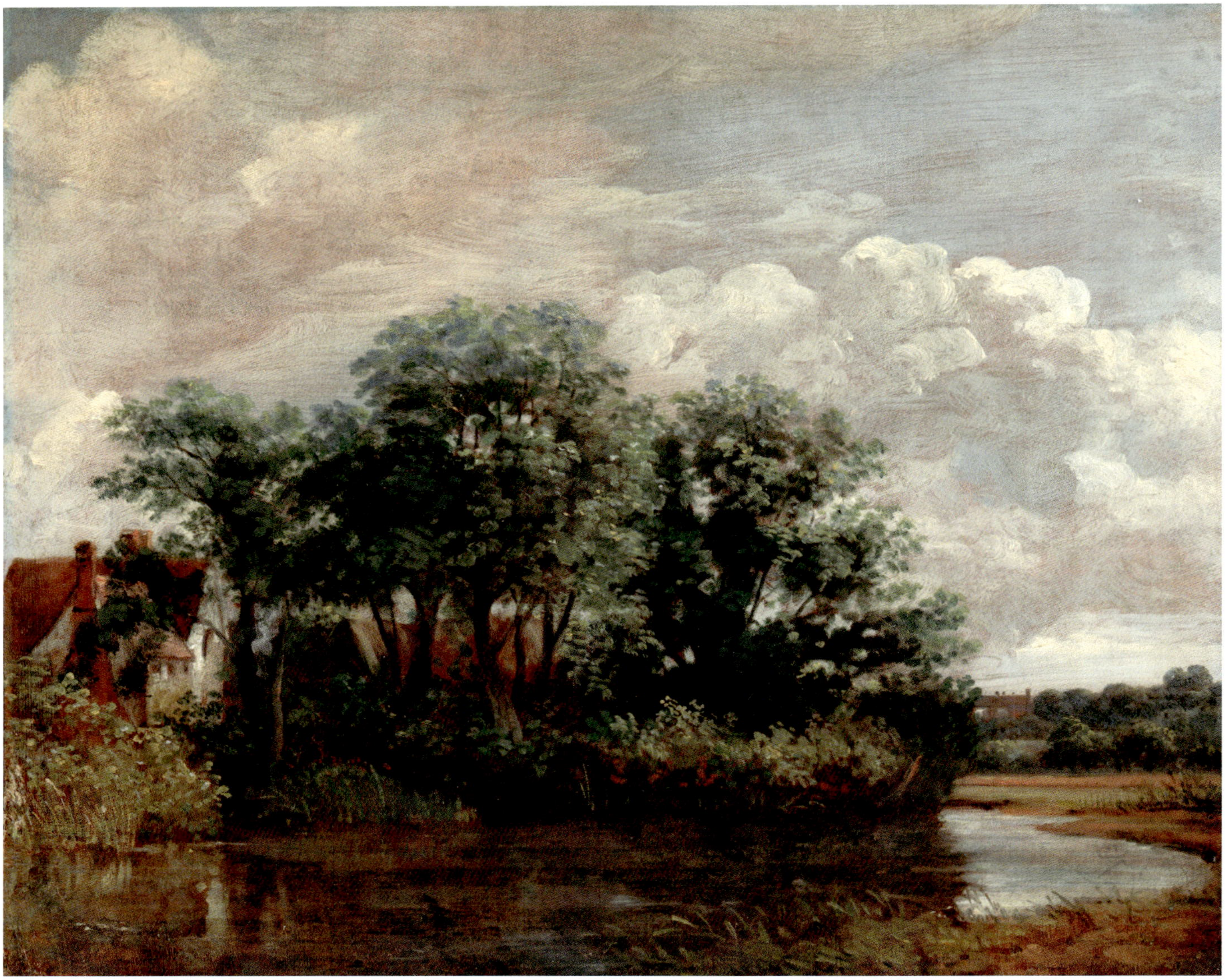

Fig. 72
Willy Lott's House, 1802
Oil on canvas, 33.7 × 42.5 cm
Clark Art Institute,
Williamstown, Massachusetts

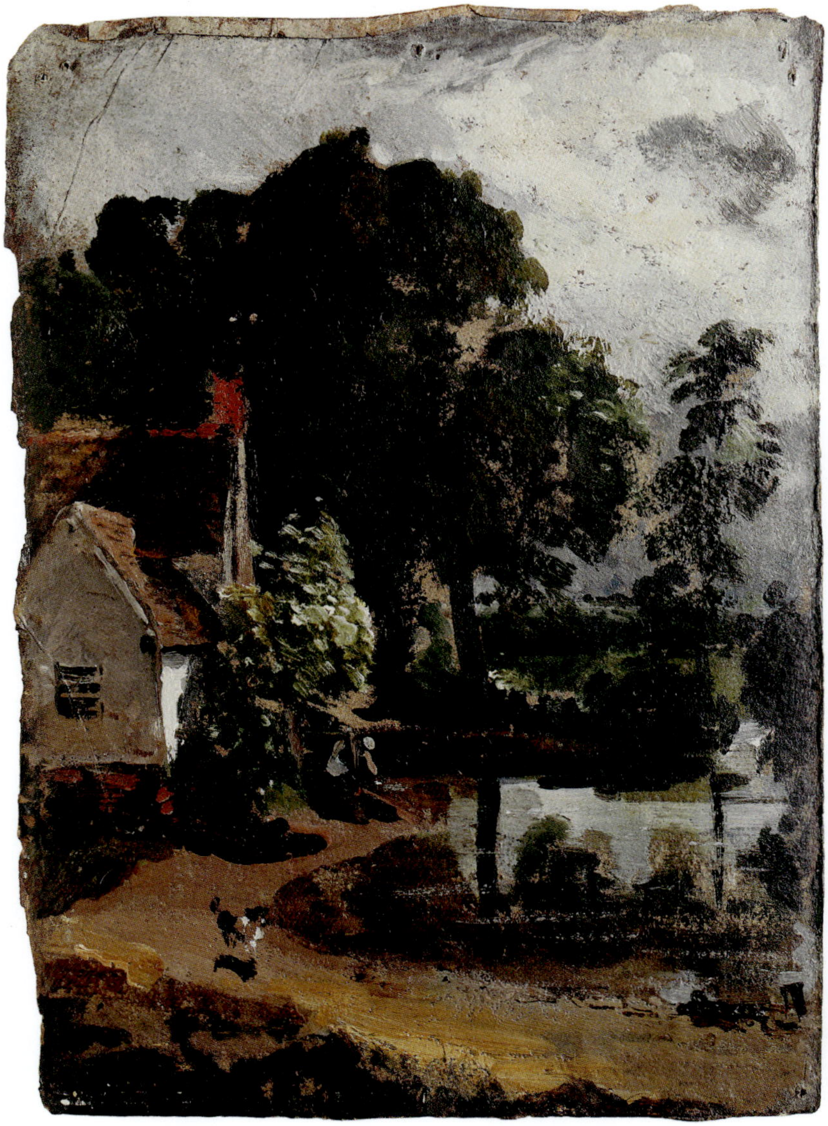

Fig. 73
Willy Lott's House, near Flatford Mill, about 1811
Oil on paper, 24.1 × 18.1 cm
Victoria and Albert Museum, London

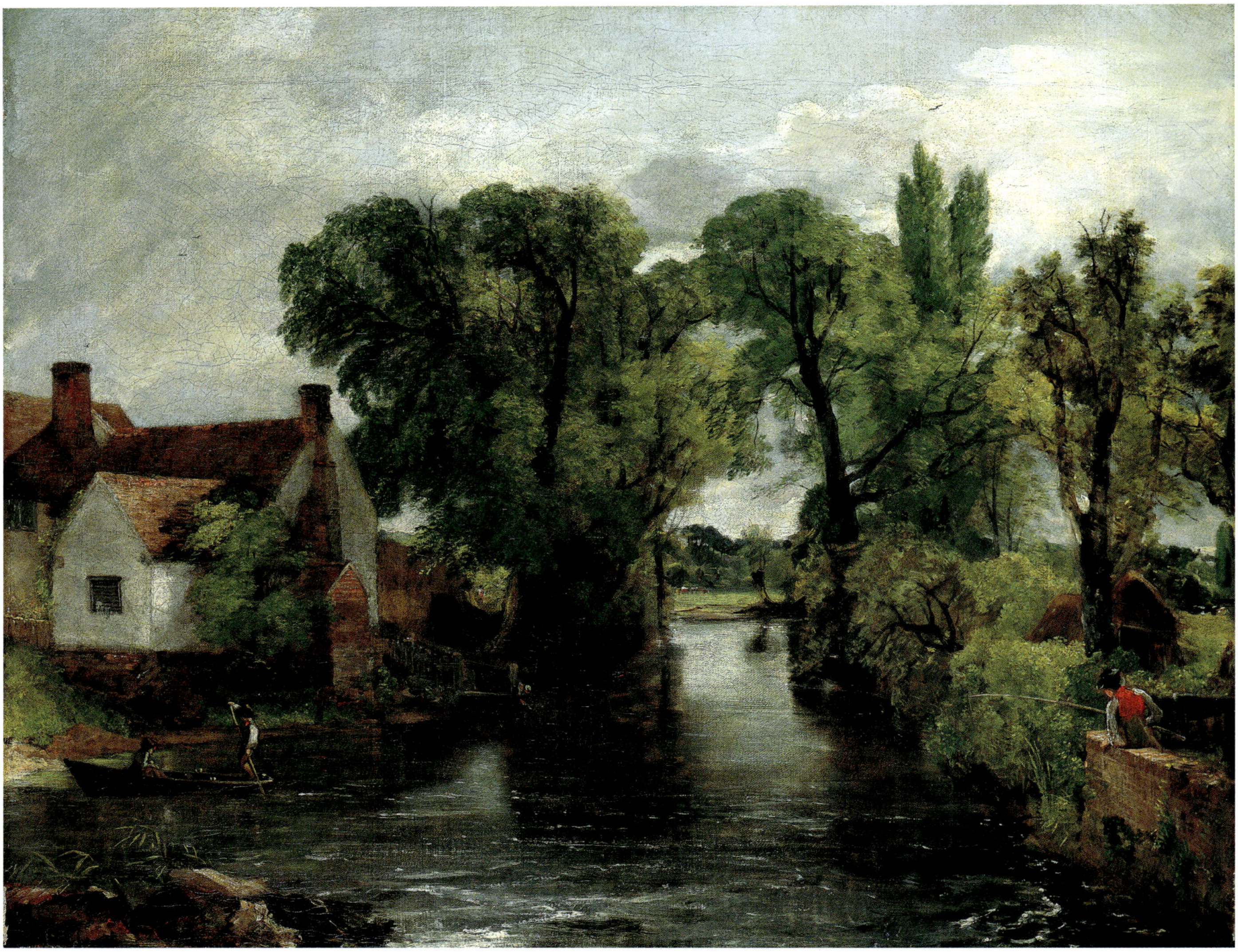

Fig. 74
The Mill Stream, 1814–15
Oil on canvas, 72 × 93.5 cm
Ipswich Borough Council
Collections: Colchester and
Ipswich Museum Service

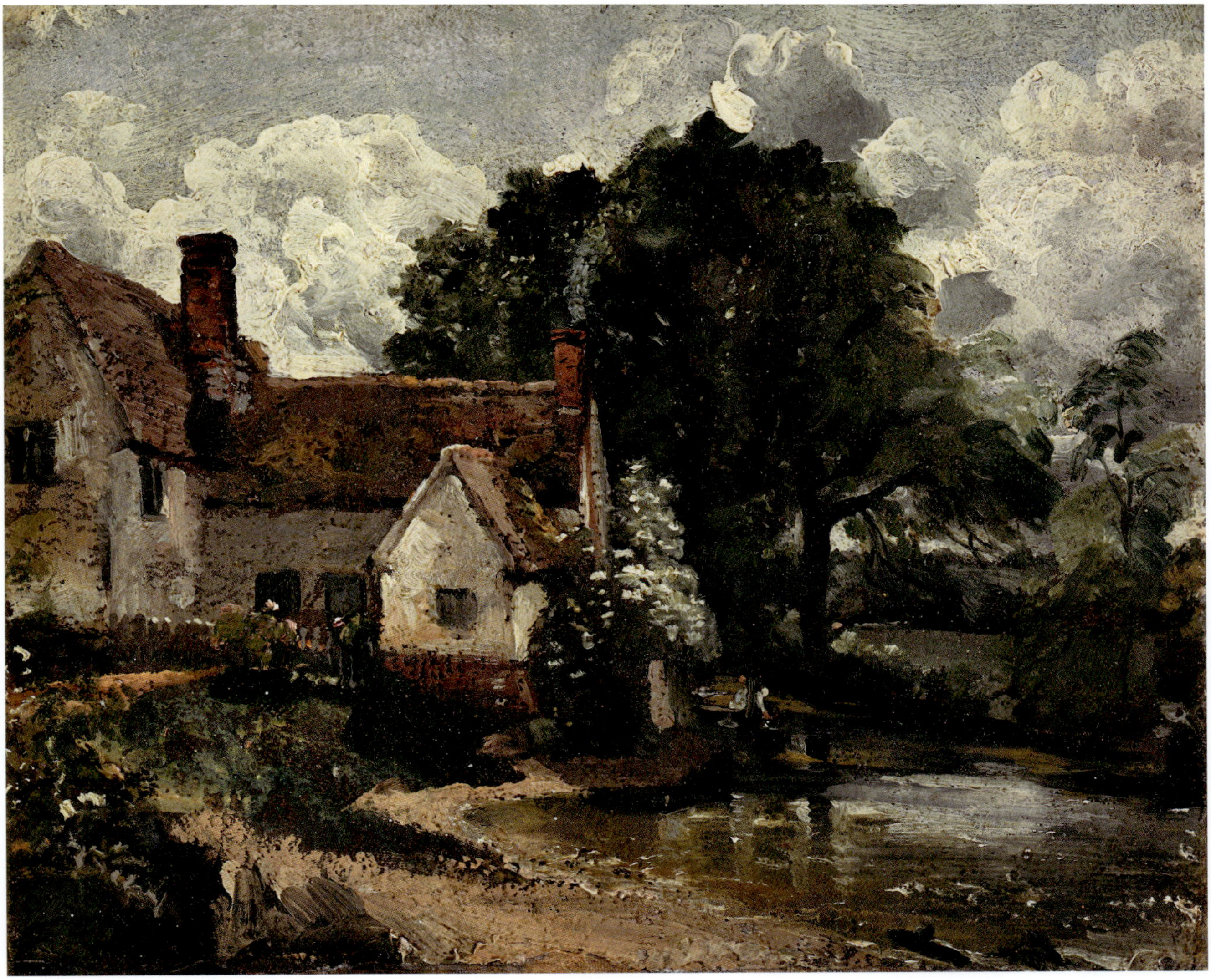

Fig. 75
Willy Lott's House, 1816
Oil on canvas, 19.5 × 24.1 cm
Ipswich Borough Council
Collections: Colchester and
Ipswich Museum Service

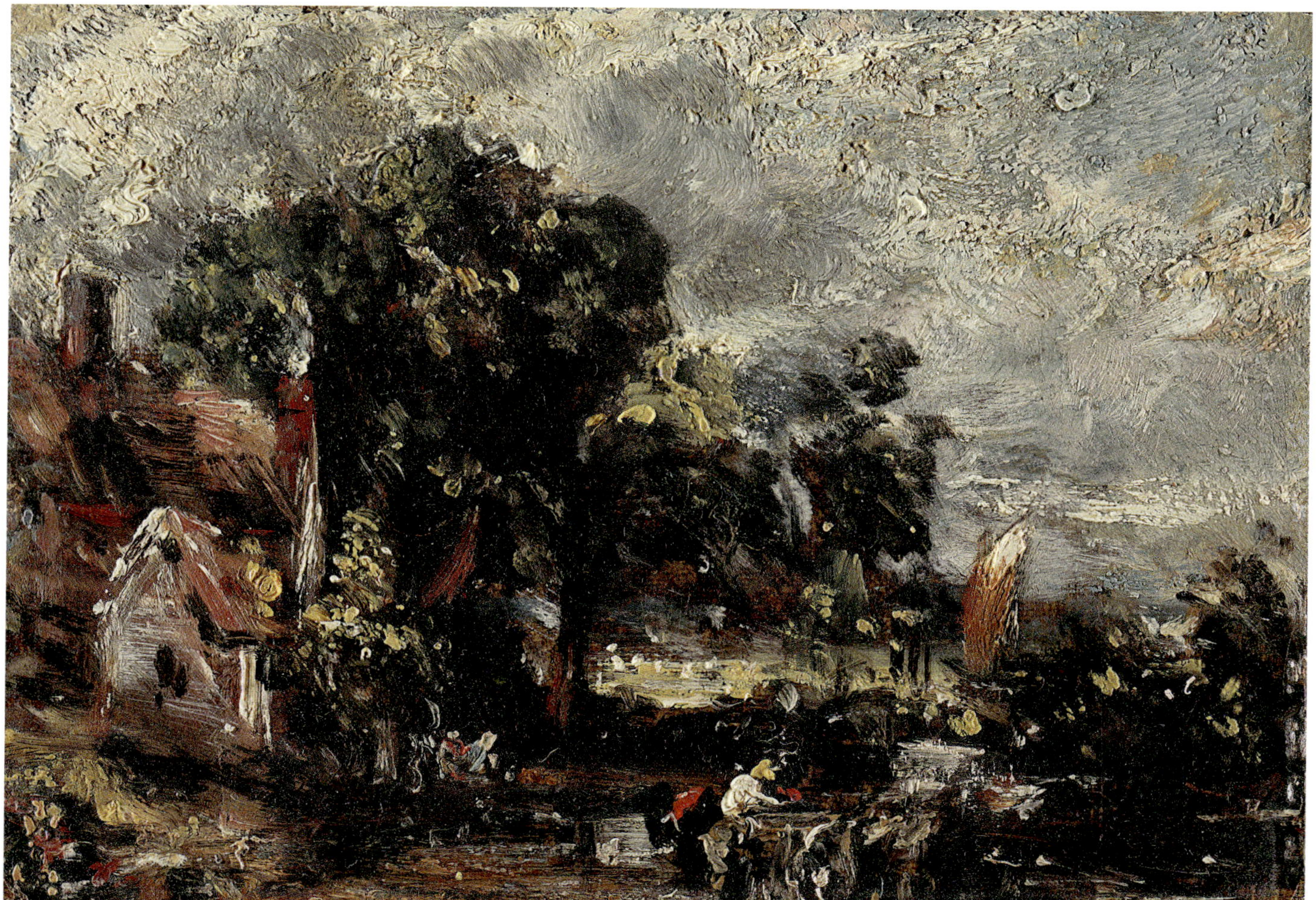

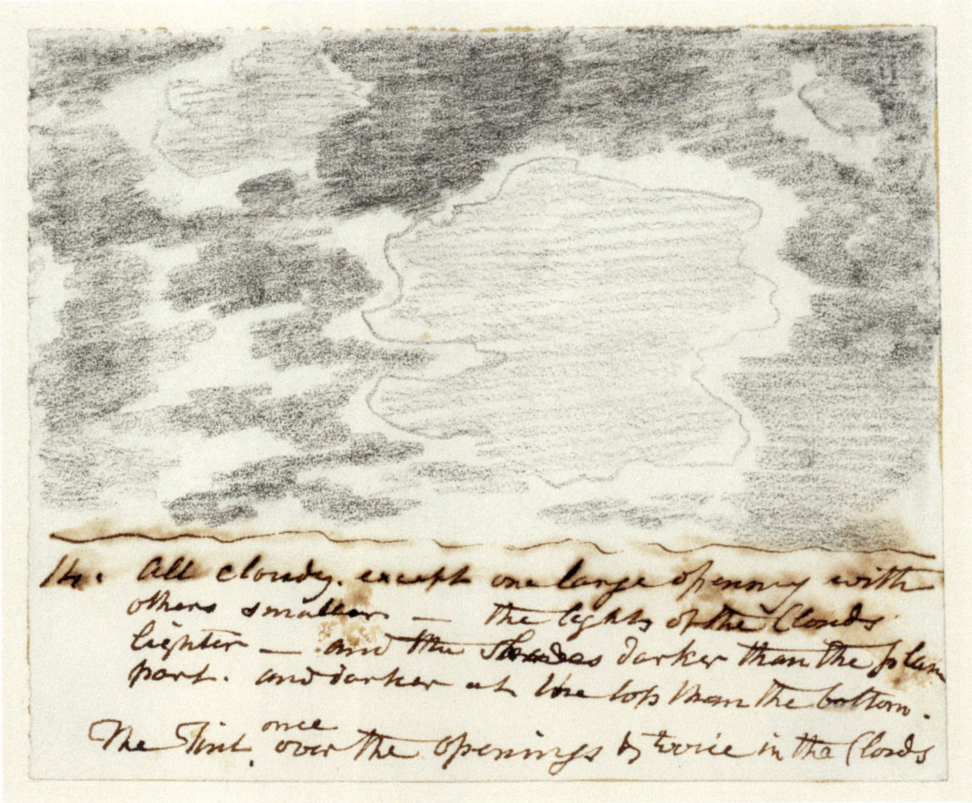

Fig. 76
Sketch for 'The Hay Wain', about 1820
Oil on canvas laid to paper, 12.4 × 17.8 cm
Yale Center for British Art, Paul Mellon Collection, New Haven

Fig. 77
John Constable, after Alexander Cozens (1717–1786)
Cloud Studies (after Cozens's 'Engravings of Skies'), about 1822–3
Graphite covered in fixative on wove paper, 9.4 × 11.5 cm
The Courtauld, London (Samuel Courtauld Trust)

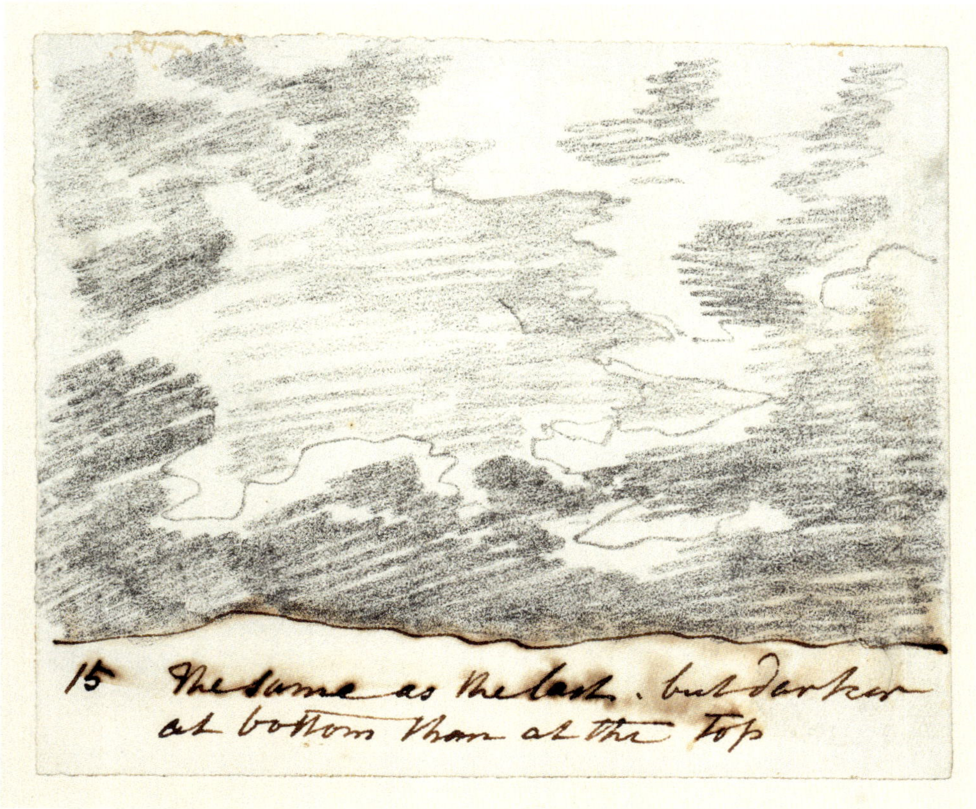

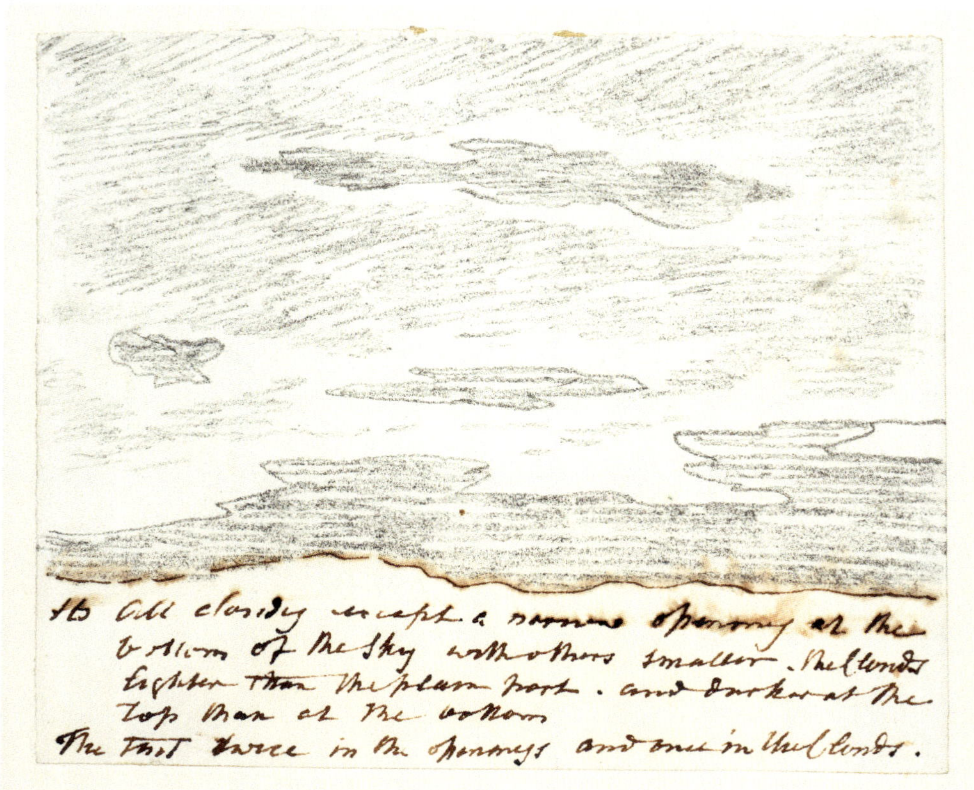

Figs 78–81
John Constable, after Alexander Cozens (1717–1786)
Cloud Studies (after Cozens's 'Engravings of Skies'), about 1822–3
Graphite covered in fixative on wove paper, 9.3 × 11.4 cm (top and opposite) and 9.2 × 11.5 cm (left)
The Courtauld, London (Samuel Courtauld Trust)

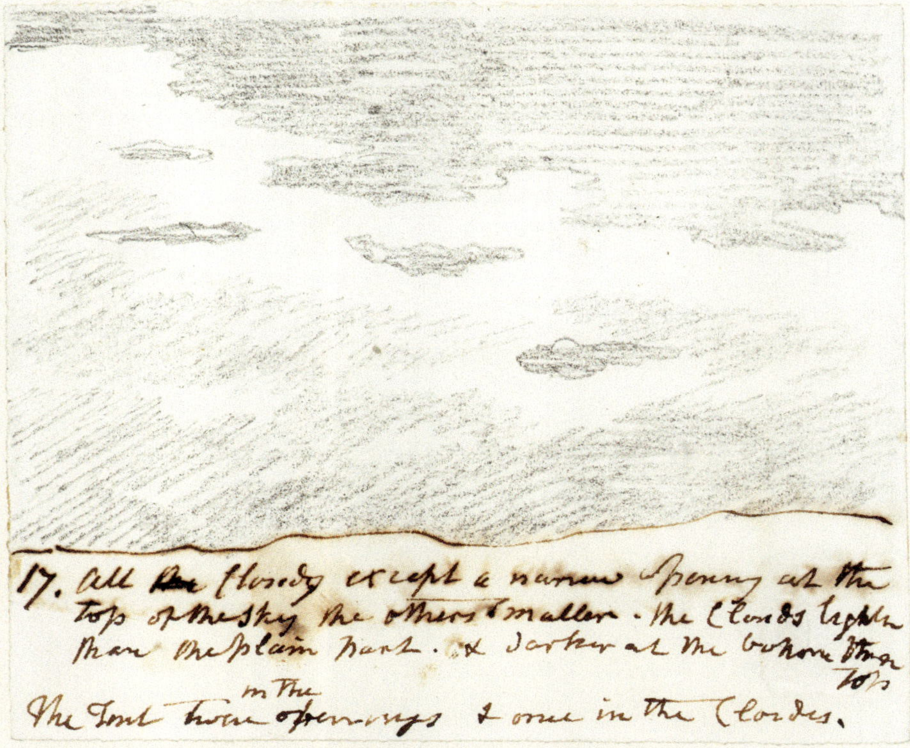
17. All Cloudy except a narrow opening at the top of the sky the others smaller - the Clouds lighter than the plain part. & darker at the bottom than top
The Tint twice in the openings & once in the Clouds.

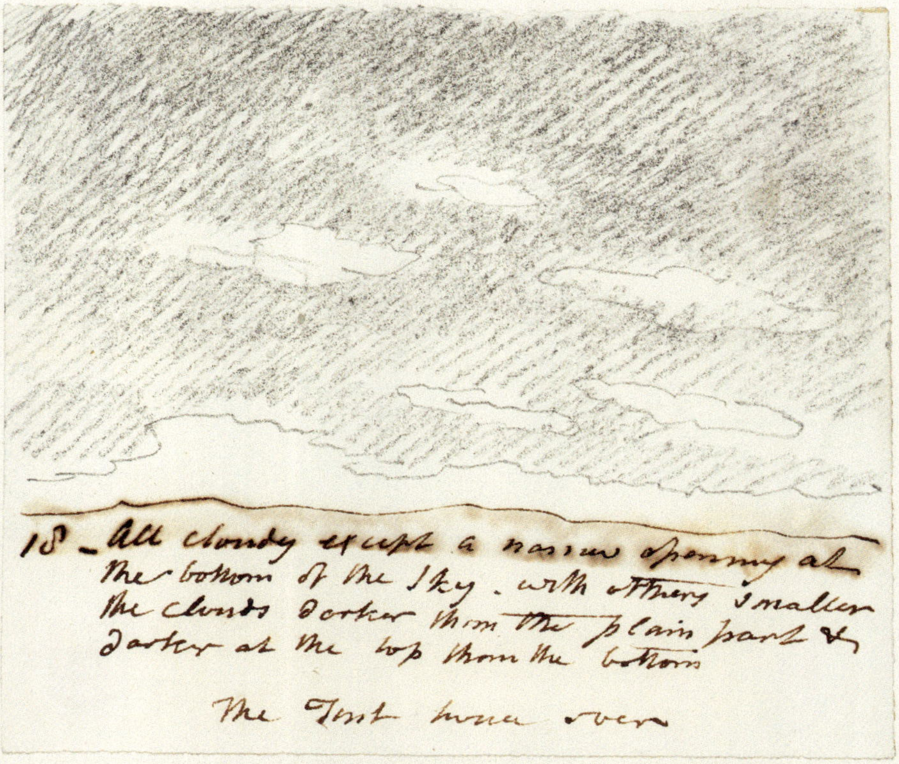
18 - All cloudy except a narrow opening at the bottom of the Sky - with others smaller the clouds darker than the plain part & darker at the top than the bottom
The Tint twice over

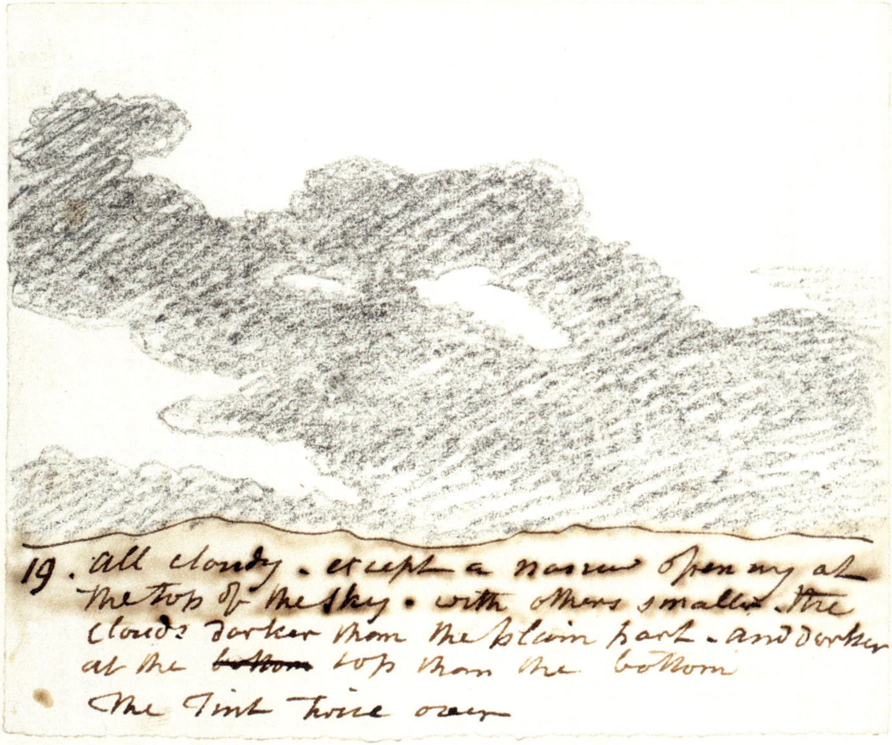

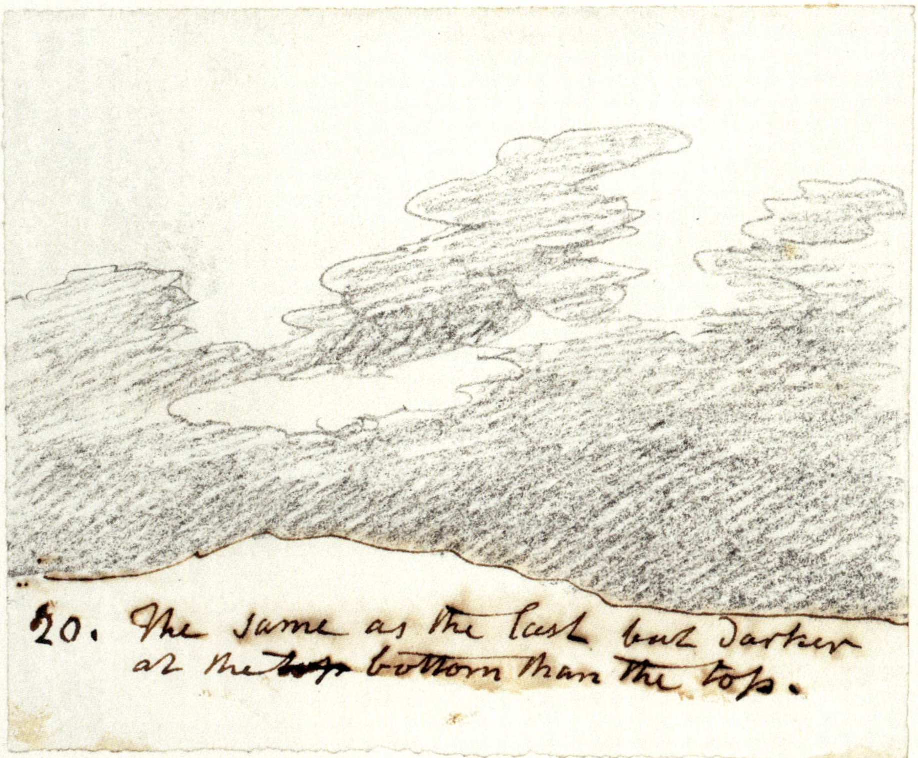

Figs 82–3
John Constable, after Alexander Cozens (1717–1786)
Cloud Studies (after Cozens's 'Engravings of Skies'), about 1822–3
Graphite covered in fixative on wove paper, 9.3 × 11.4 cm (top) and 9.3 × 11.5 cm (left)
The Courtauld, London (Samuel Courtauld Trust)

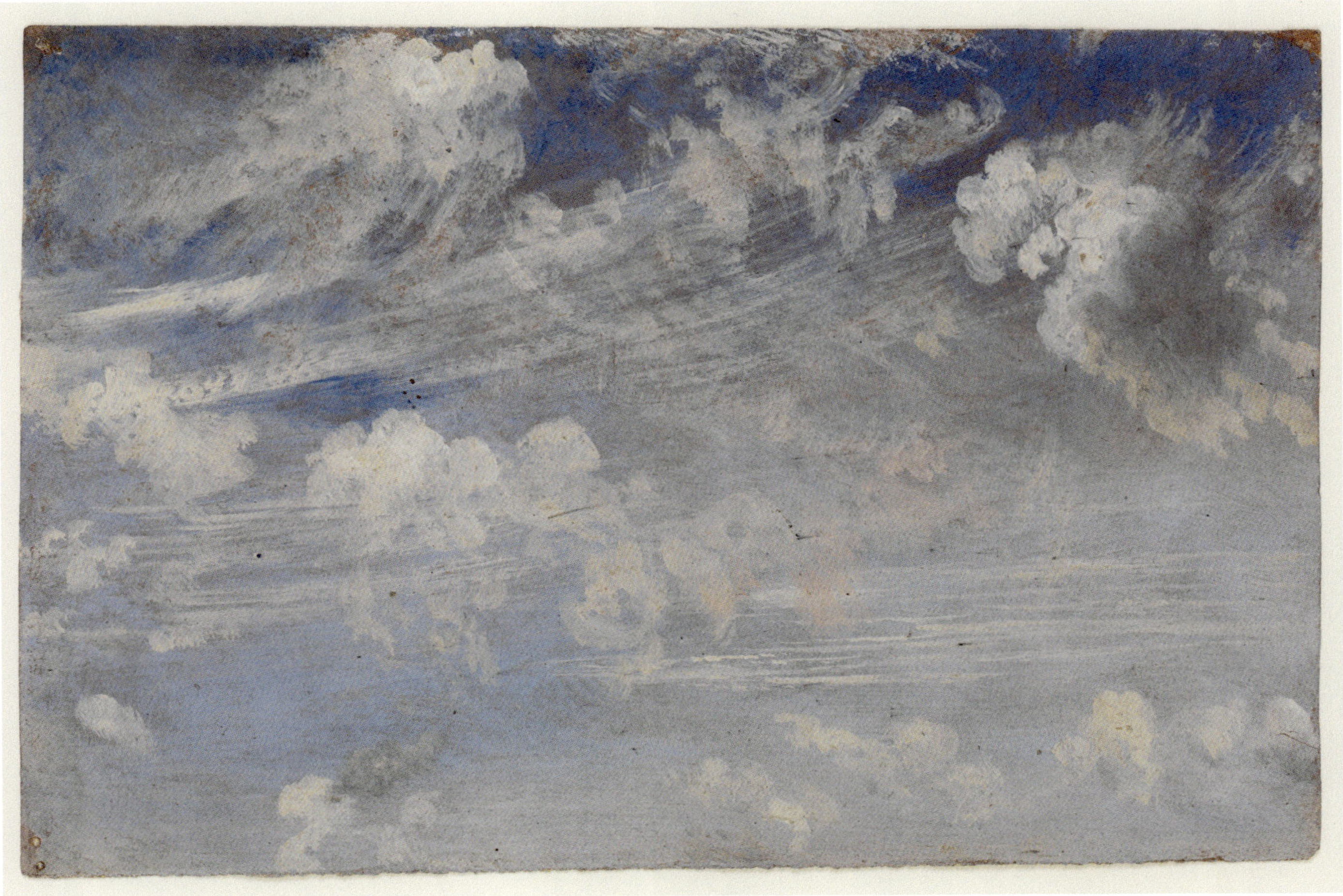

Fig. 84
Study of Cirrus Clouds, about 1822
Oil on paper, 11.4 × 17.8 cm
Victoria and Albert Museum,
London

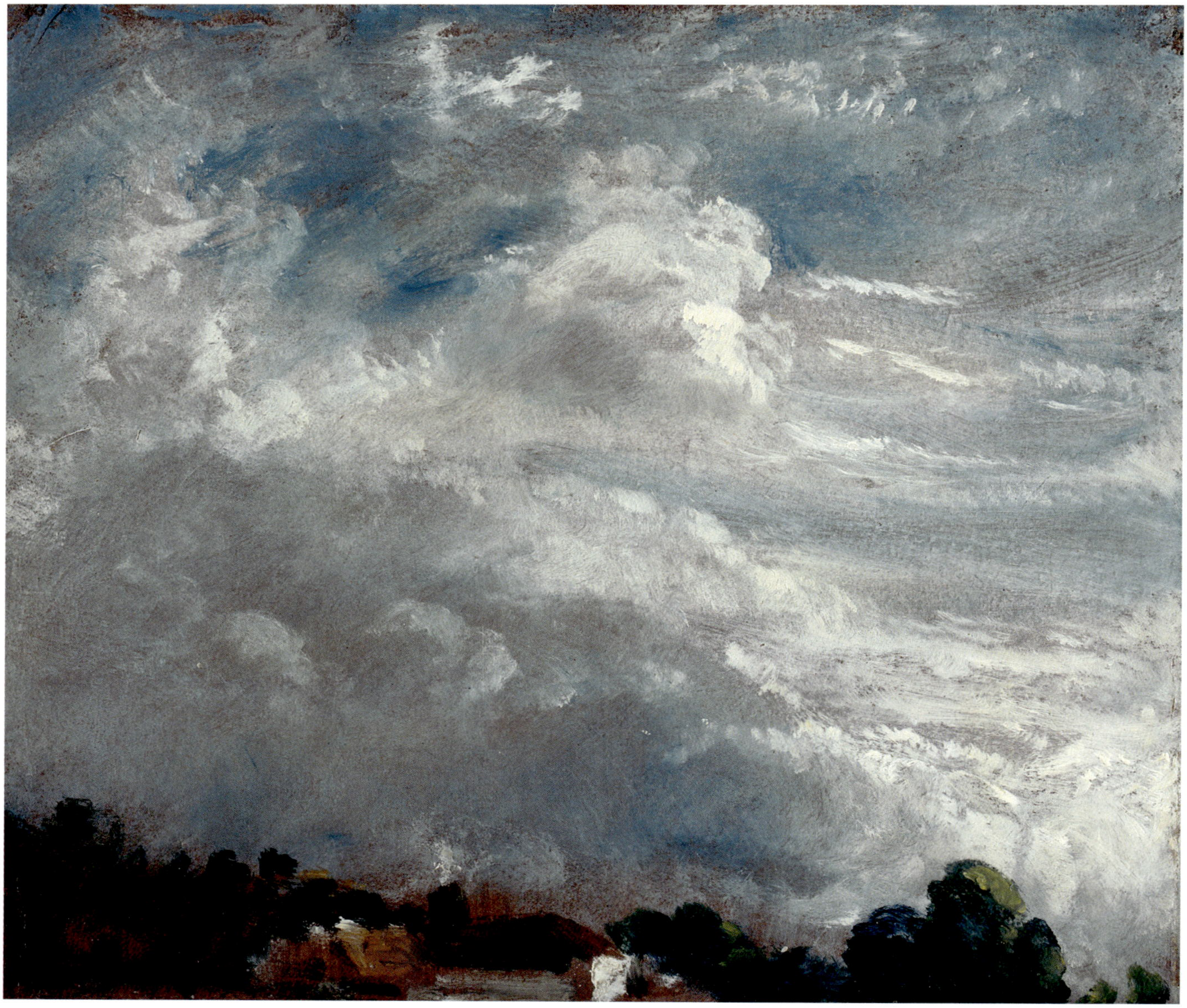

Fig. 85
Cloud Study: Horizon of Trees, 27 September 1821
Oil on paper laid on board, red ground, 25.8 × 30.5 cm
Royal Academy of Arts, London

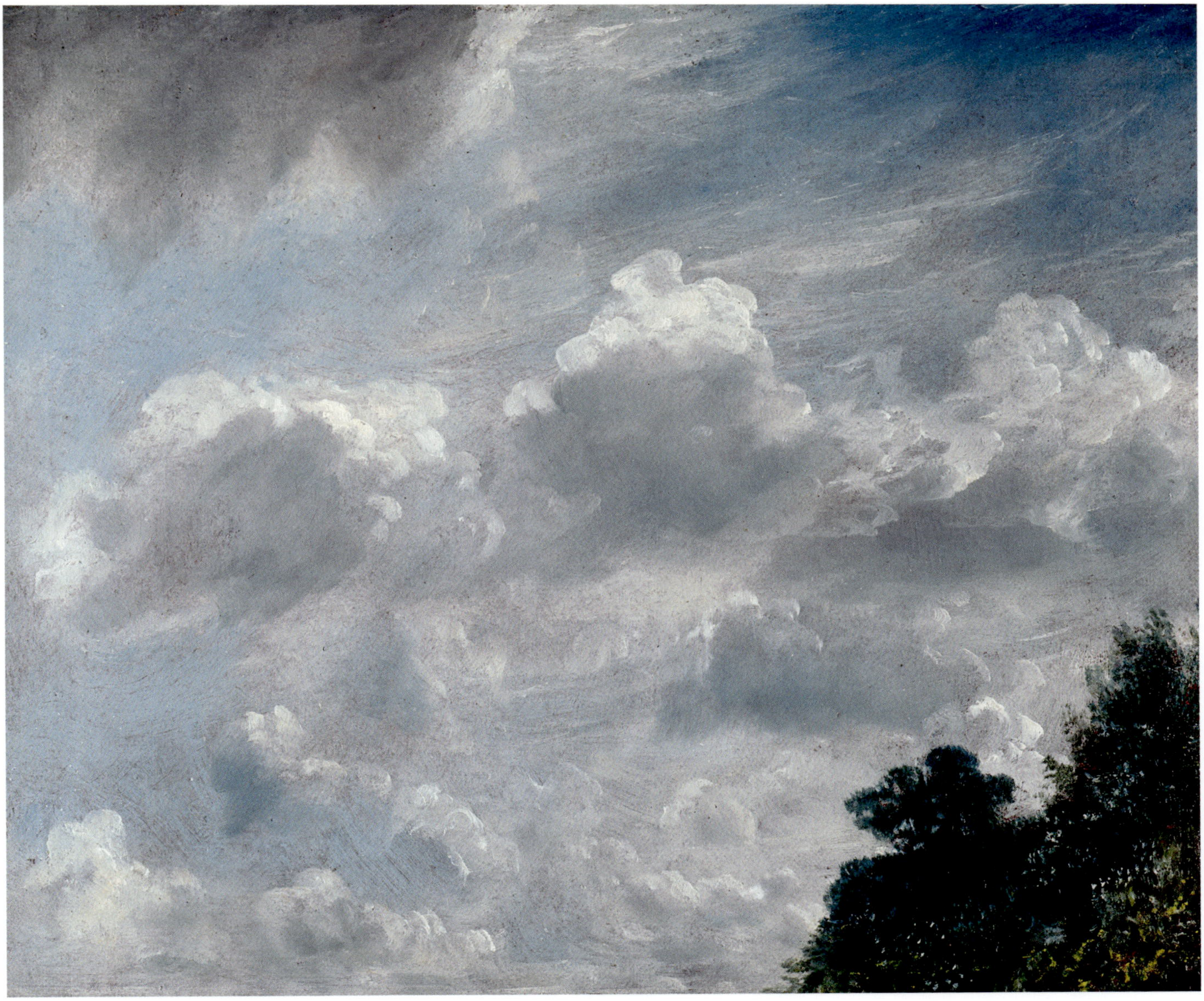

Fig. 86
Cloud Study, Hampstead, Tree at Right, 11 September 1821
Oil on paper laid on board, red ground, 24.1 × 29.9 cm
Royal Academy of Arts, London

After *The Hay Wain*

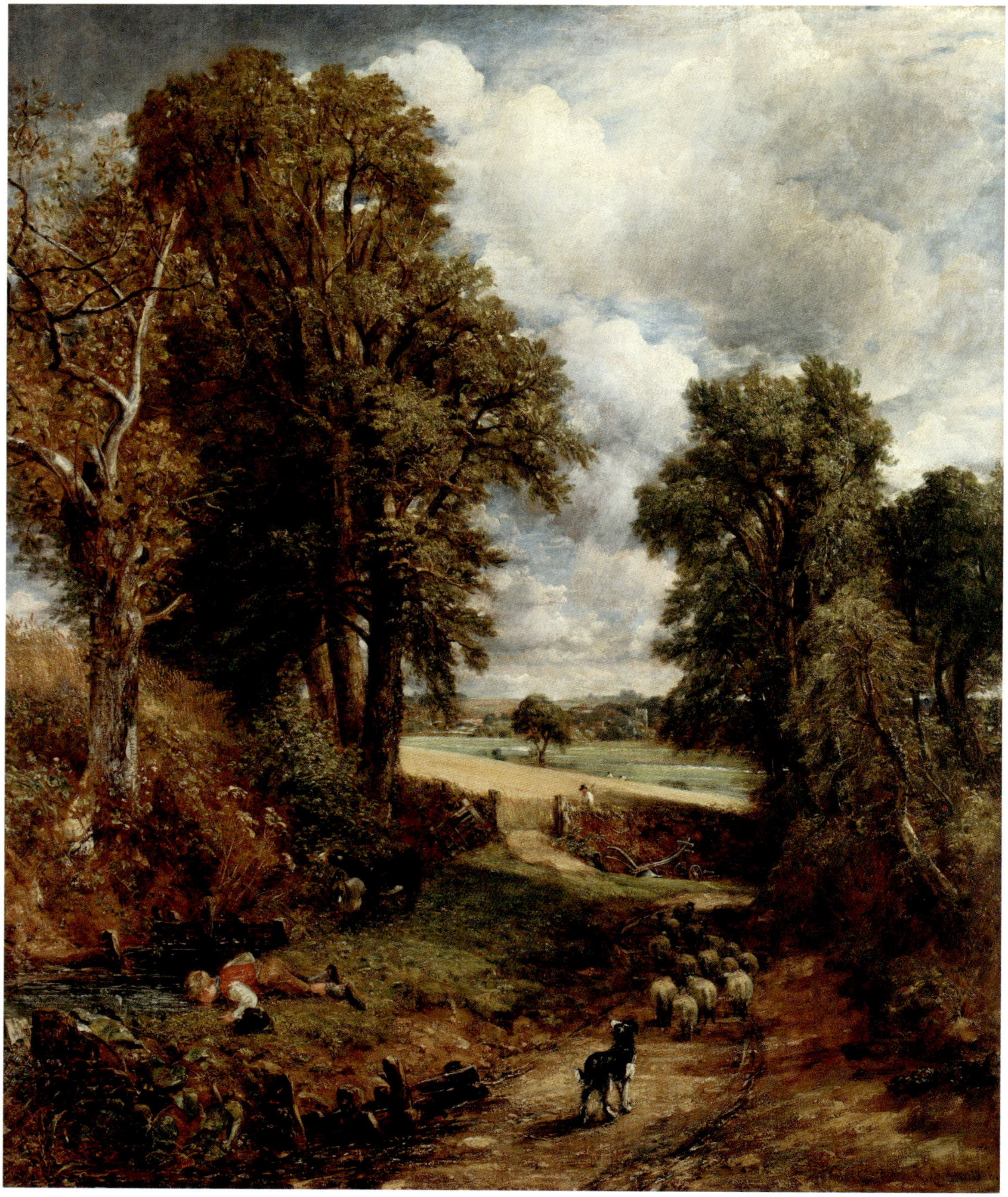

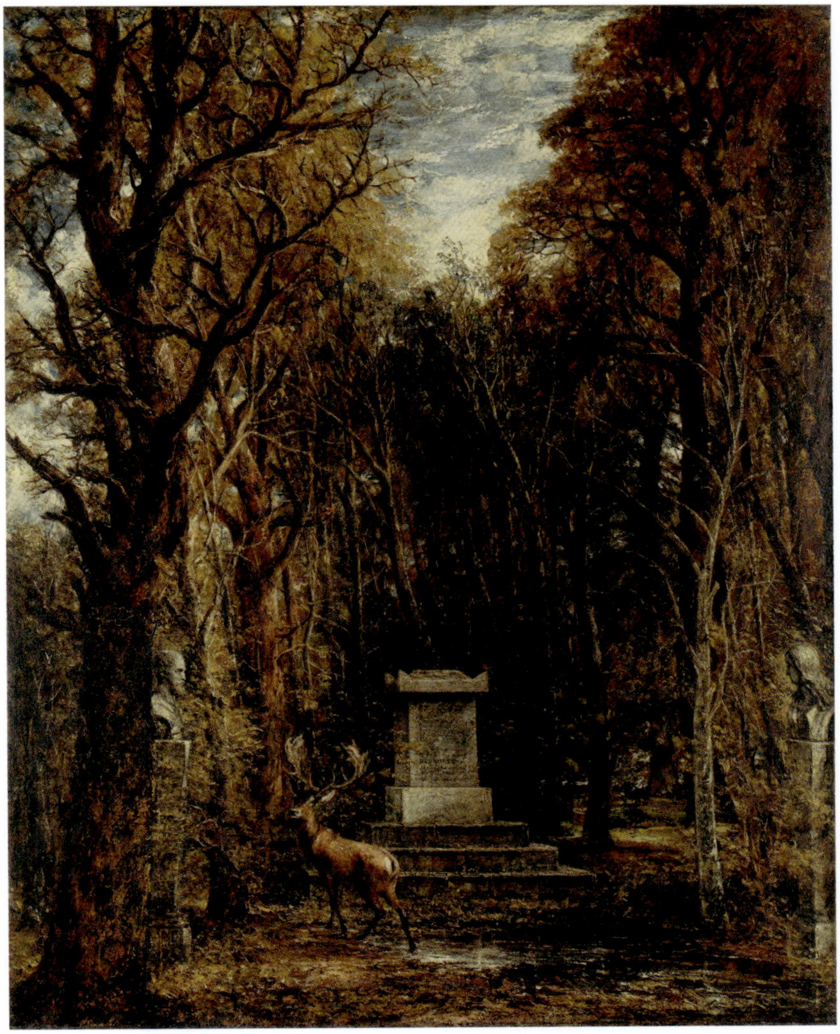

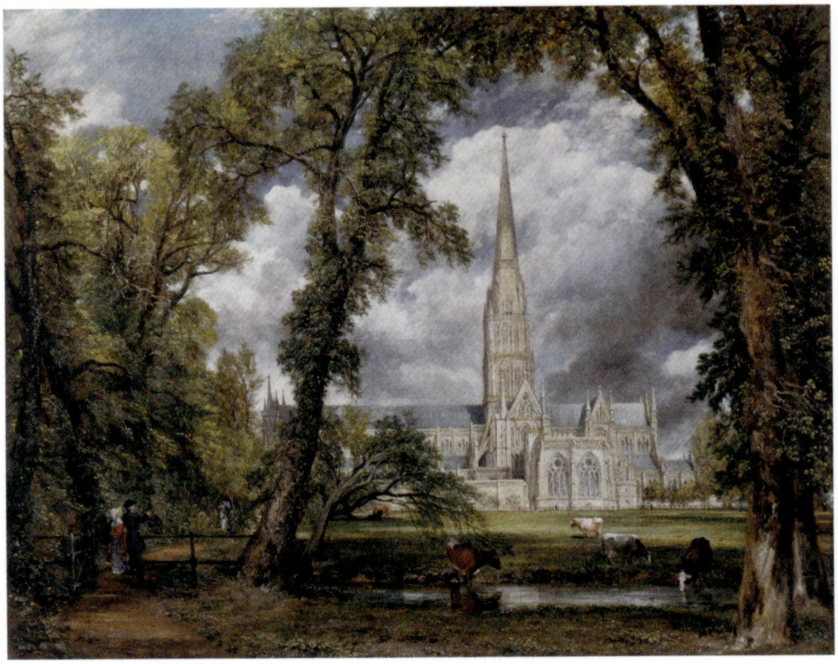

Fig. 87
The Cornfield, 1826
Oil on canvas, 143 × 122 cm
The National Gallery, London

Fig. 88
Cenotaph to the Memory of Sir Joshua Reynolds, erected in the grounds of Coleorton Hall, Leicestershire by the late Sir George Beaumont, Bt., 1833–6
Oil on canvas, 132 × 108.5 cm
The National Gallery, London

Fig. 89
Salisbury Cathedral from the Bishop's Ground, 1823
Oil on canvas, 87.6 × 111.8 cm
Victoria and Albert Museum, London

NOTES

Introduction: Nature and Nation

1 See Helsinger 1989; Vaughan 1996; Wien 2016.
2 See relevant comments from the mid-eighteenth century in Rouquet 1755, p. 22.
3 Brown 2001, p. 187.
4 Ivy 1991, pp. 4, 88–9.
5 Leslie 1896, p. 17.
6 Lambert 2005, p. 193.
7 Ivy 1991, pp. 4–5.
8 Leslie 1896, pp. 246–7.
9 Solkin 2015, p. 277.
10 Leslie 1896, p. 247.
11 Riding 2018, pp. 49, 64–7.
12 Solkin 2015, pp. 24–7.
13 Egerton 2007, p. 232.
14 Ivy 1991, p. 91.
15 Lambert 2005, p. 185.
16 In the National Gallery: Thomas Gainsborough, *The Watering Place*, before 1777, NG109.
17 Egerton 1998, p. 108.
18 New Haven 2005, pp. 3, 12, 19, no. 24.
19 Lambert 2005, pp. 165, 179.
20 Goldsmith 1770, pp. 15, 16.
21 This issue is discussed in the context of landscape and genre scenes in Chapter 5, 'Cottage Politics', in Barrell 2006, pp. 210–46.
22 Gilpin 1789, p. 124.
23 Combe 1809 (first edn, published by Rudolph Ackermann).
24 Solkin 2015, pp. 142–3.
25 Davis 2020, pp. 57–8.
26 London 2001, pp. 198–200.
27 Egerton 2007, pp. 562, 564–5.
28 Davis 2020, pp. 51–64.
29 Lambert 2005, pp. 99–104, 212–27.
30 See Essick 1999; Owens 2020, pp. 192–8.
31 Barrell 2006, p. 214.
32 Lambert 2005, pp. 93–7.
33 Cafarelli 1995, pp. 85–6.
34 Lambert 2005, p. 179.
35 London 2000, pp. 23–5.
36 London and Bristol 1988, pp. 18–22.
37 Riding 2018, pp. 3–5; Barrell 2006, pp. 2–9.
38 Avery-Quash 2023.
39 Hoock 2003, pp. 52–79; London 2013–14, pp. 103–8.
40 Hoock 2003, pp. 53, 56.
41 Egerton 1998, pp. 72, 108. *The Watering Place* was included in the British Institution's exhibition titled 'Works by Old Masters' in 1824.
42 *A Catalogue Raisonée [sic] of the Pictures now Exhibiting at the British Institution*, London [1815], lists 146 pictures, including works by Rubens and Van Dyck.
43 Riding 2018, p. 11.
44 Ibid., pp. 145–7.
45 London 1821, p. 19.
46 London 2013–14, pp. 57, 63–7; London 2000–1, pp. 39–41, 103.
47 London 2013–14, pp. 67, 88.
48 London 2006, p. 37.
49 Egerton 1998, pp. 42–9.
50 London 1821, p. 19.
51 Ivy 1991, pp. 87–91.
52 For information on the artists represented this year, see London 1821.
53 Ivy 1991, p. 89.
54 London 2011–12, pp. 99–108.
55 London 2003, pp. 109–11.
56 Riding 2018, pp. 257–83.
57 London 2003, pp. 49, 22.
58 Ivy 1991, p. 3.

'Pure nature's soul': The Emergence of a Natural Painter

1 The title of this essay is taken from a line of poetry written by Elizabeth Cobbold, Ipswich, 1825.
2 Priscilla Wakefield, in Parris, Shields and Fleming-Williams 1975, p. 129.
3 Leslie 1951, p. 3.
4 Ibid.
5 In the National Gallery: Claude, *Landscape with Hagar and the Angel*, 1646, NG61.
6 In the Tate collection: Richard Wilson, *Distant View of Maecenas' Villa, Tivoli*, about 1756–7, N00108.
7 Letter from Constable to William Wordsworth, 15 June 1836. Wordsworth Trust, Dove Cottage, Grasmere.
8 Letter from Constable to John Thomas Smith, 9 November 1796, in Beckett 1964, p. 6.
9 Letter from Constable to Smith, 7 May 1797, in ibid., pp. 11–12.
10 Letter from Constable to Smith, 18 August 1799, in ibid., p. 16.
11 Letter from Constable to Maria Bicknell, 22 June 1812, in ibid., p. 78.
12 Letter from Constable to Maria, 19 October 1815, in ibid., p. 156.
13 Letter from Constable to John Dunthorne Sr, 22 February 1814, in Beckett 1962, p. 101.
14 Letter from Constable to Maria, 14 January 1816, in Beckett 1964, p. 167.
15 Letter from Constable to Maria, 12 September 1816, in ibid., p. 203.
16 Letter from Constable to Maria, 9 May 1819, in ibid., pp. 245–6.
17 Cited in Beckett 1970, p. 69.
18 Letter from Constable to Abram Constable, 2 November 1819, in Beckett 1964, p. 189.

'Rather a more novel look than I expected': The Making of *The Hay Wain*

1 C.R. Leslie's *Memoirs of the Life of John Constable, Esq., R.A.*, was first published in 1843, a few years after Constable's death. Today the most widely consulted edition is that of 1951 (with reprints), edited by Jonathan Mayne and published by Phaidon.
2 See Kitson 1976, p. 749.
3 See London 1991, p. 197.
4 Cited in Reynolds 1984, no. 21.1, p. 68.
5 For a fuller discussion of all six river Stour landscapes and their related full-scale sketches, see London 2006.
6 See Fleming-Williams 1972; see also London 1991, p. 157.
7 This sketch, not listed in the Constable literature, featured in an episode of BBC Television's *Fake or Fortune* in August 2017: www.bbc.co.uk/iplayer/episode/b092sh3q/fake-or-fortune-series-6-1-constable (accessed 22 April 2024).
8 As suggested by Judy Egerton (Egerton 1998, p. 46).
9 Letter from Abram Constable in response to John Constable, 25 February 1821, in Beckett 1962, p. 193.
10 See St John 2000, p. 7.
11 Reynolds 1984, no. 21.1, p. 68.
12 See also London 2006, p. 140.
13 Egerton 1998, pp. 46–7.
14 Cove 2006, p. 64.
15 For a full listing of Constable's exhibits at the Royal Academy, see London 1991, pp. 39–42. The titles of Constable's exhibits tended to be rather general, and it can therefore be hard to match them today with specific works. However, the Fitzwilliam Museum painting seems a strong candidate for one of the exhibits in 1821 (see also London 1991, pp. 215–16).
16 See Cove 2006, p. 52.
17 Letter from Constable to John Fisher, 1 April 1821, in Beckett 1968, p. 65.
18 Ivy 1991, no. 21.11, p. 88.
19 Ibid.
20 The first known use of the title is in a letter dated 14 February 1821 from John Fisher to Constable when he enquires: 'And how thrives the "hay wain"?' (Beckett 1968, p. 62).
21 Thornes 1999, p. 46.
22 As suggested by Graham Reynolds (Reynolds 1984, under no. 21.1, pp. 68–9).
23 Ivy 1991, no. 21.11, p. 88.
24 Draft for lecture on the Dutch School; see Beckett 1970, p. 65.
25 Ivy 1991, no. 21.17, p. 90; 'there is much skill shewn in this performance, of which Ruysdoen [*sic*] has evidently been the model'.
26 Parris, Shields and Fleming-Williams 1975, p. 57 (annotation by engraver David Lucas made in connection with a letter from Constable to John Fisher, 20 September 1821).
27 For Constable's collecting of, and admiration for, the old masters, see London 2014–15; see also Haarlem 2020–1.
28 The two paintings were reunited in an exhibition at the Wallace Collection in 2020: *Rubens: The Two Great Landscapes* (catalogue by Lucy Davis). See also Gage 2006, pp. 21–3.
29 Tyler 1975, p. 275.
30 Gage 2006, p. 23.
31 Ivy 1991, nos 21.2 and 21.14, pp. 88–9.
32 Cove 2006, p. 63.
33 Florisoone 1957, p. 181.
34 Beckett 1966, pp. 178–81, gives a good summary of these events.
35 Whiteley 2002–3, p. 50.

'Landscape not merely as seen, but as experienced': Constable and Europe

1 Florisoone 1957, p. 181.
2 Gombrich 1950, p. 375. Readers would also have found a similar version of this narrative in 'The Natural Vision' chapter of Kenneth Clark's landmark publication *Landscape into Art*, published the previous year, with the first German and French translations in 1962.
3 Venice 1950, n.p.
4 Ibid.
5 See Beckett 1970.
6 Alfrey 2020.
7 See Paris, Washington and Berlin 1996–7, pp. 115, 118, 431.
8 See Berlin 1998, p. 20.
9 Meier-Graefe 1908, pp. 129, 143.
10 John Constable, *Landscape with a View of Dedham Vale seen from Langham*, about 1812/13, pencil and white chalk on grey paper, Statens Museum for Kunst, Inv.no. GB 6157; *Higham Village on the River Stour*, about 1804, oil on canvas, Alte Nationalgalerie, Staatliche Museen zu Berlin, Inv.no. A I 555; for example, *Dedham Vale, Suffolk, from Near East Bergholt*, about 1805, watercolour, National Gallery of Ireland, Inv.no. NGI.2056; and

The Celebration in East Bergholt of the Peace of 1814 Concluded in Paris between France and the Allied Powers, about 1824, oil on canvas, Szépművészeti Múzeum, Budapest, Inv.no. 4624.

11 For example, *Portrait of Abraham [sic] Constable*, brother of the artist, n.d., watercolour and pencil, Musée du Louvre, Inv.no. RF 6105.

12 Stuttgart 2011, p. 11.

13 Fleming-Williams and Parris 1984.

14 Hamburg, Oslo, Stockholm and Copenhagen 1949, n.p.

15 Hamburg 2002–3.

16 Madrid 2007, p. 15.

17 Groningen 2017, p. 5.

18 Haarlem 2020–1, p. 12.

19 Dordrecht 2021.

20 Rome 2014, p. 79.

21 Ghent 2007–8.

22 Cristian 2022, n.p.

23 Ibid.

24 Stuttgart 2011, p. 9.

25 See Paris 2002–3.

From 'dull replica' to 'national treasure': The Afterlife of *The Hay Wain*

1 During production of this series, the painting was held in French collections. In 1824, S.W. Reynolds proposed to go to France to engrave or supervise production of a mezzotint plate, but this plan did not come to fruition. The full title of the series was 'Various Subjects of Landscape, Characteristic of English Scenery' (1833).

2 Stephen Deuchar, 'Foreword', in London 2006, p. 12.

3 It was exhibited by Anglo-French dealer John Arrowsmith at the Salon under the title *Une charrette à foin traversant un gué au pied d'une ferme; paysage*; reputedly sold by Arrowsmith to an anonymous French collector in 1825; sold by Henry, Paris (31 March–1 April 1828); then bought by Boursault.

4 Artaria 1841, p. 285.

5 Reynolds 1984, pp. 67–9.

6 Egerton 1998, pp. 42–9.

7 The painting had previously been exhibited there by the artist in 1822.

8 Letter from Constable to John Fisher, 6 December 1822, in Beckett 1968, p. 107.

9 National Gallery Archive, NG5/32/12, Full list of subscribers for *The Cornfield*.

10 The pictures were sometimes moved to the South Kensington Museum when Marlborough House was in use.

11 *The Valley Farm*, presented by Robert Vernon in 1847, is now in Tate Britain (N00327); Waagen 1854, p. 385.

12 Egerton 1998, p. 11.

13 Manchester 1857, pp. 112–15, 208.

14 Sketchly 1857, p. 70.

15 1857 was also the year of the Turner bequest to the National Gallery Collection.

16 Henry Vaughan (1809–1899) noted that he first saw these works in 'the house of Mr. C. R. Leslie, RA. who admired them greatly': 'V&A, 987-1900 "Full-Scale Study for *The Hay Wain*"' and 'V&A, 986-1900 "*The Leaping Horse* (full-scale study)"': collections.vam.ac.uk/item/O81405/full-scale-study-for-ithe-oil-painting-constable-john-ra/ (accessed 22 April 2024).

17 Vaughan had 16 oils by Constable in his collection. Reynolds 1984, pp. 69–70; Rhyne 2006.

18 'Constable's works. By Tom Taylor – Handbook of International Exhibition – 1862. London', National Gallery Archive, NG72/49, Vaughan album, p. 5.

19 First noted in list of pictures on loan on 24 October 1862; matching frames supplied by Vaughan.

20 The sketches have been on display at the museum almost continuously ever since, formally becoming part of the V&A collection following the Vaughan bequest in 1900.

21 Gillott shared the profit from the sale with Cox; Chapel 2008, pp. 41–2.

22 The photograph was taken at Vaughan's house by Messrs Goupil, who sent the negative to Paris to be enlarged to the size of the proposed engraving. Alfred Louis Brunet-Debaines, the engraver, made a drawing in black chalk from which the etching was made. Vaughan noted it took Debaines 'about 4 years', alongside other engagements; National Gallery Archive, NG72/49, Vaughan album.

23 The Royal Academy, by the 1870s, was the primary location for organising annual old master exhibitions in London.

24 *International Exhibition of Science, Industry and Art*, Edinburgh, 6 May–30 October 1886.

25 Redgrave 1866, pp. 383–99.

26 Heaton 1880, pp. 191–205.

27 In 1881 a small sketch of *The Hay Wain* hanging in Sir Frederic Leighton's Drawing Room was described as 'the greatest treasure', hung by Leighton with a Daubigny below and a Corot 'close by', Wilfrid Meynell characterising them as 'outcomes' and 'results' of the influence of Constable; Meynell 1881, pp. 175–6.

28 Some of those works bequeathed by Isabel Constable are now in the Tate collection, such as *The Grove, Hampstead*, about 1821–2 (N01246).

29 See Grosvenor Gallery 1888; Grosvenor Gallery 1889.

30 NG72/49, album of materials compiled by Henry Vaughan, 1886–93.

31 See K. Clark, 'Foreword', in Amsterdam 1936, pp. 17–21.

32 Clark [1949] 1961, p. 77.

33 *Masterpieces of English Painting: William Hogarth, John Constable, J.M.W. Turner: Lent by His Majesty the King, the Museums and Collections of Great Britain*, Art Institute of Chicago; Metropolitan Museum of Art, New York; and Art Gallery of Toronto, 1946–7.

34 Chicago 1946, p. 14.

35 'Willy Lott's House': www.flatfordandconstable.org.uk/flatford-places/willy-lotts-house/ (accessed 22 April 2024).

36 Reynolds 1960; Reynolds 1984; Reynolds 1996.

37 London 1976.

38 This series was later presented to the Tate by Jacobson.

39 Other publications of note include Rosenthal 1983.

40 The casts were without value and the medal itself was in store. Media reports included 'Damage to "Hay Wain": National Gallery Intruder', *Daily Telegraph*, 12 July 1963; 'Artful Thief Gets ... Replica', *Daily Sketch*, 13 July 1963; and 'Constable Medallion Replica Stolen', *Ipswich Evening Star*, 12 July 1963.

41 London 1996, p. 35.

42 London 2014–15.

43 Cork and Slocombe, in Slocombe 2015.

44 Kennard's artwork even featured on the wall in the background of a television episode of *The Young Ones*.

45 Adams 2014.

46 New Haven 2022.

BIBLIOGRAPHY

Adams 2014
T. Adams, 'Frank Auerbach: Constable, Turner and me', *The Observer*, 21 September 2014: www.theguardian.com/artanddesign/2014/sep/21/frank-auerbach-constable-turner-and-me-interview (accessed 22 April 2024)

Alfrey 2020
N. Alfrey, 'John Constable and Paul Huet: Marsh and Flood', Tate Papers, no. 33 (2020): www.tate.org.uk/research/tate-papers/33/john-constable-paul-huet-marsh-flood (accessed 22 April 2024)

Amsterdam 1936
Twee Eeuwen Engelsche Kunst, exh. cat., Stedelijk Museum, Amsterdam 1936

Artaria 1841
H. Artaria, *A Descriptive Catalogue of the Gallery of Pictures, Collected by Edmund Higginson, Esq. of Saltmarsh Castle, c. 1838*, London 1841

Avery-Quash 2023
S. Avery-Quash, 'Building(s) for Art: The Evolution of Public Art Galleries in England, 1780–1840', in M. McCue and S. Thomas (eds), *The Edinburgh Companion to Romanticism and the Arts*, Edinburgh 2023, pp. 165–83

Barrell 2006
J. Barrell, *The Spirit of Despotism: Invasions of Privacy in the 1790s*, Oxford 2006

Beckett 1962
R.B. Beckett (ed.), *John Constable's Correspondence*, vol. I, Ipswich 1962

Beckett 1964
R.B. Beckett (ed.), *John Constable's Correspondence*, vol. II, Ipswich 1964

Beckett 1966
R.B. Beckett (ed.), *John Constable's Correspondence*, vol. IV, Ipswich 1966

Beckett 1968
R.B. Beckett (ed.), *John Constable's Correspondence*, vol. VI, Ipswich 1968

Beckett 1970
R.B. Beckett (ed.), *John Constable's Discourses*, vol. XIV, Ipswich 1970

Berlin 1998
C. Keisch, P.-K. Schuster and M. Wullen (eds), *Fontane und die Bildende Kunst*, exh. cat., Neue Nationalgalerie, Berlin 1998

Brown 2001
D.B. Brown, *Romanticism*, London 2001

Cafarelli 1995
A.W. Cafarelli, 'The Romantic "Peasant" Poets and their Patrons', *The Wordsworth Circle*, 26, no. 2 (1995), pp. 77–87

Chapel 2008
J. Chapel, 'The Papers of Joseph Gillott (1799–1872)', *Journal of the History of Collections*, 20, no. 1 (2008), pp. 37–84

Chicago 1946
K. Clark, 'Hogarth, Constable and Turner', in H. Huth, *Masterpieces of English Painting*, exh. cat., Art Institute of Chicago 1946, pp. 9–16

Clark [1949] 1961
K. Clark, *Landscape into Art*, Boston 1961 (reprint of London 1949 edn)

Cobbold 1825
E. Cobbold, *Poems by Mrs Elizabeth Cobbold, with a memoir of the author, 'To a Young Artist'*, Ipswich 1825

Combe 1809
W. Combe, *The Tour of Doctor Syntax in Search of the Picturesque*, London 1809

Cove 2006
S. Cove, 'The Painting Techniques of Constable's "Six-Footers"', in London 2006, pp. 50–67

Cristian 2022
D. Cristian, 'The Most Treasured Exhibition in the History of Art Safari Will Be Seen this Fall', *Business Review*, 24 August 2022: business-review.eu/bucharest-going-out/events/the-most-treasured-exhibition-in-the-history-of-art-safari-will-be-seen-this-fall-234559 (accessed 22 April 2024)

Daniels 1992
S. Daniels, 'Love and Death across an English Garden: Constable's Paintings of his Family's Flower and Kitchen Gardens', *Huntington Library Quarterly*, 55, no. 3 (1992), pp. 433–57

Davis 2020
L. Davis, *Rubens: The Two Great Landscapes*, London 2020

Dordrecht 2021
D.B. Brown et al., *In the Light of Cuyp: Aelbert Cuyp & Gainsborough – Constable – Turner*, exh. cat., Dordrechts Museum, Dordrecht 2021

Egerton 1998
J. Egerton, *National Gallery Catalogues: The British School*, London 1998

Egerton 2007
J. Egerton, *George Stubbs, Painter: Catalogue Raisonné*, New Haven, CT 2007

Essick 1999
R.N. Essick, *A Troubled Paradise: William Blake's Virgil Wood Engravings*, San Francisco 1999

Fleming-Williams 1972
I. Fleming-Williams, 'A Runover Dungle and a Possible Date for "Spring"', *Burlington Magazine*, 114 (1972), pp. 386–93

Fleming-Williams and Parris 1984
I. Fleming-Williams and L. Parris, *The Discovery of Constable*, London 1984

Florisoone 1957
M. Florisoone, 'Constable and the "Massacres de Scio" by Delacroix', *Journal of the Warburg and Courtauld Institutes*, 20, no. 1/2 (1957), pp. 180–5

Gage 2006
J. Gage, 'Constable: The Big Picture', in London 2006, pp. 18–29

Ghent 2007–8
R. Hoozee, 'Everyday Landscape', in R. Hoozee et al., *British Vision: Observation and Imagination in British Art, 1750–1950*, exh. cat., Museum of Fine Arts, Ghent 2007–8, pp. 223–42

Gilpin 1789
W. Gilpin, *Observations relative chiefly to Picturesque Beauty, made in the year 1776, on several parts of Great Britain; particularly the High-lands of Scotland*, London 1789

Goldsmith 1770
O. Goldsmith, *The Deserted Village: A Poem*, London 1770

Gombrich 1950
E.H. Gombrich, *The Story of Art*, London 1950

Groningen 2017
D. Jackson, W. Busch and J. Reynaerts, *Romanticism in the North: From Friedrich to Turner*, exh. cat., Groninger Museum, Groningen 2017

Grosvenor Gallery 1888
Sir C. Lindsay, Bart, and J.W. Beck, Secretary, The Grosvenor Gallery, Summer Exhibition 1888, 'A Century of British Art from 1737 to 1837, with notes by F.G. Stephens', London 1888

Grosvenor Gallery 1889
Sir C. Lindsay, Bart, assisted by C.W. Deschamps, The Grosvenor Gallery, Summer Exhibition 1889, 'A Century of British Art (second series) from 1737 to 1837, with notes by Walter Armstrong', London 1889

Haarlem 2020–1
C. Shields et al., *John Constable*, exh. cat., Teylers Museum, Haarlem 2020–1

Hamburg 2002–3
J.E. Howoldt, U.M. Schneede and Hamburger Kunsthalle, *Expedition Kunst: Die Entdeckung der Natur von C.D. Friedrich bis Humboldt*, exh. cat., Hamburger Kunsthalle, Hamburg 2002–3

Hamburg, Oslo, Stockholm and Copenhagen 1949
E.K. Waterhouse, *British Painting from Hogarth to Turner*, exh. cat., British Council and Hamburger Kunsthalle, Hamburg; Kunstnernes Hus, Oslo; Nationalmuseum, Stockholm; and Statens Museum for Kunst, Copenhagen 1949

Heaton 1880
The Lives of the Most Eminent British Painters by Allan Cunningham. Revised edition. Annotated and continued to the present time by Mrs. Charles Heaton, vol. III, London 1880

Helsinger 1989
E. Helsinger, 'Constable: The Making of a National Painter', *Critical Inquiry*, 15, no. 2 (1989), pp. 253–79

Hoock 2003
H. Hoock, *The King's Artists: The Royal Academy of Arts and the Politics of British Culture 1760–1840*, Oxford 2003

Ipswich 2021–2
E. Roodhouse and C. Howgego, *Creating Constable*, exh. cat., Christchurch Mansion, Ipswich 2021–2

Ivy 1991
J.C. Ivy, *Constable and the Critics, 1802–1837*, Woodbridge and Rochester, NY 1991

Kitson 1976
M. Kitson, 'The Inspiration of John Constable', *Journal of the Royal Society of Arts*, CXXIV, no. 5244 (1976), pp. 738–53

Lambert 2005
R. Lambert, *John Constable and the Theory of Landscape Painting*, Cambridge 2005

Leslie 1896
C.R. Leslie, *Life and Letters of John Constable, R.A.*, London 1896

Leslie 1951
C.R. Leslie, *Memoirs of the Life of John Constable, Composed Chiefly of his Letters*, ed. Jonathan Mayne, London 1951

London 1821
The Exhibition of the Royal Academy, exh. cat., Royal Academy of Arts, London 1821: chronicle250.com/1821 (accessed 20 May 2024)

London 1976
L. Parris (ed.), *Constable: Paintings, Watercolours & Drawings*, exh. cat., Tate, London 1976

London 1991
L. Parris and I. Fleming-Williams, *Constable*, exh. cat., Tate, London 1991

London 1996
C. Painter, *At Home with Constable's Cornfield*, exh. cat., The National Gallery, London 1996

London 2000
D.B. Brown, A. Hemingway and A. Lyles, *Romantic Landscape: The Norwich School of Painters*, exh. cat., Tate, London 2000

London 2000–1
E. Shanes et al., *Turner: The Great Watercolours*, exh. cat., Royal Academy of Arts, London 2000–1

London 2001
R. Godfrey, *James Gillray: The Art of Caricature*, exh. cat., Tate, London 2001

London 2003
P. Noon, D.B. Brown, C. Riding et al., *Constable to Delacroix: British Art and the French Romantics*, exh. cat., Tate, London 2003

London 2006
A. Lyles (ed.), *Constable: The Great Landscapes*, exh. cat., Tate, London 2006

London 2011–12
M. Myrone (ed.), *John Martin: Apocalypse*, exh. cat., Tate, London 2011–12

London 2013–14
C. Riding and R. Johns, *Turner and the Sea*, exh. cat., National Maritime Museum, London 2013–14

London 2014–15
M. Evans, *John Constable: The Making of a Master*, exh. cat., Victoria and Albert Museum, London 2014–15

London and Bristol 1988
F. Greenacre, *Francis Danby, 1793–1861*, exh. cat., Tate, London, and City of Bristol Museum and Art Gallery 1988

Madrid 2007
R. Rosenblum et al., *The Abstraction of Landscape: From Northern Romanticism to Abstract Expressionism*, exh. cat., Fundación Juan March, Madrid 2007

Manchester 1857
Catalogue of the Art Treasures of the United Kingdom, Collected at Manchester in 1857, exh. cat., Art Treasures Palace, Manchester 1857

Meier-Graefe 1908
J. Meier-Graefe, *Modern Art: Being a Contribution to a New System of Aesthetics*, vol. 1, London 1908

Meynell 1881
W. Meynell, 'The Homes of our Artists: Sir Frederick [*sic*] Leighton's House in Holland Park Road', *The Magazine of Art*, 4 (1881), pp. 169–76

New Haven 2005
O.H. Turner, *Nobleness and Grandeur: Forging Historical Landscape in Britain, 1760–1850*, exh. cat., Yale Center for British Art, New Haven, CT 2005

New Haven 2022
B. Riley, 'On Works by Constable and Delacroix', *Bridget Riley: Perceptual Abstraction*, digital exh. cat., Yale Center for British Art, New Haven, CT 2022: bridget-riley.publications.britishart.yale.edu/c-and-d/ (accessed 22 April 2024)

Owens 2020
S. Owens, *Spirit of Place: Artists, Writers and the British Landscape*, London 2020

Paris 2002–3
L. Freud, *Constable : Le Choix de Lucian Freud*, exh. cat., Galeries nationales du Grand Palais, Paris 2002–3

Paris, Washington and Berlin 1996–7
C. Keisch and M.U. Riemann-Reyher (eds), *Adolph Menzel, 1815–1905: Das Labyrinth der Wirklichkeit*, exh. cat., Musée d'Orsay, Paris; National Gallery of Art, Washington, DC; and Nationalgalerie im Alten Museum, Berlin 1996–7

Parris, Shields and Fleming-Williams 1975
L. Parris, C. Shields and I. Fleming-Williams (eds), *John Constable: Further Documents and Correspondence*, Ipswich 1975

Redgrave 1866
R. Redgrave and S. Redgrave, *A Century of Painters of the English School; with critical notices of their works, and an account of the progress of art in England*, London 1866

Reynolds 1960
G. Reynolds, *Victoria and Albert Museum: Catalogue of the Constable Collection*, London 1960

Reynolds 1984
G. Reynolds, *The Later Paintings and Drawings of John Constable*, New Haven, CT, and London 1984

Reynolds 1996
G. Reynolds, *The Early Paintings and Drawings of John Constable*, New Haven, CT, and London 1996

Rhyne 1990
C. Rhyne (ed.), *John Constable: Toward a Complete Chronology*, Portland, OR 1990

Rhyne 2006
C. Rhyne, 'The Remarkable Story of the "Six-Foot-Sketches"', in London 2006, pp. 40–9

Riding 2018
J. Riding, *Peterloo: The Story of the Manchester Massacre*, London 2018

Rome 2014
A. Wilton, 'Turner and Constable: Poetics and Technique', in C. Brook and V. Curzi (eds), *Hogarth, Reynolds, Turner: British Painting and the Rise of Modernity*, exh. cat., Fondazione Roma, Rome 2014, pp. 79–87

Rosenthal 1983
M. Rosenthal, *Constable: The Painter and his Landscape*, New Haven, CT, and London 1983

Rosenthal 2006/7
M. Rosenthal, 'Constable and Englishness', *The British Art Journal*, 7, no. 3 (2006/7), pp. 40–5

Rouquet 1755
J.A. Rouquet, *The Present State of the Arts in England*, London 1755

Sketchly 1857
P. Sketchly, 'British Landscape Painters, No. 1', in *The Art-Treasures Examiner: A Pictorial, Critical, and Historical Record of the Art-Treasures Exhibition, at Manchester, in 1857*, Manchester 1857, pp. 69–71

Slocombe 2015
R. Slocombe, 'Protest and survive: why Peter Kennard is political dynamite', *The Guardian*, 1 May 2015: www.theguardian.com/artanddesign/2015/may/01/blair-selfie-peter-kennard-political-dynamite (accessed 22 April 2024)

Solkin 2015
D.H. Solkin, *Art in Britain 1660–1815*, New Haven, CT 2015

St John 2000
I. St John, *Flatford: Constable Country*, Ipswich 2000

Stuttgart 2011
C. Conrad, 'Constable und Deutschland: Etappen einer Annäherung', in M. Evans et al. (eds), *John Constable: Maler der Natur: Ölskizzen und Zeichnungen aus dem Victoria and Albert Museum, London*, exh. cat., Staatsgalerie Stuttgart 2011, pp. 9–11

Thornes 1999
J. Thornes, *John Constable's Skies: A Fusion of Art and Science*, Birmingham 1999

Tyler 1975
R.E.G. Tyler, 'Rubens and "The Hay-Wain"', *The Connoisseur*, CLXXIX (1975), pp. 270–5

Vaughan 1996
W. Vaughan, 'Constable's Englishness', *Oxford Art Journal*, 19, no. 2 (1996), pp. 17–27

Venice 1950
British Council et al., *Exhibition of Works by John Constable, Matthew Smith, Barbara Hepworth*, exh. cat., Venice Biennale, Venice 1950

Waagen 1854
Dr [G.F.] Waagen, *Treasures of Art in Great Britain: Being an account of the chief collections of paintings, drawings, sculptures, illuminated MSS., &c &c. in three volumes*, vol. I, London 1854

Whiteley 2002–3
L. Whiteley, 'Constable et le Salon de 1824', in Paris 2002–3, pp. 47–51

Wien 2016
I. Wien, 'The Opaque Nature of John Constable's Naturalism', *RACAR: Revue d'art canadienne/Canadian Art Review*, 41, no. 2 (2016), pp. 44–61

LIST OF EXHIBITED WORKS

The Hay Wain, 1821
Oil on canvas, 130.2 × 185.4 cm
The National Gallery, London.
Presented by Henry Vaughan, 1886
Fig. 2

Cenotaph to the Memory of Sir Joshua Reynolds, erected in the grounds of Coleorton Hall, Leicestershire by the late Sir George Beaumont, Bt., 1833–6
Oil on canvas, 132 × 108.5 cm
The National Gallery, London.
Bequeathed by Miss Isabel Constable as the gift of Maria Louisa, Isabel, and Lionel Bicknell Constable, 1888
Fig. 88

Thomas Gainsborough (1727–1788)
Cornard Wood, near Sudbury, Suffolk, 1748
Oil on canvas, 122 × 155 cm
The National Gallery, London.
Bought (Lewis Fund), 1875
Fig. 47

The Cornfield, 1826
Oil on canvas, 143 × 122 cm
The National Gallery, London.
Presented by subscribers, 1837
Fig. 87

Alexis Joseph Depaulis (1792–1867)
Gold medal awarded by Charles X of France to John Constable, 1824
Gold or gold-plated with silk ribbon, 4.5 × 4.5 cm
The National Gallery, London. Presented by Sir Charles Wakefield, 1927
Page 8

James Gillray (1756–1815)
'Connoisseurs examining a collection of George Morland's', 1807
Hand-coloured etching and aquatint on paper, 43 × 33 cm
Omek and Linda Marks Family Collection
Fig. 49

Thomas Rowlandson (1756–1827)
'Rural sports. Or a pleasant way of making hay', 1814
Etching with contemporary hand colouring on wove paper, 38.8 × 26.2 cm
Nicholas J.S. Knowles
Fig. 50

Thomas Rowlandson (1756–1827)
'The Sign of the Four Alls', 1810
Etching with contemporary hand colouring on wove paper, 24.5 × 34.5 cm
Nicholas J.S. Knowles
Fig. 51

Joseph Mallord William Turner (1775–1851)
The Vale of Ashburnham, 1816
Watercolour on paper, 38 × 56.4 cm
British Museum, 1910,0212.272.
George Salting Bequest, 1910
Fig. 57

Willy Lott's House, East Bergholt, about 1812–13
Graphite on three sheets of wove paper joined together, 20.1 × 28.4 cm
The Courtauld, London (Samuel Courtauld Trust)
Fig. 70

Rowing Boat moored beneath a Bank, around 1809
Graphite on blue-grey laid paper, 9 × 12.5 cm
The Courtauld, London (Samuel Courtauld Trust)
Fig. 71

John Constable, after Alexander Cozens (1717–1786)
Cloud Studies (after Cozens's 'Engravings of Skies'), about 1822–3
Graphite covered in fixative on wove paper, 9.4 × 11.5 cm
The Courtauld, London (Samuel Courtauld Trust)
Fig. 77

John Constable, after Alexander Cozens (1717–1786)
Cloud Studies (after Cozens's 'Engravings of Skies'), about 1822–3
Graphite covered in fixative on wove paper, 9.3 × 11.4 cm
The Courtauld, London (Samuel Courtauld Trust)
Fig. 78

John Constable, after Alexander Cozens (1717–1786)
Cloud Studies (after Cozens's 'Engravings of Skies'), about 1822–3
Graphite covered in fixative on wove paper, 9.2 × 11.5 cm
The Courtauld, London (Samuel Courtauld Trust)
Fig. 79

John Constable, after Alexander Cozens (1717–1786)
Cloud Studies (after Cozens's 'Engravings of Skies'), about 1822–3
Graphite covered in fixative on wove paper, 9.3 × 11.4 cm
The Courtauld, London (Samuel Courtauld Trust)
Fig. 80

John Constable, after Alexander Cozens (1717–1786)
Cloud Studies (after Cozens's 'Engravings of Skies'), about 1822–3
Graphite covered in fixative on wove paper, 9.3 × 11.4 cm
The Courtauld, London (Samuel Courtauld Trust)
Fig. 81

John Constable, after Alexander Cozens (1717–1786)
Cloud Studies (after Cozens's 'Engravings of Skies'), about 1822–3
Graphite covered in fixative on wove paper, 9.3 × 11.4 cm
The Courtauld, London (Samuel Courtauld Trust)
Fig. 82

John Constable, after Alexander Cozens (1717–1786)
Cloud Studies (after Cozens's 'Engravings of Skies'), about 1822–3
Graphite covered in fixative on wove paper, 9.3 × 11.5 cm
The Courtauld, London (Samuel Courtauld Trust)
Fig. 83

William Blake (1757–1827)
The Blighted Corn; 'Nor Fox, nor Wolf, nor Rat among our Sheep'; Sabrina's Silvery Flood; and Colinet's 'Fond Desire Strange Lands to Know', 1821
Wood-engraving and letterpress printed on laid paper, 3.3 × 7.4 cm (each image)
From R.J. Thornton, *The Pastorals of Virgil*, 3rd edn, London 1821: vol. 1, p. 15
Lent by the Royal Academy of Arts, London
Fig. 54

Palette owned by John Constable, RA, date unknown
23 × 40 cm
Lent by the Royal Academy of Arts, London
Fig. 68

Cloud Study, Hampstead, Tree at Right, 11 September 1821
Oil on paper laid on board, red ground, 24.1 × 29.9 cm
Lent by the Royal Academy of Arts, London
Fig. 86

Cloud Study: Horizon of Trees, 27 September 1821
Oil on paper laid on board, red ground, 25.8 × 30.5 cm
Lent by the Royal Academy of Arts, London
Fig. 85

George Robert Lewis (1782–1871)
Sketchbook, about 1815
Pen and wash drawing, with pencil sketch underneath, on paper
Victoria and Albert Museum
Fig. 55

Sketchbook owned by John Constable, 1814
Pencil and watercolour on paper
Victoria and Albert Museum. Given by Isabel Constable, daughter of the artist
Fig. 67

Willy Lott's House, near Flatford Mill, about 1811
Oil on paper, 24.1 × 18.1 cm
Victoria and Albert Museum.
Given by Isabel Constable
Fig. 73

Full-scale study for *The Hay Wain*, about 1821
Oil on canvas, 137 × 188 cm
Victoria and Albert Museum.
Bequeathed by Henry Vaughan
Fig. 1

Salisbury Cathedral from the Bishop's Ground, 1823
Oil on canvas, 87.6 × 111.8 cm
Victoria and Albert Museum. Given by John Sheepshanks, 1857
Fig. 89

Study of Cirrus Clouds, about 1822
Oil on paper, 11.4 × 17.8 cm
Victoria and Albert Museum.
Given by Isabel Constable
Fig. 84

John Linnell (1792–1882)
Woody Landscape, 1824
Oil on panel, 24.7 × 32.2 cm
Brighton & Hove Museums
Fig. 60

Francis Danby (1793–1861)
Clifton Rocks from Rownham Fields, about 1821
Oil on panel, 40 × 50.8 cm
Courtesy of Bristol Museums: Bristol Museum & Art Gallery
Fig. 58

Francis Danby (1793–1861)
A Scene in Leigh Woods, 1822
Oil on panel, 35.2 × 50.4 cm
Courtesy of Bristol Museums: Bristol Museum & Art Gallery
Fig. 59

Attributed to John Constable
East Bergholt Singers, about 1800
Carved and painted wood with textile, 15.5 × 28.5 × 12.6 cm
Ipswich Borough Council Collections: Colchester and Ipswich Museum Service
Fig. 69

Golding Constable's Flower Garden, 1815
Oil on canvas, 33.1 × 50.7 cm
Ipswich Borough Council Collections: Colchester and Ipswich Museum Service
Fig. 63

Golding Constable's Kitchen Garden, 1815
Oil on canvas, 33.4 × 51.1 cm
Ipswich Borough Council Collections: Colchester and Ipswich Museum Service
Fig. 64

The Mill Stream, 1814–15
Oil on canvas, 72 × 93.5 cm
Ipswich Borough Council Collections: Colchester and Ipswich Museum Service
Fig. 74

Willy Lott's House, 1816
Oil on canvas, 19.5 × 24.1 cm
Ipswich Borough Council Collections: Colchester and Ipswich Museum Service
Fig. 75

William Mulready (1786–1863)
The Farrier's Shop, after 1820
Oil on canvas, 40.9 × 52.1 cm
The Syndics of the Fitzwilliam Museum, University of Cambridge. Bequeathed by Joseph Prior in 1919
Fig. 61

John Crome (1768–1821)
Marlingford Grove, about 1815
Oil on canvas, 136.5 × 100.5 cm
National Museums Liverpool, Lady Lever Art Gallery
Fig. 56

George Stubbs (1724–1806)
The Reapers, 1783
Oil and enamel on panel (oak), 91.4 × 137.3 cm
National Trust Collections, Upton House (The Bearsted Collection)
Fig. 46

A Cottage in a Cornfield, 1817
Oil on canvas, 31.5 × 26.3 cm
Lent by Amgueddfa Cymru – Museum Wales. Purchased with the assistance of the Art Fund
Fig. 65

Charles Williams (active 1796–1830)
'Political Balance', 1816
Hand-coloured etching on paper, 23.7 × 34 cm
Fagan Collection of Political Prints and Caricatures, Pol P 25. University of Nottingham Manuscripts and Special Collections
Fig. 52

George Morland (1763–1804)
The Coming Storm, Isle of Wight, 1789
Oil on canvas, 51.5 × 64.6 cm
Courtesy of Wolverhampton Art Gallery
Fig. 48

The Wheat Field, 1816
Oil on canvas, 54.6 × 78.1 cm
Clark Art Institute, Williamstown, Massachusetts, USA, gift of the Manton Art Foundation in memory of Sir Edwin and Lady Manton
Fig. 66

Willy Lott's House, 1802
Oil on canvas, 33.7 × 42.5 cm
Clark Art Institute, Williamstown, Massachusetts, USA, acquired by the Clark with support from the Manton Foundation
Fig. 72

Print made by William Blake (1757–1827)
Songs of Innocence and of Experience, Plate 4, 'The Shepherd' (Bentley 5), 1789
Relief etching printed in green ink, with watercolour, pen and black ink on wove paper, 11.1 × 7 cm
Yale Center for British Art, Paul Mellon Collection
Fig. 53

Sketch for 'The Hay Wain', about 1820
Oil on canvas laid to paper, 12.4 × 17.8 cm
Yale Center for British Art, Paul Mellon Collection
Fig. 76

Richard Parkes Bonington (1802–1828)
A Wooded Lane, about 1825
Oil on millboard, 27.9 × 22.9 cm
Yale Center for British Art, Paul Mellon Collection
Fig. 62

LIST OF LENDERS

Brighton
Brighton & Hove Museums

Bristol
Bristol Museums: Bristol Museum & Art Gallery

Cambridge
The Fitzwilliam Museum

Cardiff
Amgueddfa Cymru – Museum Wales

Ipswich
Ipswich Borough Council Collections: Colchester and Ipswich Museum Service

Liverpool
National Museums Liverpool, Lady Lever Art Gallery

London
The British Museum
The Courtauld
Omek and Linda Marks Family Collection
The National Gallery
Royal Academy of Arts
Victoria and Albert Museum

New Haven, Connecticut
Yale Center for British Art, Paul Mellon Collection

Nottingham
Fagan Collection of Political Prints and Caricatures, University of Nottingham

Private collection
Nicholas J.S. Knowles

Warwickshire
National Trust Collections, Upton House (The Bearsted Collection)

Williamstown, Massachusetts
Clark Art Institute

Wolverhampton
Wolverhampton Art Gallery

ACKNOWLEDGEMENTS

I proposed the idea for an exhibition focusing on *The Hay Wain* in 2020 primarily because the painting had caused a sensation at the Paris Salon in 1824, the year the National Gallery was founded. It therefore seemed the perfect subject for the Gallery's Bicentenary. However, as the Covid crisis deepened from March onwards with its sequence of lockdowns, access to nature and being in the landscape had never felt so important. Consequently, Constable's much-cherished image of rural England struck a chord with visitors to the National Gallery in ways that were unthinkable just a year before. As this exhibition and accompanying publication demonstrate, *The Hay Wain* has again and again shown a remarkable ability to absorb and reflect multiple cultural, social and political meanings and concerns. I have no doubt that it will continue to do so for many decades to come.

My deep gratitude goes to Gabriele Finaldi, Director, and Jane Knowles, Director of Public Engagement, for their enthusiastic support for the *Discover Constable & The Hay Wain* exhibition from the outset. The whole project has benefitted enormously over the last two years from the input, research and ideas of Mary McMahon, co-curator of this exhibition and a specialist in British art.

During the spring of 2022, the painting and its frame underwent conservation treatment that greatly improved our ability to appreciate Constable's masterly technique and composition. It also offered us the opportunity to reintroduce to the frame itself the recto and verso copies of the gold medal that Constable was awarded in Paris. We are deeply indebted to Paul Ackroyd, Conservator, and Isabella Kocum, Frame Conservator, both acknowledged experts in their respective fields, for their vital contributions. We also owe a great debt to the contributors to this catalogue, Jenny Gaschke and Emma Roodhouse, who were additionally instrumental in selecting and agreeing important loans from their respective institutions, and to Anne Lyles, for sharing her unparalleled knowledge of Constable's life and career. I am also indebted to Jacqueline Riding for her advice and thoughtful comments on my introductory essay.

This exhibition would not have been possible without the generosity of our lenders. We are indebted to the following institutions: Brighton & Hove Museums, Bristol Museum & Art Gallery, British Museum, Clark Art Institute, Colchester and Ipswich Museum Service, The Courtauld, The Fitzwilliam Museum, Museum Wales, National Museums Liverpool, National Trust and Upton House, Royal Academy of Arts, University of Nottingham, Victoria and Albert Museum, Wolverhampton Art Gallery and the Yale Center for British Art. We are also grateful to Nicholas J.S. Knowles and Omek and Linda Marks for enriching the exhibition with works from their own collections.

At the National Gallery, I wish to thank Alice Cox, Julie Firth, Sunnifa Hope, Jonathan King, Laura Lappin, Eleanor Richards and Per Rumberg for their advice and support. My colleagues in Press and Public Affairs, Alexandra Moskalenko and Neil Evans, devised a wonderful press trip to 'Constable Country', which included my first opportunity to see inside Willy Lott's House at Flatford, courtesy of Claire Madder from the Field Studies Council. Special thanks go to Simon Peachey and David Piper from the National Trust who led the tours, imparting their immense knowledge and enthusiasm for this famous site and its environs. My gratitude also goes to Dana Mokaddem for her brilliant management of the exhibition, to Alessandra Isolan and Sonia D'Orsi for their sensitive exhibition design, and to Minnie Scott for her thoughtful interpretation brief. This catalogue has been expertly overseen by Catherine Hooper, Project Editor, with the care and attention of Diana Adell, Suzanne Bosman, Jane Hyne, Jenny Wilson and Sandra Zellmer.

My sincere thanks go to the following individuals: Esther Bell, Mark Bills, Alice Briggs, Julia Carver, Hugo Chapman, Tim Clayton, Ollie Douglas, Martina Droth, Lucy Faithful, Melissa Gustin, Charlotte Keenan, Allan King, Michelle Leake, Rachel Loan, Rebecca Lyons, Clare Marlow, Jane Munro, Alysson Pollard, Andrew Renton, Rachel Sloan, Kathryn Steenson, Luke Syson, Carol Thompson and Edward Town.

Finally, this book is dedicated to my late mother, Patricia Betty Riding.

Christine Riding

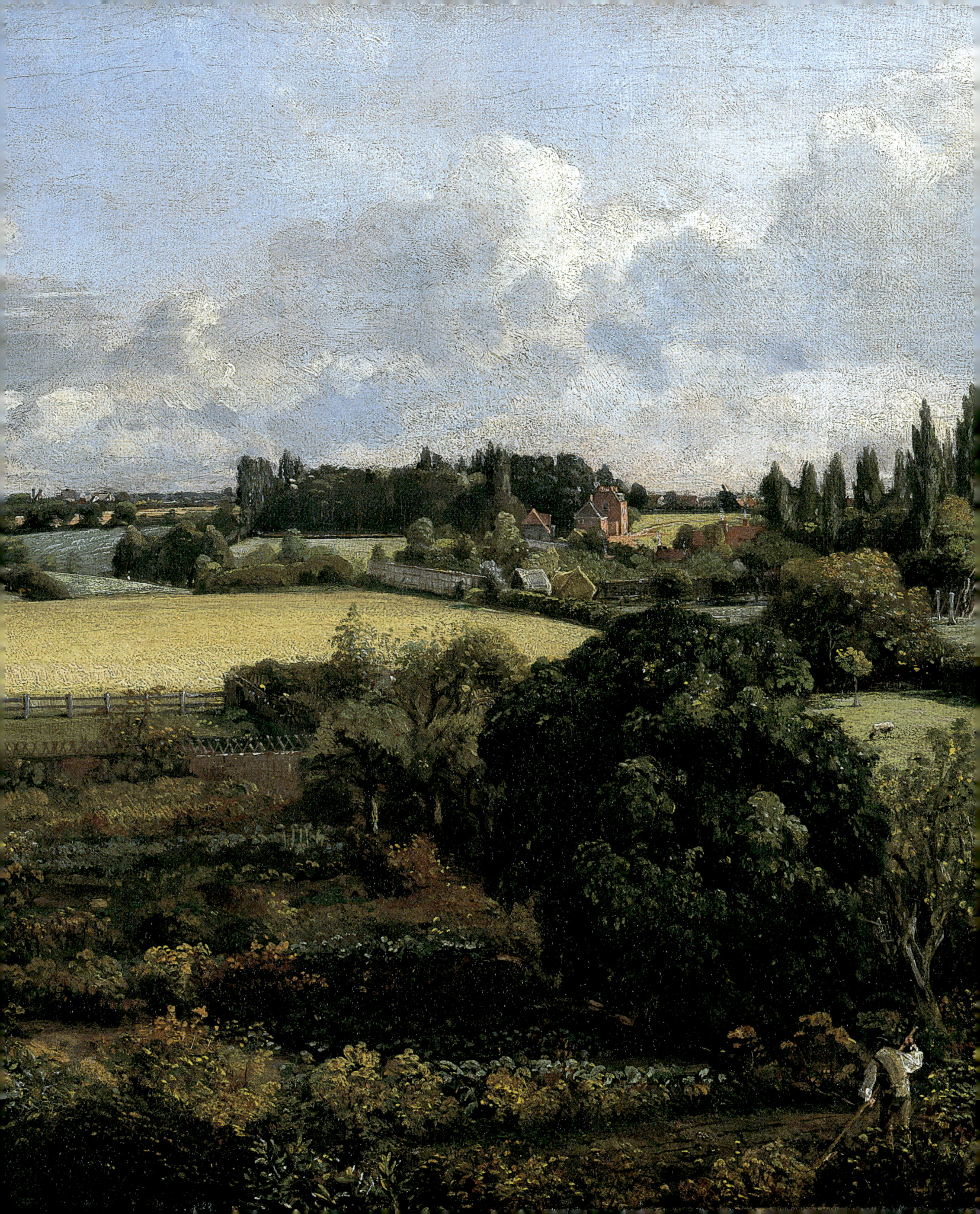

PHOTOGRAPHIC CREDITS

Berlin
Nationalgalerie, Staatliche Museen zu Berlin © Photo Scala, Florence/ bpk, Bildagentur für Kunst, Kultur und Geschichte, Berlin / Photo: Andres Kilger: fig. 31.

Boston, Massachusetts
Museum of Fine Arts, Boston, Massachusetts. Photograph © Museum of Fine Arts, Boston. All rights reserved. Warren Collection. William Wilkins Warren Fund / Bridgeman Images: fig. 19.

Brighton
© Brighton Museum and Art Gallery: fig. 60.

Bristol
© By Permission of Bristol's City Museum & Art Gallery, Bristol: figs 58, 59.

Cambridge
© Fitzwilliam Museum, Cambridge: fig. 61; © Fitzwilliam Museum, Cambridge / Bridgeman Images: fig. 25.

Cardiff
© Amgueddfa Cymru – National Museum Wales: fig. 65.

Dedham
The Trustees of the Constable Trust/ Dedham Church © The Trustees of the Constable Trust: fig. 17.

Edinburgh
Scottish National Gallery © National Galleries of Scotland/Bridgeman Images: fig. 30.

Haarlem
© Teylers Museum, Haarlem: fig. 32.

Høvikodden
Henie Onstad Kunstsenter, Høvikodden. Photo: Øystein Thorvaldsen / Henie Onstad Kunstsenter: fig. 34.

Ipswich
© Ipswich Borough Council Collections: Colchester and Ipswich Museum Service: figs 12, 13, 63, 64, 69, 74, 75.

Liverpool
Lady Lever Art Gallery, Port Sunlight. Board of Trustees of the National Museums and Galleries on Merseyside © Board of Trustees of the National Museums and Galleries on Merseyside: fig. 56.

London
The British Library, London © By Permission of The British Library, London / Bridgeman Images: fig. 5.
The British Museum, London © The Trustees of the British Museum: fig. 57.
The Samuel Courtauld Trust, The Courtauld Gallery, London © The Courtauld, London / Bridgeman Images: figs 70, 71, 77, 78, 79, 80, 81, 82, 83.
© Daily Express, photo courtesy CPRE: fig. 41.
© Museum of London: fig. 20.
© The National Gallery, London: figs 2, 8, 24, 27, 29, 36, 37, 40, 47, 87, 88; © Frank Auerbach / photo The National Gallery, London: fig. 44.
© Royal Academy of Arts, London: figs 54, 68, 85, 86.
© Royal Collection Enterprises Limited 2024 | Royal Collection Trust: fig. 26.
© Tate: figs 3, 7, 9, 16; © Peter Kennard / photo Tate: fig. 42; © Chris Shaw / photo Tate: fig. 45.
Victoria and Albert Museum, London © V&A Images / Victoria and Albert Museum, London: figs 1, 11, 14, 22, 33, 55, 67, 73, 84, 89.

New Haven, Connecticut
© Yale Center for British Art, New Haven, Connecticut: figs 4, 6, 10, 35, 53, 62, 76.

New York
The Frick Collection, New York, Image © The Frick Collection: fig. 21.

Nottingham
The Fagan Collection of Political Prints and Caricatures. University of Nottingham Manuscripts and Special Collections: fig. 52.

Private collections
© David Hockney: fig. 39.
Nicholas JS Knowles © Photo courtesy of the owner: figs 50, 51.
Omek & Linda Marks Family Collection © Photo courtesy of the owner: fig. 49.
Private collection © Photo courtesy of the owner: fig. 23.
Private collection © Cold War Steve: fig. 43.
Private collection © the artist's estate / photo courtesy of Swann Auction Galleries: fig. 38.

San Marino, California
The Huntington Library, Art Museum, and Botanical Gardens © courtesy of the Huntington Library, Art Museum, and Botanical Gardens, San Marino, California: fig. 28.

Sudbury
Constable Family on loan to Gainsborough's House © Photo courtesy of the owner: fig. 15.

Swindon
Upton House, National Trust © National Trust Images / Angelo Hornak: fig. 46.

Williamstown, Massachusetts
© Sterling and Francine Clark Art Institute, Williamstown, Massachusetts, USA: fig. 66; © Sterling and Francine Clark Art Institute, Williamstown, Massachusetts, USA, image courtesy of Lowell Libson Ltd: fig. 72.

Wolverhampton
Image courtesy of Wolverhampton Art Gallery: fig. 48.